Economic Impact and Recovery Following a Global Health Crisis

Brian W. Sloboda
University of Maryland Global Campus, USA

Yaya Sissoko
Indiana University of Pennsylvania, USA

A volume in the Advances in Finance, Accounting, and Economics (AFAE) Book Series

IGI Global
PUBLISHER of TIMELY KNOWLEDGE

Published in the United States of America by
IGI Global
Business Science Reference (an imprint of IGI Global)
701 E. Chocolate Avenue
Hershey PA, USA 17033
Tel: 717-533-8845
Fax: 717-533-8661
E-mail: cust@igi-global.com
Web site: http://www.igi-global.com

Library of Congress Cataloging-in-Publication Data

Names: Sloboda, Brian W., 1968- editor. | Sissoko, Yaya, 1961- editor.
Title: Economic impact and recovery following a global health crisis / Brian Sloboda, and Yaya Sissoko, editors.
Description: Hershey, PA : Business Science Reference, 2021. | Includes bibliographical references and index. | Summary: "The COVID-19 pandemic has triggered a massive spike in concerns and uncertainties and raised challenges in assessment of the macroeconomic and microeconomic impacts, so this book assesses the economic impacts of the COVID-19 pandemic, covering macroeconomic and microeconomic impacts of COVID-19"-- Provided by publisher.
Identifiers: LCCN 2021004521 (print) | LCCN 2021004522 (ebook) | ISBN 9781799869009 (hardcover) | ISBN 9781799869016 (paperback) | ISBN 9781799869023 (ebook)
Subjects: LCSH: Macroeconomics. | Microeconomics. | International trade. | COVID-19 (Disease)--Economic aspects.
Classification: LCC HB172.5 .E28 2021 (print) | LCC HB172.5 (ebook) | DDC 330.9--dc23
LC record available at https://lccn.loc.gov/2021004521
LC ebook record available at https://lccn.loc.gov/2021004522

This book is published in the IGI Global book series Advances in Finance, Accounting, and Economics (AFAE) (ISSN: 2327-5677; eISSN: 2327-5685)

British Cataloguing in Publication Data
A Cataloguing in Publication record for this book is available from the British Library.

For electronic access to this publication, please contact: eresources@igi-global.com.

Advances in Finance, Accounting, and Economics (AFAE) Book Series

Ahmed Driouchi
Al Akhawayn University, Morocco

ISSN:2327-5677
EISSN:2327-5685

MISSION

In our changing economic and business environment, it is important to consider the financial changes occurring internationally as well as within individual organizations and business environments. Understanding these changes as well as the factors that influence them is crucial in preparing for our financial future and ensuring economic sustainability and growth.

The **Advances in Finance, Accounting, and Economics (AFAE)** book series aims to publish comprehensive and informative titles in all areas of economics and economic theory, finance, and accounting to assist in advancing the available knowledge and providing for further research development in these dynamic fields.

COVERAGE

- Fiscal Policy
- Auditing
- Wages and Employment
- Economics of Agriculture and Biotechnology
- Statistical Analysis
- Economics of Migration and Spatial Mobility
- Economic Downturn
- Finance
- Investments and Derivatives
- Corporate Finance

IGI Global is currently accepting manuscripts for publication within this series. To submit a proposal for a volume in this series, please contact our Acquisition Editors at Acquisitions@igi-global.com or visit: http://www.igi-global.com/publish/.

The Advances in Finance, Accounting, and Economics (AFAE) Book Series (ISSN 2327-5677) is published by IGI Global, 701 E. Chocolate Avenue, Hershey, PA 17033-1240, USA, www.igi-global.com. This series is composed of titles available for purchase individually; each title is edited to be contextually exclusive from any other title within the series. For pricing and ordering information please visit http://www.igi-global.com/book-series/advances-finance-accounting-economics/73685. Postmaster: Send all address changes to above address.

Titles in this Series

For a list of additional titles in this series, please visit: http://www.igi-global.com/book-series

FinTech Development for Financial Inclusiveness
Muhammad Anshari (Universiti Brunei Darussalam, Brunei) Mohamad Nabil Almunawar (Universiti Brunei Darussalam, Brunei) and Masairol Masri (Universiti Brunei Darussalam, Brunei)
Business Science Reference • © 2022 • 269pp • H/C (ISBN: 9781799884477) • US $225.00

Evaluating Trade and Economic Relations Between India and Southeast Asia
Anita Medhekar (Central Queensland University, Australia) and Harpreet Kaur (Central Queensland University, Australia)
Business Science Reference • © 2022 • 347pp • H/C (ISBN: 9781799857747) • US $195.00

Handbook of Research on Global Aspects of Sustainable Finance in Times of Crises
Ibrahim Yasar Gok (Süleyman Demirel University, Turkey & Freie Universität Berlin, Germany)
Business Science Reference • © 2022 • 442pp • H/C (ISBN: 9781799885016) • US $285.00

Handbook of Research on Developing Circular, Digital, and Green Economies in Asia
Patricia Ordóñez de Pablos (The University of Oviedo, Spain)
Business Science Reference • © 2022 • 521pp • H/C (ISBN: 9781799886785) • US $225.00

Handbook of Research on Climate Change and the Sustainable Financial Sector
Odunayo Magret Olarewaju (Durban University of Technology, South Africa) and Idris Olayiwola Ganiyu (University of KwaZulu-Natal, South Africa)
Business Science Reference • © 2021 • 573pp • H/C (ISBN: 9781799879671) • US $295.00

CSR and Management Accounting Challenges in a Time of Global Crises
Ionica Oncioiu (Titu Maiorescu University, Romania)
Business Science Reference • © 2021 • 278pp • H/C (ISBN: 9781799880691) • US $215.00

IGI Global
PUBLISHER of TIMELY KNOWLEDGE

701 East Chocolate Avenue, Hershey, PA 17033, USA
Tel: 717-533-8845 x100 • Fax: 717-533-8661
E-Mail: cust@igi-global.com • www.igi-global.com

Table of Contents

Detailed Table of Contents

The subject and purpose of this study is to examine the new type of coronavirus disease (COVID-19), which has turned into a global epidemic, with an economic-political approach. There are twin crises in the form of a health crisis (high human deaths) and an economic crisis (recession). Trillion-dollar aid packages from governments and international financial organizations also show that this global public health crisis has created an economic crisis. In the context of these crises, G-20 countries that did not intervene in their transmission channels in a timely manner showed the worst situations. This epidemic, calculated with the SIR model, is global, but the measures are local. What makes a clean, masked, and socially distant life obligatory against the risk of contamination is that this epidemic locks or restricts the whole economy, especially trade, education, and tourism. Measures called "new normalization" have started to relax in order to prevent further increase in unemployment and poverty.

The pandemic offers numerous applications of very basic microeconomics concepts and their extension to other aspects of economic life. It also creates an opportunity for better understanding of how the market works and its effects on the economy and society. Allocation of a scarce resource is the definition of economics. There have been countless examples of scarcity (toilet paper, vaccines). How do we decide how to allocate those goods, especially when the market fails? The pandemic is a classic illustration of tradeoffs. In particular, there are tradeoffs between shutting (or re-opening) the economy and loss of human life; a rational decision would compare the costs and the benefits. Lastly, there are countless examples of the unequal economic effects of the virus and their implications for public policy.

The emergence and spread of severe acute respiratory syndrome corona virus 2 (SARS-CoV-2) with its attendant coronavirus disease in late 2019 (COVID-19) have brought untold social and economic hardships on the global society but with severe impacts on the sub-Saharan African households. The social and economic impacts were severe given that lifestyle in Africa is largely characterised by poor infrastructure development and social amenities. This situation increased food insecurity arising from complete loss or temporary halt of means of livelihood of the continent's households. Alongside this is loss of social security with resultant psychological stress and anxieties. This notwithstanding, developed resilience and social protection support have strengthened the African households to cope and possibly recover from the negative impacts of the COVID-19 pandemic.

The author suggests a range of public policies that the Thai government should employ so as to help Thai nationals and smaller-size businesses weather the storm of the pandemic. As the Thai economy is significantly tied to its tourism development, it is not pragmatic for Thai authorities and nationals to aim at full economic recovery in the short- and mid-term. In the short-term, Thai authorities should help local businesses and nationals to satisfy household subsistence. Then, the Thai government should create more job opportunities for the Thai workforce and financially support local businesses in the short- and mid-term. Concurrently, the Thai government should expand their delivery of social protection schemes to Thai nationals, helping local populations obtain basic social welfare services that are conducive to their survival. In the longer-term, the Thai government should welcome international tourisms in phases, and co-build transport infrastructures with neighbouring countries in order to prepare a full re-opening of national borders in due course.

It is possible to define the concept of risk in various ways. Risk is the deviation possibility of the realized value from the expected value. It has two components, nonsystematic risk and systematic risk. Despite this, pandemics are risk factors that cannot be anticipated. They have deeply affected economies and financial markets under every condition. The importance of the detection of the COVID-19 pandemic comes from the selection of monetary and fiscal policies to be applied by governments during the rehabilitation process of economies. Equity share markets provide important information regarding the future of a company or economy. The reason for this is that the current value of an equity share is dependent on the deducted calculation of the cash flows of the equity share to be provided in the future. The actual price of the equity share is determined according to supply and demand under market conditions.

This study investigates the relationship between the COVID-19 crisis and economic inequalities in some developed and developing countries. Many institutions, like OECD, ILO, and UNDP, have released several reports deal with the relationship between COVID-19 and different kinds of inequalities. These reports generally emphasize the same problem. This study includes some indicators about the situation of education and gender inequalities in OECD countries. These indicators purely reveal that COVID-19 has negative effects on both education and gender inequalities in most of developed and developing countries. The main contribution of the study is to point out the importance of recovery policies the cover the inequality problems.

As the COVID-19 pandemic continues to evolve even beyond a second wave, there is an urgent need for business organisations to rethink and reconfigure their strategies for long-term sustainability beyond the pandemic. Many organisations are already making changes in the way they run their businesses and the way they make decisions to emerge stronger. It can be observed that the pandemic has seriously affected the way business organisations are being operated. However, this research suggests

of causing the stagnation of growth, miniscule firms have been losing their weight rapidly among the entrants. It revives lost hopes for the future of the economy and also motivates questions regarding the other determinants of such transformation in new firm formation.

Foreword

Even though public health experts have been warning for several years that there was a danger of a viral pandemic, the crisis caused by Sars-Cov-2 (COVID-19) has been a shock to governments and the people. The chaotic and dissimilar way in which governments have reacted has shown that they were not prepared to take the appropriate measures or engage in effective political communication.

From the perspective of academic research, the literature on the COVID-19 pandemic has seen a steep development. The researcher can discover different perspectives for analyzing this global health crisis: political science, economic, social-demographic, environmental, sociological, anthropological, cultural, human rights, and so on. All these perspectives have a common denominator: the recognition that the pandemic has caused a major change in the approach to the World Order (Brands et al., 2020) and public policy. If the 1990s and beyond were the period of strengthening a globalist agenda, even despite the criticism and sovereignist challengers, the year of 2020 has allowed the world to observe the benefits and costs of globalization in the context of a pandemic with transnational effects.

The COVID-19 pandemic has brought several social issues to the surface that have been inevitable with a myriad of limiting measures: marginalization, discrimination, ageism, isolation (Lupton & Willis, 2021). This pandemic period has introduced a "new normal" that manifests itself in "new common" (Aarts et al., 2021) in different fields: education, health, information management, migration, environment, artificial intelligence, economy, and governance.

Each state has provided its own narrative about the crisis, which reflects its own political system, but also perceptions of leadership and its performance (Lillekert et al., 2021). However, what the spread of the COVID-19 virus has shown is that we are in a truly global society (Giordano, 2020), and the solution to such a crisis can only be global. From the perspective of the individual or group, the crisis has brought to the surface the social, perception, mental health or even existential risks, and the increasing need to develop a "resilience society" (Vos, 2021).

This volume, coordinated by Brian Sloboda and Yaya Sissoko, approaches the COVID-19 pandemic issue from an economic perspective. This book is structured into nine chapters authored by academics from different countries. A brief description of each chapter intends to emphasize the main arguments built by contributors in this volume.

The first chapter, authored by Irfan Kalaycı (Inönü University), addresses the political economy effects of the COVID-19 Pandemic analyzed as a double crisis: a health crisis (high human deaths) and an economic crisis (recession). This essay contrasts the traditional pattern of intervention by G20 countries during economic crises with the approach taken during the current crisis when economic recovery measures were taken locally. Obviously, the question that remains is if this new approach represents the "new normalization."

In the second chapter, Nancy Ruth Fox (Saint Joseph's University) highlights the compromises that accompany the pandemic: "shutting (or re-opening) the economy and loss of human life." This approach fits into the model of the rational actor who can assess the costs and benefits of his potential decisions. What the author intends to indicate is that the COVID-19 pandemic helps us better understand how the basic mechanisms of an economy and a society work.

The emergence and widespread prevalence of severe acute respiratory syndrome coronavirus 2 (SARS-CoV-2), with its attendant coronavirus disease in 2019 (COVID-19), have brought untold social and economic hardships on the global society as presented by Okanlade Adesokan Lawal-Adebowale in the third chapter.

Jason Jung (Cambridge University) offers a case study of Thailand's economy in the context of the pandemic in the fourth chapter. This is an example of a country's government policy in attempting to stem the economic effects of the pandemic.

In the fifth chapter, Hakan Altin (University of Aksaray) discusses the effects that the pandemic is having on international stock exchanges. The analysis of the impact of the pandemic goes beyond non-systematic and systematic risks. In general, the unanticipated nature of a pandemic deeply affects both economies and financial markets but makes it difficult to select appropriate monetary and fiscal policies to facilitate the recovery process of national economies.

Inevitably, the COVID-19 pandemic has also exacerbated economic inequalities between countries. The study proposed by Eren Yildirim (Hitit University) in the sixth chapter of this book uses relevant indicators from the reports of some main institutions (OECD, ILO, and UNDP) to reveal that the problems of inequality must also be considered in post-pandemic recovery policies.

Chabi Gupta (Christ University) suggests in the seventh chapter of this book that "a transformational change" is needed in the organization of the business post-COVID-19 pandemic. In this sense, artificial intelligence and financial analytics will be the tools of this "transformational change." Changing the vision of leadership can be the opportunity that a crisis brings to the fore.

In the eighth chapter, Sebak Kumar Jana (Vidyasagar University), Subrata Naru (Vidyasagar University), and Pranjit Kr Paul (Vidyasagar University) examined the impacts of COVID-19 on migrant workers in India. The spread of the COVID-19 and the subsequent nationwide lockdown in India that begain in March 2020 to control its further outbreak of the virus brought turmoil in the lives of millions who are primarily involved in the informal sector. These disruptions were quite significant and the authors in this chapter examined the economic and social impacts on migrant workers.

The ninth or the final chapter, written by Yigit Aydogan (Kirklareli University), looks at how new firms in Turkey have been affected by the COVID-19 pandemic. The chapter intends to identify the determining factors that contributed to the revival of small businesses.

This book provides a complement to an economic perspective on the impact that the COVID-19 pandemic has on society and relations between nations. Contributors to this book reveal the same idea: the world was not ready for the changes that the pandemic has brought, and societies are trying to find their own ways to survive. The studies of this volume contribute to the building of a complex puzzle that will eventually reveal the image of the post-pandemic world. Finally, the researcher will seek to discover whether the elements that characterized the pre-pandemic world helped avoid a collapse or became lessons for the reconstruction of the post-pandemic world with a new normality.

Mihai Alexandrescu
Babes-Bolyai University, Romania

REFERENCES

Aarts, E., Fleuren, H., Sitskoorn, M., & Wilthagen, T. (2021). *The New Common: How the COVID-19 Pandemic is Transforming Society*. Springer. doi:10.1007/978-3-030-65355-2

Basu, R. (2021). *Democracy and Public Policy in the post-COVID-19 World: Choices and Outcomes*. Routledge.

Brands, H., & Gavin, F. J. (Eds.). (2020). *COVID-19 and World Order. The Future of Conflict, Competition, and Cooperation*. John Hopkins University Press.

Giordano, P. (2020). *Contagio*. Giulio Einaudi.

Lilkert, D., Coman, I., Gregor, M., & Novelli, E. (Eds.). (2021). *Political Communication and COVID-19. Governance and Rhetoric in Times of Crisis*. Routledge. doi:10.4324/9781003120254

Lupton, D., & Willis, K. (Eds.). (2021). *The COVID-19 Crisis: Social Perspective*. Routledge. doi:10.4324/9781003111344

Vos, J. (2021). *The Psychology of COVID-19: Building Resilience for Future Pandemics*. SAGE Publications. doi:10.4135/9781529757156

Preface

INTRODUCTION

Before the COVID-19 crisis began in late 2019 with an outbreak on China, most economies in Asia, North America, and Europe experienced a long period of economic stability and prosperity. After the declaration of the global pandemic in February 2020 by the World Health Organization (WHO), the world changed suddenly. Many countries throughout the world reacted to this shock, and these governments began to implement various policies to prevent a sudden decline in their economies. Since March 2020, the effects of the COVID-19 pandemic have had a profound impact on these economies, and the economic damage from these effects could linger for many years after the formal end of the pandemic by the World Health Organization (WHO). There is still a push for innovative policies to ameliorate from the negative impacts of the COVID-19 pandemic on their economies.

In this volume, we solicited chapters that examine the economic impact of the COVID-19 pandemic and the potential longer-term impacts. We encouraged authors to investigate problems of society from different economic perspectives. In addition, we wanted to explore the damaging effects of the COVID-19 pandemic and the lingering influences of the COVID-19 pandemic. Stated differently, we attempted (we hope!) to explore paths to recovery and the new opportunities that this crisis could bring as well as improve our stance as a modern civilization.

To this end, the COVID-19 pandemic raised and continues to raise challenges in the assessment of macroeconomic and microeconomic impacts. More importantly, the impacts of COVID-19 on the macroeconomic and microeconomic levels of an economy as well as the current and future economic tendencies have yet to be fully realized. The impact of COVID-19 research holds limitless potential, but the necessary research for professionals to understand these economic impacts is lacking and unclear because the pandemic is still ongoing.

Economic Impact and Recovery Following a Global Health Crisis presents the economic impacts of the COVID-19 pandemic. We hope that the range of topics - from stock market behavior to impacts on the tourism sectors - would give some breadth as to the potential impacts from the COVID-19 pandemic, which as of this publication date is still ongoing. *Economic Impact and Recovery Following a Global Health Crisis* would be ideal for policymakers, researchers, instructors, and students in economics and noneconomic disciplines.

CHAPTERS PRESENTED IN THIS VOLUME

In Chapter 1, İrfan Kalaycı examines the new type of coronavirus disease (COVID-19), which has turned into a global epidemic, with an economic-political approach. There are twin crises in the form of a health crisis (high human deaths) and an economic crisis (recession). Trillion-dollar aid packages from governments and international financial organizations also show that this global public health crisis has created an economic crisis. In the context of these crises, G-20 countries did not intervene in their transmission channels in a timely manner to lessen the impacts of the pandemic. This epidemic, calculated with the SIR (Suspectible-Infection-Recovery) model, is global, but the measures are local. What makes a clean, masked, and socially distant life obligatory against the risk of contamination is that this epidemic locks or restricts the whole economy, especially trade, education, and tourism. Measures called "new normalization" have started to be relaxed to prevent further increases in unemployment and poverty.

In Chapter 2, Nancy Fox delves offers numerous applications of very basic microeconomics concepts and their extension to other aspects of economic life during the pandemic. The pandemic also creates an opportunity for better understanding of how the market works and its effects on the economy and society. Allocation of a scarce resource is the definition of economics. There have been countless examples of scarcity (toilet paper, vaccines). How do we decide how to allocate those goods, especially when the market fails? The pandemic is a classic illustration of tradeoffs. In particular, tradeoffs exist between shutting (or re-opening) the economy and loss of human life; a rational decision would compare the costs and the benefits. Lastly, there are countless examples of the unequal economic effects of the virus and their implications for public policy. The content of this chapter is readily applicable to the current debates about the vaccination process.

The emergence and widespread prevalence of severe acute respiratory syndrome coronavirus 2 (SARS-CoV-2), with its attendant coronavirus disease in 2019 (COVID-19), have brought untold social and economic hardships on the global society as presented by Okanlade Adesokan Lawal-Adebowale in Chapter 3. Although countries across Asia, Europe, and America have been the hotspots of the COVID-19 spread, the severity of impacts of the global pandemic is more pronounced in sub-Saharan Africa. Thus, this article reflects the antecedent of COVID-19 emergence, extent of spread, dimension of impacts, and adopted resiliencies by households in the continent for protection and survival. A meta-analysis of the COVID-19 situation in Africa shows that confirmed death cases from the viral disease were relatively lower in the continent, but spikes increased food insecurity as a result of complete loss or temporary halt of the households' means of livelihood. Alongside this is loss of social security with resultant psychological stress and anxieties. This notwithstanding, developed resiliencies and social protection support have strengthened the African households to cope and possibly recover from the negative impacts of the COVID-19 pandemic.

In Chapter 4, Jason Hung suggests a range of public policies that the Thai government should employ to help Thai nationals and smaller-size businesses weather the storm of the pandemic. As the Thai economy is significantly tied to its tourism development, it is not pragmatic for Thai authorities and nationals to aim at full economic recovery in the short- and mid-term. In the short-term, Thai authorities should help local businesses and nationals satisfy household subsistence. Then, the Thai government should create more job opportunities for the Thai workforce and financially support local businesses in the short- and mid-term. Concurrently, the Thai government should expand its delivery of social protection schemes to Thai nationals, helping local populations obtain basic social welfare services that are conducive to their survival. In the longer term, the Thai government should welcome international tourisms in phases and co-build transport infrastructures with neighboring countries in order to prepare a full re-opening of national borders in due course.

Hakan Altin in Chapter 5 presents the impacts of the pandemic on international stock exchanges. As presented by Altin, it is possible to define the concept of risk in various ways. Risk is the deviation possibility of the realized value from the expected value. It has two components: nonsystematic risk and systematic risk. Despite this, pandemics are risk factors that cannot be anticipated. They have deeply affected economies and financial markets under every condition. The importance of the detection of COVID-19 pandemic comes from the selection of monetary and fiscal policies to be applied by governments during the rehabilitation process of economies. Equity share markets provide important information regarding the future of a company or economy. The reason for this is that the current value of an equity share is dependent on the deducted calculation of the cash flows of the equity share to be provided in the future. The actual price of the equity share is determined according to supply and demand under certain market conditions.

In Chapter 6, Ahmet Eren Yıldırım investigated the relationship between COVID-19 crisis and economic inequalities in some developed and developing countries. Many institutions, such as OECD, ILO, and UNDP, have released several reports that address the relationships between COVID-19 and different kinds of inequalities. These reports generally emphasize the same problem. This study includes some indicators about the situation of education and gender inequalities in OECD countries. These indicators purely reveal that the COVID-19 crisis has a negative effect on both education and gender inequalities in most developed and developing countries. The main contribution of this chapter is the importance of recovery policies that carefully address these inequality problems.

Chapter 7 presents the theme of artificial intelligence by Chabi Gupta which is an emerging topic in economics and the social sciences. As the COVID-19 pandemic continues to evolve even beyond a second wave, there is an urgent need for business organizations to rethink and reconfigure their strategies for long-term sustainability beyond the pandemic. Many organizations are already making changes in the way they run their businesses and the way they take decisions to emerge stronger. It can be observed that the pandemic has seriously affected the way business organizations were being operated. However, this research suggests during the discussion that what is required is a transformational change rather than a directed one for any business organization. In the current scenario, AI is being seen as a key enabler for business organizations to be on the path to recovery. What will be the 'modus operandi' beyond the pandemic, is a relevant issue for businesses indicating further need of research in this area. Using financial analytics and AI in combination will bring in a transformational change that might be viewed as the 'game changer' for businesses beyond the pandemic.

In Chapter 8, Sebak Kumar Jana, Subrata Naru, and Pranjit Kr Paul examined the impacts of COVID-19 on migrant workers in India. The spread of the COVID-19 and the subsequent nationwide lockdown in India that commenced March 22, 2020 to control its further outbreak brought turmoil in the lives of millions who are primarily involved in the informal sector. A primary survey was conducted in the District of South 24 Pgs. in the state of West Bengal India to examine the effects of COVID-19 on rural livelihood, particularly of the migrant workers. The types of disruptions of rural livelihood of the households have been explored in the study. Furthermore, the perceptions of the effects of shocks of COVID-19 on the rural households have been assessed in terms of the following variables: loss of assets, loss of income, food insecurity/shortage, death of livestock, decline in consumption, declines in health conditions, socialization, effects on education, and problems in accessing health facilities. Types of government support provided to the households have been examined for the study area. The role of the government in overcoming the crisis of livelihood has also been assessed.

In the final chapter by Yigit Aydogan, the author explored the new surge in new firm registrations that has been one of the most intriguing outcomes of the economic turbulence caused by the COVID-19 pandemic. Turkey followed a similar pattern to many other economies that observed an initial drop and a rapid V-shaped recovery of entry when the virus hit the country. However, the size distribution of new firms has been very different. While others experience a strong rise in smaller entrants, larger firms have dominated the pack in Turkey. As a widely known, long-term problem of the Turkish economy which has been accused of the stagnation of growth, minuscule firms have been rapidly losing their weight among the entrants. It revives lost hopes for the future of the economy and motivates questions regarding the other determinants of such transformation in new firm formation.

ENDING THOUGHTS

Two things hampered the preparation of this edited volume. First, we are not epidemiologists, so we had to absorb the material hastily about the potential economics of the COVID-19. Our goal was to present the pertinent economic issues as the pandemic continued to transpire. Second, the events of the pandemic were constantly evolving because governments were implementing policies and reissuing new policies at a quick pace. More importantly, scientists were constantly learning about the virus and the implications of COVID-19 on the health and wellbeing of people. The COVID-19 pandemic was ever changing and continues to be. But if this volume is going to be relevant a month after publication, let alone in one year, we could not be overly judgmental about the content of these chapters because no one really knows for sure how this pandemic will end or when it will end.

We would like to thank our colleagues for enabling us to pursue this evolving project. Additionally, we needed something more to do while in lockdown and having to social distance from others to keep our minds busy from the perils of the evolving COVID-19 pandemic. We would also like to thank the reviewers for their reviews of their assigned chapters. Special recognition goes to Chandra Putcha (California State University, Fullerton), Rolando Santos (Lakeland Community College, Ohio), and Sami Ullah Khan (Gomal University, Dera Ismail Khan, Pakistan) for kindly volunteering to review more chapters. Their help was immensely appreciated as a means to ensure this project is completed. Finally, we owe a special debt to Katie McLoughlin and the IGI Global team for their assistance in seeing that this project comes to a successful end!

Brian W. Sloboda
Yaya Sissoko

Introduction

We are now experiencing a whole new level of uncertainty as questions only the virus can answer complicate the outlook. Jerome Powell, Chairman of the Federal Reserve, May 21, 2021

As stated by Jerome Powell, economies throughout the world must deal with massive uncertainty concerning the trajectory of the COVID-19 pandemic, including the infectiousness of the virus. Since the coronavirus, which is the SARS-CoV-2 virus, was first detected in China in late 2019, the virus spread quickly throughout the world. Many countries throughout the world experienced a global public health emergency, and significant economic damage occurred. The economic damage was witnessed in the macroeconomic indicators, including gross domestic product (GDP), industrial production, unemployment rate, and others. To prevent the spread of the virus, many countries attempted to flatten the curve through social distancing measures and lockdowns. Consequently, these draconian measures triggered supply and demand shocks, which disrupted most economies. From these experiences, the consequences from these actions were detrimental to most world economies.

Eighteen months later, the consequences of the pandemic still persist. We recovered from the first significant virus from 2020, but the emergence of the Delta variant began to take hold in late 2020 and spread quickly throughout the world. Consequently, worries over the pandemic's effects on the economy have also reemerged as mentioned via a recurring survey by McKinsey (McKinsey, 2021). McKinsey periodically conducted a survey of business leaders to take a pulse of their thoughts concerning the effects of the pandemic on economic recovery. In June 2021, 36 percent of the business leaders believed that the pandemic would harm economic growth. In October 2021, 49 percent of business leaders have said the same which exceeded the 42 percent in July 2021. In addition to the worries about the economic impacts from the COVID-19, new worries over the supply-chain disruptions are now becoming a looming threat to economic growth. We expect some research will evolve concerning the emerging supply chain issues to take shape in the near term.

The Spanish Flu pandemic that occurred nearly a century ago offers a useful point of comparison to the current COVID-19 pandemic. Barro et al. (2020) estimated that the Spanish Flu killed about 40 million people worldwide which was about 2.1 percent of the world's population. The worldwide deaths attributed to COVID-19 as of November 22, 2021 are about 5.15 million[1] on a global population base of 7.7 billon, yielding a global mortality rate of less than 0.10 percent. However, the number of deaths attributed to COVID-19 continues to rise because of the persistence of the Delta variant. When the pandemic concludes, the death toll will no doubt be higher.

As mentioned, the COVID-19 pandemic resulted in a major economic shock as measured by GDP. Because of this sudden shock, global GDP declined by approximately 4% in 2020. This decline is larger than any decline recorded in the last six decades (Appendix Figure A4, International Monetary Fund, 2020). In comparison to other economic disruptions, global GDP declined approximately 2 percent during the Great Recession of 2009 and was largely flat during the 1973-4 Oil Embargo. Most importantly, the COVID-19 pandemic has resulted in a higher number of people living in poverty, and the number of people living in poverty has increased by nearly 100 million (which returns to levels last seen in 2015). Consequently, the pandemic has undone poverty reduction of the past decade (Gerszon Mahler et al., 2021).

In the literature, there is also a growing assessment that the adverse effects of the pandemic - both in terms of COVID-19 morbidity and mortality itself as well as the damage from the lockdowns - exceed the potential economic impacts. Stated differently, there are distributional consequences that adversely affect women, low-income and migrant workers, and other groups. In addition, there are the broader impacts on societal welfare (e.g., educational, physical, and mental healthcare) and increases in crime, especially domestic violence (Miguel, 2021). These distributional effects will continue to be studied well after the pandemic concludes because these impacts could affect these groups both economically and socially.

This brief introductory discussion highlights the range of research that has been conducted about the economic impacts of the COVID-19 pandemic. There is no shortage of research about the COVID-19 pandemic. There is also no clear, expected outcome for the COVID-19 pandemic as this pandemic continues to evolve. In this context, this volume provides a variety of research in different contexts and examines a range of related themes pertaining to the impacts of the COVID-19 pandemic. It is also worth noting that the economic and broader impacts were less in developing countries (lesser in Africa) than in developed countries. No one knows precisely when and how the COVID-19 pandemic will end, but the economic impacts and related transformations will be felt for many years to come.

Brian W. Sloboda
University of Maryland Global Campus, USA

Yaya Sissoko
Indiana University of Pennsylvania, USA

REFERENCES

Barro, R. J., Ursua, J. F., & Weng, J. (2020). *The Coronavirus and the Great Influenza Pandemic: Lessons from the 'Spanish Flu' for the Coronavirus's Potential Effects on Mortality and Economic Activity*. NBER Working Paper 26866.

Gerszon Mahler, D., Yonzan, N., Lakner, C. R., Castaneda Aguilar, A., & Wu, H. (2021). *Updated Estimates of the Impact of COVID-19 on Global Poverty: Turning the Corner on the Pandemic in 2021?* World Bank Blogs. Retrieved November 21, 2021 from, https://blogs.worldbank.org/opendata/updated-estimates-impact-covid-19-global-povertyturning-corner-pandemic-2021

International Monetary Fund. (2020). *A Crisis Like No Other, An Uncertain Recovery*. World Economic Outlook Update. Retrieved November 21, 2021, from https://www.imf.org/en/Publications/WEO/Issues/2020/06/24/WEOUpdateJune2020

McKinsey. (2021). *The coronavirus effect on global economic sentiment*. Retrieved November 21, 2021, from https://www.mckinsey.com/business-functions/strategy-and-corporate-finance/our-insights/the-coronavirus-effect-on-global-economic-sentiment

Miguel, E. (2021). The economics of the COVID-19 pandemic in poor countries. *Annual Review of Economics*, 14.

ENDNOTE

1 The number of deaths was obtained from https://www.worldometers.info/coronavirus/.

Chapter 1
An Essay on the Political Economy Effects of the COVID-19 Pandemic as Twin Crises

Irfan Kalaycı
İnönü University, Turkey

ABSTRACT

The subject and purpose of this study is to examine the new type of coronavirus disease (COVID-19), which has turned into a global epidemic, with an economic-political approach. There are twin crises in the form of a health crisis (high human deaths) and an economic crisis (recession). Trillion-dollar aid packages from governments and international financial organizations also show that this global public health crisis has created an economic crisis. In the context of these crises, G-20 countries that did not intervene in their transmission channels in a timely manner showed the worst situations. This epidemic, calculated with the SIR model, is global, but the measures are local. What makes a clean, masked, and socially distant life obligatory against the risk of contamination is that this epidemic locks or restricts the whole economy, especially trade, education, and tourism. Measures called "new normalization" have started to relax in order to prevent further increase in unemployment and poverty.

DOI: 10.4018/978-1-7998-6900-9.ch001

INTRODUCTION

The first fatal case of the new type of corona[1] virus was detected in Wuhan, China, in October 2019. At the end of the year, the disease rapidly spread across the country and from there to the whole world with the diagnosis of "COVID-19". After it was declared as a global pandemic by the World Health Organization (WHO) on 1/3/2020, governments immediately began to take medical and economic-political measures to combat the epidemic. Despite this, there were unexpectedly high casualties. Since the epidemic and vaccination processes have not yet ended, human losses and economic damages continue in every country it is transmitted to.

COVID-19 is the last link - for now - added to the history of the world epidemic chain.[2]

The countries of the G-20 (Group 20), which dominates eighty percent of the world economy, covers the 20 richest economies of the world by gross domestic product (GDP) size and is an advisory summit, have affected at different levels by COVID-19, depending on the rapid measures and priorities they take.

Globally, as of August 16 2021, there have been 207.173.086 confirmed cases of COVID-19, including 4.361.996 deaths, reported to World Health Organization (WHO). On the same date, a total of 4.452.111.864 vaccine doses have been administered in the whole world. the USA, India and Brazil ranked in the top three on the basis of positive cases, while Turkey ranked 5th after France. But China, where Covid was first seen, fell to the bottom.

The death of more than four millions people from COVID-19- for now - means the deletion of an "X district" of Istanbul with a population of this size or a "city Y" of Turkey or a "country Z" of the world within a year. This description has been made to reveal the dimensions of the global drama. When the epidemic is over, these maps will become clearer.

The world has almost entered the process of the 3rd World War (WWIII). All the countries of the world stand on one side (allied powers) and COVID-19stands alone on the other (only enemy). The general characteristics of this enemy are that, as an invisible 20-50 micron virus, it attacks the lungs and collapses immunity, is deadly and rapidly infectious. World allies, who have been in quarantine for a long time, have three weapons against the virus: "Contactless life + Diagnosis by testing + Monitoring of treatment." The problem is globalized, but the solution continues with global cooperation and local-level measures. Undoubtedly, the world, which is highly experienced in epidemics, will also emerge victorious from the war with COVID-19. Because no virus is stronger than human beings and their rational, determined and sustainable measures.

The virus is contagious, but human beings are also inventive. Accordingly, the epidemic caused by COVID-19, the whole world was mobilized to find vaccines against mass fear and to reassure its citizens, and achieved significant success. Both the risk and the mobilization are not over yet.

COVID-19, one of the coronavirus, seems to confirm the population theory of Malthus.[3] According to this theory, when the world's scarce resources cannot sufficiently feed the growing population, wars and epidemics are needed for balance.

The main purpose of this study, which prefers to define the COVID-19 epidemic as a twin crisis in the form of a global public health crisis and an economic crisis, is to draw attention to the complex political economy dimension of the epidemic. In the study, based on the literature background, first of all, the SIR model was accepted as a theoretical framework for the calculation of the epidemic, then a scales metaphor was built for the overall major harms and minor benefits of the epidemic, and also various concrete distances against the epidemic were listed, and finally a series of political economy predictions and recommendations were presented in the fight against the epidemic.

BACKGROUND

Scientific studies focusing on the political economy dimension of COVID-19 have increasingly begun to enter the literature. Below is a brief summary of selected studies.

Hendrix (2021) states that the success of OECD countries in controlling the COVID-19 pandemic has varied greatly and explanations for the differences fall into four broad categories (political/economic, cultural/social, demographic/geographic, and policy-oriented). The author used the Bayesian mean of the model to assess the explanatory power of 21 potential covariates. According to him, standard political economy variables that predict more investment in public health, such as GDP per capita and level of democracy; both general and pandemic disease-specific measures of government activity; and demographic factors that predict increased vulnerability, such as the share of the elderly or obese population, do not explain the differences in outcomes. The key factors s/he points out are prohibitibility (the ability to tightly control borders and effectively restrict or monitor those entering at a limited number of ports), the early adoption of stronger international travel restrictions, and a female head of government appears to be. It was found that the simple Bayesian model, which includes these three variables, has an R2 value of 0.78 and is robust among the estimators.

Using the background of COVID-19, Bagus and colleagues (2021) point out that negative information that is repeatedly disseminated through government related mass media and digital media can adversely affect public health in the form of nocebo effects and mass hysteria: The resulting mass hysteria is a response to governments' health recommendations. may have contributed to non-compliant policy errors. The authors show that while mass hysteria can occur in societies with a minimal state, certain self-correcting mechanisms, such as sacred private property rights, and the limits of harm do exist. According to them, however, when negative information comes from an authoritative source, when the media is politicized, and when social networks make negative information ubiquitous, mass hysteria can exacerbate and self-reinforce. They concluded that the negative long-term effects of mass hysteria are exacerbated by the size of the state.

Lipsey (2020) argues that COVID-19 politics is a politics of crisis that forces leaders to take high risks and whose humanitarian and political consequences are often intertwined: The politics of crises in economic globalization and climate change and certain problems such as finance, energy, natural disasters and pandemics are at the center of attention of international political economy. He explores the great puzzles surrounding the ‘causal sources’ (uncertainty as a barrier to crisis prevention, prevention of contagion through international cooperation), ‘reactions’ (uncertainty and first-mover disadvantage, threat perceptions and manipulations, leadership and ad hoc decision-making) and ‘transformations’ (crisis characteristics and transformational change, political volatility, and public perceptions of crisis response) of crisis politics.

Barbieri and Bonini (2021), reminding that many governments have implemented social distance and quarantine measures to prevent the spread of COVID-19, examined the political side of the application in Italy: According to Italy’s provincial data, the political disbelief associated with protesting the rules limits the effectiveness of government policy. One of the findings of the study is that bipartisan support and national responsibility are necessary to implement and manage social distancing effectively; the other shows that partisan politics and discontent with the political class can significantly affect human health and the economy.

Kaplan, Lefler, and Ziberman (20121) evaluated the economic and health costs of Covid and the political responses to Covid: As they point out, significant differences in death rates between the US and other countries are due to population density, climate, exposure and investment policies. So while some developing countries initially took drastic and expensive measures, perhaps motivated by political economy, regions that were able to contain the disease early experienced fewer deaths and lower economic losses.

Bergsen (2020) emphasizes that the COVID-19 pandemic has led to unprecedented measures of economic support from governments in Europe, but the crisis nevertheless provides an opportunity for the ability to implement a market-balanced “protective state” policy and provide services.

Bump and colleagues (2021) point to aspects of the political economy of COVID-19 linked to racial discrimination, marginalization and colonialism. The burden of Covid has increased as it marginalized people and deepened the rich-poor gap, economic inequalities and vulnerability. According to their observations, the increasing competitiveness of some countries and progress in public health have brought about governance reforms in multilateral institutions and international redistribution mechanisms.

Smith et al (2021) evaluated the gendered effects of the COVID-19 pandemic in terms of feminist political economy. In China, Hong Kong, Canada and the United Kingdom, they found that the epidemic had effects in the form of financial discrimination, crisis in care and unequal risks. The varying results due to gender inequality point to transnational structural conditions that place women at the forefront of the pandemic at work and at home, while depriving them of health, economic and personal security.

Phiri (2021) argues that contemporary approaches to South Africa's social, domestic, and foreign policy responses should be viewed through the theoretical lenses of racial capitalism—a racially hierarchical political economy constituting war, militarism, imperialist accumulation, expropriation by domination, and labour super exploitation. According to writer, South Africa's pandemic responses are enveloped in a global financial architecture that champions the markets. As s/he wishes, if power and resources are shared democratically with the opportunity to fight Covid, the slave / master relationship that underpins South Africa's public policy will be disrupted.

Boettke and Powell (2021) reveal what COVID-19 strategies might be if politicians adopt the measures that standard welfare economics would suggest: The economic rationale for any public policy to mitigate the Covid epidemic depends on the presence of externalities. In their view, an alternative but complementary approach for a welfare economist to deal with the COVID-19 externality is to undertake policies that reduce the cost of the externality, rather than simply trying to limit activities that lead to virus transmission. These policies should include government funds to expand hospital capacity and purchase supplies and equipment, and research funds to accelerate the discovery of new medical treatments and vaccines. It may also include removing regulatory barriers to medical capacity and the development of drugs and vaccines.

Baum and colleagues (2021) discuss in the context of the Global Health Security Index (GHSI) factors that predict the success of national response to COVID-19 and affect future pandemic preparedness: They recommend that the GHSI consists of the following 10 critical factors: i-Limited consideration of globalization, geography, and global governance; ii-Bias to high income countries; iii-Failure to assess health system capacity; iv-Role of political leadership; v-Importance of context overlooked; vi-Limits of national wealth as predictive factor; vii-No examination of inequalities within countries; viii-Importance of social security provisions; ix-Civil society capacity not assessed; x-Gap between capacity and its application not assessed.

A BRIEF DISCUSSION FOR THE SIR MODEL

SIR models, whose epidemiological origins date back to the beginning of the 20th century and have become popular again with the COVID-19 epidemic, are used with differential or stochastic equations to predict how and how long the disease spreads and to find the most effective control technique by making a limited number of vaccines in a certain population.

WHO calculated the rate of spread (R0) of COVID-19 to be between 2-2.5 (this value may vary in each type of epidemic). When it first appeared, the *R*-coefficient was 8: that is, 1 person transmitted the virus to 8 people, and the infected patient increased with the geometric index. It plateaued after the *R0* 15-16 summit in Spain and Italy. If the *R0* curve, which flattens and tends to decrease, falls below 1, it is understood that the epidemic is about to end “under control”. There is also a “SIR model” that describes the population-transmission relationship developed since the Spanish flu in three groups (*S*, healthy people with potential to get sick; *I*, those who are infected and contagious; *R*, those who become immune / die by recovering). Here, as *I* increase, R0 also increases (BBC, 20/5/2020).

Cooper et al (2020) developed the classical SIR model that can accommodate fluctuations in the susceptible population. Their SIR model is based on a simple three-order differential equation (ODE) system, identical to the classical SIR model, which can be easily applied and used to better understand how the COVID-19 virus spreads in populations of variable populations around the world. The model here is designed to usefully remove, both quantitatively and qualitatively, many of the complexities associated with the real-time evolution of virus spread. It is a dynamic system given by three combined ODEs that describe the time evolution of the following three populations:

1. *Susceptible individuals, S (t):* These are people who are not infected but can become infected.
2. *Infected individuals, I (t):* These are people who have already been infected by the virus and can transmit it to susceptible persons.
3. *Removed individuals, Rm (t):* These are individuals who have recovered from the virus and are presumed immune, with Rm (t) or deceased, D (t). Based on these assumptions, the rates of change of the three populations are governed by the following ODE system, which creates the SIR model used in this study, where *a* and *b* are real, positive, parameters of the initial exponential growth and final exponential decay of the infected population *I*.

According to this SIR model of Cooper et al, the rate of increase in the number of infections depends on the product of the number of infected and susceptible individuals. Above eq. explains the staggering increase in the infection rate around the world. During a surge period, millions infected people traveling around the world has led to the increase in infected numbers and this results in a further increase in the susceptible population. This has given rise to a positive feedback loop leading to a very rapid rise in the number of active infected cases as a finding of this model.

Moein, et al (2021), after drawing attention to the alternative SEIR (Susceptible-Exposed-Infectious-Recovered) model, joined the discussion of SIR-based models through a study they conducted for Iran and explaining the failure of these models to predict the COVID-19 pandemic for the following reasons: First, the oversimplified SIR models ignore some factors that have a major impact on the course of the disease, such as socio-cultural behavior change and air pollution. Second, modeling is based on assumptions that are not necessarily correct because while in these models the population was considered closed, most regions did not follow complete isolation, making them vulnerable to changes in neighboring communities. Third, it is assumed that recovered individuals have been vaccinated in SIR models that are no longer susceptible, which contradicts recent findings suggesting that there is a possibility of reactivation of the virus or reinfection of previously infected individuals. The authors say that the pandemic characteristics are not compatible with the SIR modeling framework, and the dynamics of this epidemic are under the influence of various parameters for which quantitative information is not yet available. According to their suggestion, more sophisticated modeling approaches compatible with more precise epidemiological and biomedical data are urgently needed to predict the pandemic well.

COVID-19 SCALE

Whatever the benefit of a pandemic killing people, the "net damage" it causes is always enormous, and COVID-19 is no exception. If the major damages and small benefits of COVID-19 are put in two separate panes, the harm side of the scale will undoubtedly suffer (Figure 1).

People in every country and in Turkey were quarantined with the slogan "Life Fits in the House" ("Hayat Eve Sığar", HES, in Turkish) and put serious distances from business, street, education and entertainment activities as a result of the constant official warnings against the fear of the COVID-19 epidemic and the psychology of the transmission. While the people staying at home were bored on the one hand, they also had the opportunity to get closer to their nuclear family.

Figure 1. Social benefits and losses of Covıd-19

Source: Author's. (See also: Ratten, 2020; Walque et al, 2020; Shah, et al, 2020; Qian and Fan, 2020; Kim and Katelyn, 2021.)

Note: The author has created this metaphor of scales based on his personal observations and opinions that can be adapted to many countries of the world, starting from his own country.

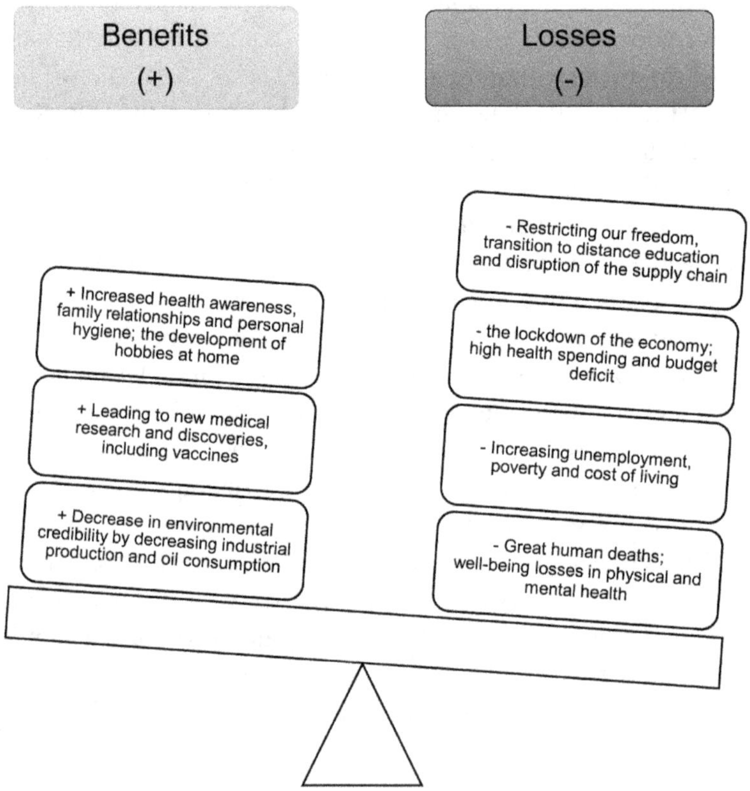

During this period: i- It was seen that family fights, unwanted pregnancies and divorce decisions constituted the "opportunity-alternative costs" of the quarantine. ii- As another development, oil consumption and carbon emissions that pollute the environment / air decreased while limiting intercity and urban transportation. iii- While cleaning products are frequently used, the importance of cleaning has updated and as the consumption of masks increases, its production has turned into a serious sub-sector. iv- While the supply supply chain in the economy deteriorated, the social health chain was strengthened. v- As unemployment and impoverishment increased, unemployment insurance fund, short employment allowances, and "people's municipality" were put into action, as well as "national solidarity campaigns". vi- As fear and panic grew, so did government-community cooperation to seek and build trust. vii- Medical drugs and equipment were used excessively in health institutions that were declared "pandemic hospitals" for infected patients. viii- The resulting gigantic viral dump was presented to the recycling of nature in a way that threatens sustainable growth / development, which is very closely related to the lives of future generations (how much soil and water is contaminated will be determined later).

On the other hand, some epidemiologists say that in this catastrophic conjuncture, half of the world's population may be infected with this virus and 2% of the world's population may die. Some economic-political experts also observe and compare which states autocratically hide cases (declaring them openly in a democratic way), which ones are insufficient (adequate) to take precautions, or which countries' health and financial systems collapse (remain intact) during the COVID-19 process (Wyplosz, 2020).

Figure 2. Five types of distance to Covıd-19
Source: Author's.

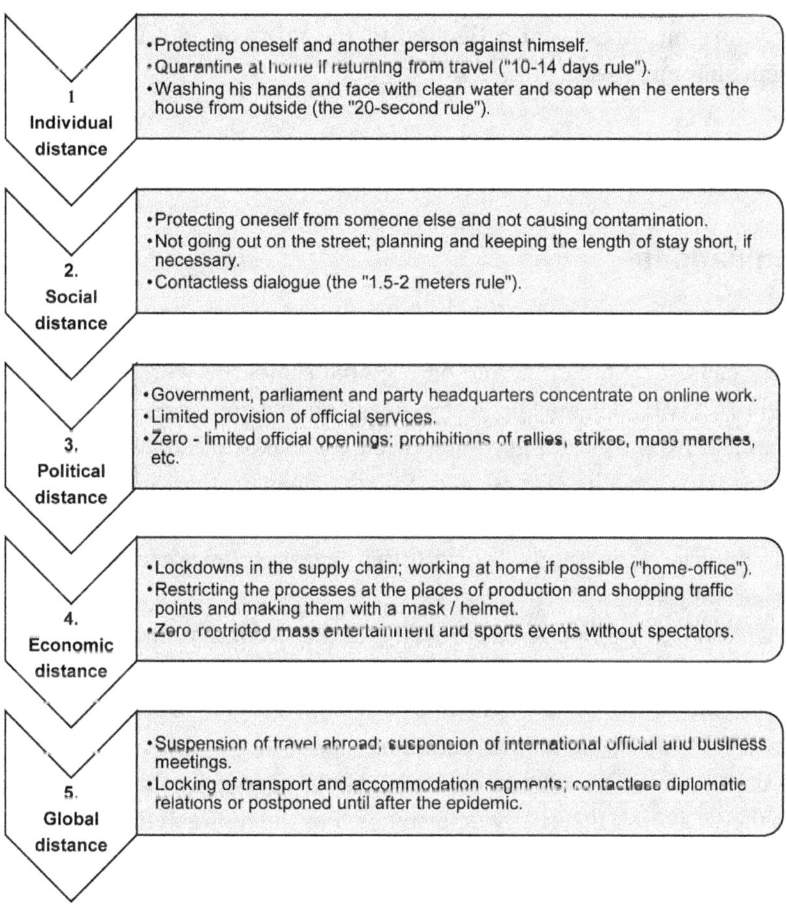

In the first year of the epidemic, the socio-economic and economic-political response of developed countries, such as those of developing and underdeveloped countries, was not homogeneous, but in this second year, the reactions began to resemble. Among them, there are still countries that show more positive and more negative political economy behaviors and that are marginal with this feature. In the beginning, the states that had to open their customs gates to the virus with the effect of globalization blamed China for being the homeland of the virus, but now every society has accepted the reality of the virus on a material and moral level, and they are accustomed to national policies, although they sometimes find it unpleasant and unnecessary.

With the assumption that the 2nd / 3rd and other waves of the COVID-19 epidemic may emerge, at this stage where the "abnormal" situation is transitioning to the "new normalization" state, the "various distances" formed during the epidemic process (Figure 2) are continuing and also the new economic- political costs are encountered.

On the other hand, the epidemic process has also led to the emergence of different theses. A Table (1) regarding some theses, antitheses and their synthesis regarding the target, origin, spread and reflection of the virus on international integration movements has emerged.

CONCLUSION

Determinations

There is an ironic situation: Given the high loss of life and economic-political instability caused by the epidemic on a global scale, the workforce in China, the epicenter of COVID-19, may be "very cheap" and its goods may be of poor quality, but the spread from this country ('imported') The cost of the virus to the world is "quite expensive" and its effects seem to be permanent for a long time. It will not be right to upload the entire cost to China during the epidemic process, because modern countries that cannot act with the necessary awareness and precautions have a share in this.

The COVID-19 pandemic has proven that the strength of a chain is as strong as the strength of the weakest link. It was understood that not only the underdeveloped countries of the world, but even the most developed regions such as North America and Western Europe were helpless and not very strong in the face of the "invisible enemy" corona virus. No matter how strong all the other links that make up the chain are, it is the weak link that really determines. For the moment the weak link breaks away, all the other strong links have neither meaning nor any function.

Table 1. Target, source and spread of COVID-19: theses, antitheses and synthesis

	→	←	↔
Event / Phenomenon	*Theses*	*Anti-theses*	*Synthesis*
Target of the Virus	The virus (Sars2-nCoV) targeted everyone regardless of age, gender and class	Virus mostly targeted at immunocompromised male adults and under-nourished poor class, rather than children	The virus and its transformation into an epidemic may have led to a suspicion of selectivity in the target.
Source of the Virus	The virus may have originated naturally, but it certainly originated in China because it spread from there and began to shake the world. According to one claim, the Chinese government should pay compensation for causing global disaster by neglecting to inform the world early.	It may originate from China, but this is not what he desires. Moreover, he lost thousands of people as a society. If the compensation is to be paid, the big and wealthy Western countries that have globalized China should also pay, and they should make this payment primarily to poor and underdeveloped countries.	Establish an international pandemic fund: One of the financial resources should be the reduction of armament expenditures. Let the financiers be Western capitalist states, especially China, Russia and the USA, and the petro-dollar rich Arab states. Because they usually transfer the blessings of globalization to themselves and their burdens to poor and underdeveloped countries.
Spread of the Virus	The virus spread through contact, tourism, and negligence of cleanliness. If the virus is out, it will spread and this is inevitable.	Now that the ways the virus spreads are known, serious and sustainable bans had to be imposed. Foreign travels should be stopped, and quarantines, lack of contact and cleaning measures should be implemented before the virus arrives at our door.	In a globalizing world, it is difficult to prevent tourism immediately, but determination could be shown in quarantine / isolation.
Reflection to International Integration Movements	International integration movements such as the EU and the Shanghai Cooperation Organization (SCO) can be loosened and disintegrated. Brexit examples could multiply in the EU.	In fact, in such global health crises, international cooperation will increase at the institutional / organizational level. It was seen that the bombs and missiles of military organizations (NATO, SCO, etc.) were helpless against COVID-19.	Outbreaks and crises are testing and breaking points for integrated structures. Regional strategic organizations should also be reconstructed to combat such future epidemics.

Source: Author created this.

Predictions

The world, which has experienced both hot war and cold war periods in the last century, has entered a "warm war" period, this time with the COVID-19 epidemic. According to this prediction, where the "unknown" is known, the world may shift from various good (democratic) situations to oppressive-bad (autocratic) situations in areas such as socio-cultural, economic-political, diplomatic.

In the context of the national defense-external security problem, COVID-19 has shown that the enemy can enter the borders as a virus and / or biological weapon instead of "conventional weapons" (soldiers, gun-rifles, fighter jets) and nuclear missiles. From now on, assuming that a similar hazard is always possible, every country should plan and provide in advance the production and distribution of emergency products such as adequate masks, respirators, disinfectants.

On the other hand, according to a narrative review prepared by Hasnain et al (2020) based on dozens of studies on the COVID-19 epidemic, its spread in Wuhan, where the epidemic first started in China, was controlled by combined measures, and some of these measures were even taken as an example for the United States and Europe. In this context, the following findings/recommendations were obtained: i-Quarantine may need to be an international priority, along with combined measures to reduce fatal human casualties. ii- High surveillance and appropriate biosecurity procedures should be used in public and private institutions conducting virus research. iii- Collaboration between domestic and foreign health stakeholders in developed and developing countries can be enhanced by providing them with more resources to pursue high-quality and competitive research in accordance with pandemic-related public health standards. iv- Diagnosis and treatment methods for the epidemic should be used according to quality standards as well as a regulatory framework.

Suggestions

In particular, some contemporary states have been subjected to populist solidarity and beggar criticisms that can evolve into a nationalist political demonstration by collecting money from the public through donation campaigns during the epidemic process. Central banks should print money[4] against these criticisms and the astronomical costs of the epidemic and transfer money to households and small-weak businesses according to fair criteria, thus contributing to social-economic state practice.

This epidemic process has drawn our attention to the need to restore the free, transparent and independent identity of the media called "4th force" against false, biased and incomplete information (disinformation). Judging by the protests in and outside of China[5], it is clear that the public pays the bill for hiding the epidemic crisis from the public.

"Virus-microbe literacy" issues[6] should be explained in schools in terms of meeting the epidemic process and new medical terminology.

Governments should refrain from increasing the type, amount and rate of taxes on the pretext of the epidemic crisis. If the public health is disrupted by this financial maneuver of the government, on the grounds of democracy and justice, that government party should not have the luxury of taking power again in the first elections.

International integration organizations such as the EU should be redesigned not only in terms of economic, political and military content, but also in terms of health-medical equipment. Such a developed design would make it possible for member countries and the other countries they will help to suffer less losses against this and possible future outbreaks. Given the extraordinary adverse effects of COVID-19, it is clear that military weapons can never be more powerful than medical weapons against epidemics.

REFERENCES

Aktan, S. (2020). Tarihteki en ölümcül salgın hastalıklar neden ortaya çıktı ve nasıl sona erdi? *Euornews.* https://tr.euronews.com/2020/05/12/tarihteki-en-olumcul-salginlar-hangileriydi-neden-olustular-ve-nasil-sona-erdiler

Bagus, P., Peña-Ramos, J. A., & Sánchez-Bayón, A. (2021). A. COVID-19 and the Political Economy of Mass Hysteria. *International Journal of Environmental Research and Public Health, 18*(4), 1376. doi:10.3390/ijerph18041376 PMID:33546144

Barbieri, P. N., & Bonini, B. (2021). Political orientation and adherence to social distancing during the COVID-19 pandemic in Italy. *Economics and Politics, 38*(2), 483–504. doi:10.100740888-021-00224-w

Baum, F., Freeman, T., Musolino, C., Abramovitz, M., De Ceukelaire, W., Flavel, J., Friel, S., Giugliani, C., Howden-Chapman, P., Huong, N. T., London, L., McKee, M., Popay, J., Serag, H., & Villar, E. (2021). Explaining COVID-19 performance: What factors might predict national responses? *BMJ (Clinical Research Ed.), 372*, n91. Advance online publication. doi:10.1136/bmj.n91 PMID:33509924

BBC. (2020). *Virüs bulaştırma katsayısı R0 nedir, nasıl hesaplanır?* bbc.com/turkce/haberler-dunya-52197229

Bergsen, P. (2020). A new political economy for Europe post-COVID-19. *European View., 19*(2), 131–137. doi:10.1177/1781685820968301

Boettke, P., & Powell, B. (2021). The political economy of the COVID-19 pandemic. *Southern Economic Journal*, *87*(4), 1090–1106. doi:10.1002oej.12488 PMID:33821055

Bump, J. B., Baum, F., Sakornsin, M., Yates, R., & Hofman, K. (2021). Political economy of COVID-19: Extractive, regressive, competitive. *BMJ (Clinical Research Ed.)*, n73. Advance online publication. doi:10.1136/bmj.n73 PMID:33483317

Convay, E. (2018). Gerçekten Bilmeniz Gereken 50 Ekonomi Fikri. İstanbul: Domingo Yayınevi.

Cooper, I., Mondal, A., & Antonopoulos, C. G. (2020). A SIR model assumption for the spread of COVID-19 in different communities. *Chaos, Solitons, and Fractals*, *139*, 110057. doi:10.1016/j.chaos.2020.110057 PMID:32834610

Hasnain, M., Paşa, M. F., & Gani, I. (2020). Combined measures to control the COVID-19 pandemic in Wuhan, Hubei, China: A narrative review. *Journal of Biosafety and Biosecurity.*, *2*(2), 51–57. doi:10.1016/j.jobb.2020.10.001 PMID:33521592

Hendrix, C. S. (2021). *The Political Economy of Pandemic Preparedness and Effectiveness.* PIIE Working Paper.

Kaplan, S., Lefler, J., & Zilberman, D. (2021). The political economy of COVID-19. *Applied Economic Perspectives and Policy*, 1–12. doi:10.1002/aepp.13164 PMID:34230850

Kayhan, M. (2020). İnsanlık Tarihinin Seyrini Değiştiren 11 Salgın Hastalık. *Arkeofili.* https://arkeofili.com/insanlik-tarihinin-seyrini-degistiren-11-salgin-hastalik/

Kim, H. H.-S., & Katelyn Kim, H.-J. (2021). Income inequality, emotional anxiety, and self-rated health in times of the coronavirus pandemic: Evidence from a cross-national survey. *Research in Social Stratification and Mobility*, *75*, 100640. Advance online publication. doi:10.1016/j.rssm.2021.100640 PMID:34385741

Lipscy, P. Y. (2020). *COVID-19 and the Politics of Crisis.* Cambridge University Press. doi:10.1017/S0020818320000375

Moein, S., Nickaeen, N., Roointan, A., Borhani, N., Heidary, Z., Javanmard, S. H., Ghaisari, J., & Gheisari, Y. (2021). Inefficiency of SIR models in forecasting COVID-19 epidemic: A case study of Isfahan. *Scientific Reports*, *11*(1), 4725. doi:10.103841598-021-84055-6 PMID:33633275

Phiri, M. Z. (2021). *South Africa's COVID-19 Responses: Unmaking the Political Economy of Health Inequalities. ORF Issue Brief 445*. Observer Research Foundation.

Qian, Y., & Fan, W. (2020). Who loses income during the COVID-19 outbreak? Evidence from China. *Research in Social Stratification and Mobility*, *68*, 100522. Advance online publication. doi:10.1016/j.rssm.2020.100522

Ratten, V. (2020). *Coronavirus (COVID-19) and social value co-creation. International Journal of Sociology and Social Policy*. doi:10.1108/IJSSP-06-2020-0237

Shah, G.H., Shankar, P., Schwind, J.S., & Sittaramane, V. (2020). The Detrimental Impact of the COVID-19 Crisis on Health Equity and Social Determinants of Health. *Journal of Public Health Management and Practice*, *26*(4). doi:10.1097/PHH.0000000000001200

Smith, J., Davies, S. E., Feng, H., Gan, C. C. R., Grépin, K. A., Harman, S., Herten-Crabb, A., Morgan, R., Vandan, N., & Wenham, C. (2021). More than a public health crisis: A feminist political economic analysis of COVID-19. *Global Public Health: An International Journal for Research, Policy and Practice*, *16*(8-9), 1364–1380. Advance online publication. doi:10.1080/17441692.2021.1896765 PMID:33705248

Tunçdemir, C. (2020). Çin'e virüs komplosunu kim kurdu? *T24*.

Walque, D., Friedman, J., Gatti, R., & Mattoo, A. (2020, April). How Two Tests Can Help Contain COVID-19 and Revive the Economy. *Research & Policy Briefs*, (29), 8. doi:10.1596/33583

WHO. (2021). *WHO Coronavirus disease (COVID-19) pandemic*. https:// www.who.int/ emergencies/diseases/novel-coronavirus-2019

Wyplosz, C. (2020). The good thing about Coronavirus. In Economics in the Time of COVID-19. CEPR Press.

ADDITIONAL READING

Ajbar, A., Alqahtani, R. T., & Boumaza, M. (2021). Dynamics of an SIR-Based COVID-19 Model With Linear Incidence Rate, Nonlinear Removal Rate, and Public Awareness. *Frontiers in Physics*, *9*, 634251. doi:10.3389/fphy.2021.634251

Alanazi, S. A., Kamruzzaman, M. M., Alruwaili, M., Alshammari, N., Alqahtani, S. A., & Karime, A. (2020). Measuring and Preventing COVID-19 Using the SIR Model and Machine Learning in Smart Health Care. *Hindawi -. Journal of Healthcare Engineering*, *2020*, 1–12. Advance online publication. doi:10.1155/2020/8857346 PMID:33204404

Bernards, N. (2021). COVID-19 and the International Political Economy of Risk and Resilience. *Global Perspectives*, *2*(1), 23665. doi:10.1525/gp.2021.23665

Telles, R. C., Lopes, H., & Franco, D. (2021). SARS-COV-2: SIR Model Limitations and Predictive Constraints. *Symmetry*, *13*(4), 676. doi:10.3390ym13040676

KEY TERMS AND DEFINITIONS

COVID-19: New type of corona virus disease that emerged in China at the end of 2019.

COVID-19 Scale: A prototype political economy approach, developed for this text that compares the good and bad effects of the coronavirus disease.

Global Health Security Index (GHSI): It is the first comprehensive assessment and benchmarking of health security and related capabilities across the 195 countries that make up the States Parties to the International Health Regulations (IHR, 2005; see https://www.ghsindex.org/)

New Normalization: Returning to the pre-epidemic by loosening the restrictions applied to control the epidemic.

Political Economy: As a derivative of moral philosophy, the discipline that studies the relationship of production, consumption, and commerce with law and the state.

Third World War: Ironic analogy for COVID-19 for its potentially quite dire global implications.

Twin Crises: A deadly public health crisis and a recession-type economic crisis that countries experience simultaneously due to COVID-19.

Virus-Microbe Literacy: Learning scientific-technical concepts that need to be known for the diagnosis and treatment of germ-virus-borne diseases systematically (lecture or seminar) in or out of school.

ENDNOTES

1 Corona means "crown" originating from Latin.

2 The first was the Typhus-Athens plague presumably BC, let alone the ones dating back to the 11th century, since the 12th century there have been many global epidemics that resulted in mass deaths of different bacterial (b) and viral (v) origin (some of them repeat at other times. should not forget): Flower (v, 12th c.); Lepra (b, 13th c.); Black Plague (b / v, 14th c.); Syphilis (b, 15th c.); Dysentery (b / v, 16th c.); Tuberculosis (b, 17th c.); Cholera (b, 19-20th c.); Typhus (World War I); Spanish flu (v, after WWI); Crimean Congo Hemorrhagic Fever (19th c., 2011); HIV / AIDS (v, 20th c.); Ebola (1976), H5N1-Avian flu (2005-2008; H1N1-Swine flu (2009); Deli Dana (1987, 2015); SARS (v, 2003); MERS (v, 2012); Zika (v, 2015) Bacterial outbreaks were treated with antibiotics, viral outbreaks with vaccine + mixed drugs (see Aktan 2020; Kayhan 2020).

3 T. Malthus, one of the classical economists of the 18th century, stated that the human population increased geometrically (exponentially 2, 4, 16, 32) and food resources increased by arithmetic index (2, 4, 6, 10, etc.) and therefore natural (drought and epidemic).) or artificial (such as war) methods, if birth rates are not reduced, hunger and poverty will be encountered. This thesis is known as the "Malthusian trap" and it was put forward when the world population was not even 1 billion. According to those who try to refute this view, the world population, which will reach 9 billion in 2050, does not increase geometrically, it tends to stabilize after a certain point, and thanks to advanced technology, births decrease as prosperity increases. In addition, although this thesis gives the New Malthusians the idea that the apocalypse was postponed for several centuries (Conway 2018), it still continues to draw attention to the danger of excessive consumption to states and societies against underproduction.

4 It can be argued that the central bank's printing of money in this context will not pose an inflationary risk as it will not pump excessive demand or expenditure. In addition, it can be thought that printing money is a more rational option than borrowing to the IMF, making monetary swaps, buying dollars from the FED, or domestic borrowing of the treasury through open market operations (bond sales).

5 Much of the dramatic bill the world has paid during the COVID-19 process is based on the mistakes (including not notifying WHO in a timely manner) that China made during the SARS virus outbreak in 2003 but promised not to repeat once again. According to Tunçdemir (2020), some of these mistakes are as follows: The prosecution of the doctor who first saw and explained the danger in China; attempting the world record for mass catering; declaring that

transmission is not transmitted from person to person at the beginning; wasting time with a perception operation that the Chinese economy was conspired and a biological war started because it was a rival to the United States; late engagement of the central communist authority; most importantly, the censorship of the media that wants to publish the truth by law enforcement.

6 During this period, the following medical terminology filled the public's agenda: For example; nCoV, infected, infectious, pandemic, endemic, filection, algorithm, virology, N95 mask, pcr test kit, intube, social distance, peak, isolation, quarantine, disefenktan, plasma transplantation, antibody, etc. If noticed, almost all of these words are foreign; the disease itself is also foreign. However, globalization has epidemicized COVID-19, and the epidemic and the words related to it have become "national" enough to cost everyone, regardless of the nation, religion and language.

Chapter 2
Your Money or Your Life: Microeconomic Lessons From the Pandemic

Nancy Ruth Fox
Saint Joseph's University, USA

ABSTRACT

The pandemic offers numerous applications of very basic microeconomics concepts and their extension to other aspects of economic life. It also creates an opportunity for better understanding of how the market works and its effects on the economy and society. Allocation of a scarce resource is the definition of economics. There have been countless examples of scarcity (toilet paper, vaccines). How do we decide how to allocate those goods, especially when the market fails? The pandemic is a classic illustration of tradeoffs. In particular, there are tradeoffs between shutting (or re-opening) the economy and loss of human life; a rational decision would compare the costs and the benefits. Lastly, there are countless examples of the unequal economic effects of the virus and their implications for public policy.

INTRODUCTION

Much of the media coverage, as well as most scholarly research about COVID-19, focuses on the macroeconomic effects, especially unemployment, recession, and economic recovery. This is not surprising, given the unprecedented and global impact of the virus. The author believes that these are not the most interesting economic topics related to the pandemic. There are numerous applications of very basic microeconomic concepts and their extension to other aspects of economic life,

DOI: 10.4018/978-1-7998-6900-9.ch002

as well as the opportunity for better understanding of how the market works and its effects on the economy and society.

In this chapter, the author analyzes three microeconomic applications of the pandemic. Part I is a discussion of the allocation of a scarce resource, *the* definition of economics. The pandemic provides examples of how the market can do this when it should not, which expands and changes the meaning of scarcity. Part II is an analysis of tradeoffs. In particular, there are tradeoffs between shutting (or re-opening) the economy and loss of human life; a rational decision maker would compare the costs and the benefits. Part III is a discussion of how the pandemic has affected certain sectors of the economy more profoundly than others and intensified existing income inequality.

ALLOCATION OF A SCARCE RESOURCE

Shortages in the Early Days of the Pandemic

Economics is fundamentally about the allocation of scarce resources. During the early days of the pandemic, there was a significant increase in demand for many items—Clorox wipes, masks, and meat. The item that grabbed the headlines was toilet paper. With an increase in demand for toilet paper used at home, a shortage developed.

Unlike many other goods that were hard to find, there is really no substitute for toilet paper on the demand side. On the supply side, the production of residential toilet paper is much different from the production of toilet paper for commercial use, such as in retail establishments and offices. The excess supply of toilet paper for commercial use could not be used to meet increased at-home demand, creating a shortage (Nyugen, 2020).

If the market had adjusted as expected, we would have seen an increase in the prices of goods whose demand increased, because at the pre-pandemic price, the quantity demanded was bigger than the quantity supplied—an economist's definition of a shortage. At a higher, market price, there would be no shortage, as defined by economists—firms could sell all their goods at that price, and consumers who were willing and able (often skipped in economic texts), could buy the good at that price. Many people call this "price gouging," raising prices in times of crisis and taking advantage of the situation. There have been examples, such as eggs selling in some places for three times the pre-pandemic price (Garcia and Vanek Smith, 2020). Many states have laws that forbid price gouging, which were enforced with significant financial penalties (Garcia and Vanek Smith, 2020).

Many stores used rationing (and still do on some items), and many people's initial reaction is that rationing is fair. But that is far from obvious. Is it fair that a person who lives alone can buy the same amount of toilet paper in one trip as her neighbor, where four people live? The neighbors need more toilet paper than the person who lives alone. A market solution would allow her neighbors to pay more for more toilet paper and to buy as much as they wanted (and could afford). When toilet paper is rationed, the neighbor must make more trips to the store to get enough, creating more risk of exposure to the virus. More fundamentally, rationing and other non-market methods of allocating scarce resources do not solve the basic problem—there is still a shortage. Allowing the price to adjust upwards creates an incentive for firms to find and/or produce more of the good.

Nobel Laureate Richard Thaler noted that the laws of supply and demand have not applied in many cases during the pandemic. In particular, he observed that large retail chains did not raise prices in response to dramatic increases in demand. His explanation was "summed up with a single word, one you won't find in the standard supply-and-demand models: fairness. Basically, it just isn't socially acceptable to raise prices in an emergency" (Thaler, May, 2020). He believes this type of behavior is part of these firms' business model. "In the current crisis, large retail chains have responded to the shortages of toilet paper not by raising the price but by limiting the amount each customer can buy. And Amazon and eBay prohibited what was viewed as price gouging on their sites" (Thaler, May, 2020).

He illustrates with the following example:

As soon as a storm ends, there is typically enormous demand for goods like bottled water and plywood. Big retailers like Home Depot and Walmart anticipate this, sending trucks loaded with supplies to regions just outside the danger zone, ready to be deployed. Then, when it is safe, the stores provide water for free and sell the plywood at the list price or lower. (Thaler, May 2020)

This is in contrast to the behavior of what Thaler calls "entrepreneurs." Two brothers in Tennessee bought up huge quantities of hand sanitizer at the beginning of the pandemic with the intention of selling them to the highest bidder. They avoided prosecution (but not public shaming) when they agreed to donate their supply (Vigdor, 2020).

Higher prices serve a purpose—they create an incentive for firms to supply more and consumers to buy less. Anti-price gouging laws, which limit large price increases in times of crisis, can contribute to hoarding. With artificially low prices and no rationing, consumers who are shopping on a first come, first served basis have an incentive to buy more.

How to Allocate the Scarce Resource: The Vaccine

In early 2021, the scarce resource in the news is the vaccine.[1] Although eventually there will be enough to vaccinate the 80-85% of the population necessary to eradicate the virus, there was not even close to enough when the FDA first authorized the vaccine for emergency use.[2] Federal officials estimate that there will be enough doses of the vaccine for one-third of Americans by late February 2021 (Silberner, 2020).

This is a classic example of the problem of allocating a scarce resource. People seemed quick to agree that a market solution (whoever is willing and able to pay the highest price) was not appropriate. It is difficult to think of any other good or service where this is true, where ability to pay is not the determining factor in acquiring a good across the board. Covid testing might be the closest example. There were promises of "free Covid testing." Demand exceeded supply, and people lined up for hours at testing sites. Schools were closed because there was not enough testing available, and it took a long time to get results (Thompson, 2020). In January 2021, Philadelphia reported testing at about 143 tests per 100,000 people daily. In order to achieve the suppression target, "using testing to catch outbreaks before they happen…" would have required 1,951 daily tests per 100,000, according to a tool designed by experts at the Brown University School of Public Health and the Harvard Global Health Institute (Piper, 2021).

Yet in June 2020, the NBA was able to test every "player and essential team staff" every other day so that they could make sure that no one entered the Orlando "bubble" who had the virus (Grasso, 2020). They claimed that they would be able to test the NBA players without decreasing the number of tests available to others. "The NBA has partnered with Quest Diagnostics to provide the tests and has assured that the tests the league use (*sic*) won't take away from the tests necessary for front-line health care workers, first responders or symptomatic patients in each team's city" (Bontemps and Lowe, 2020). But the principle of scarcity, as well as the documented shortage of tests, says otherwise. The NBA was able to obtain the tests because of its financial resources—resources that many schools and other organizations did not have access to. In this sense, the scarce resource of Covid testing was, to some extent, allocated by the market mechanism.

What is distinct about the vaccine? Perhaps the pandemic has finally enlightened the general public about the economic concept of externalities. If the person in line at the grocery store has Covid, you might catch it. And while higher income might make that more difficult (with sufficient resources, you could pay someone to buy your groceries or have them delivered so you don't have to stand next to someone in line), unless you stay home and never venture out, there is a chance you could get sick.

You don't have to care about the person in line at the grocery story to want them to get vaccinated; you only have to care about your own health, an example of acting in one's self-interest. We don't have to appeal to principles of Catholic Social Teaching that health care is a basic human right to advocate for universal and free vaccination against Covid (Wilde and Van Eshenbach, 2020). Covid may be the most dramatic example of externalities, but it is puzzling that we don't see that awareness to other aspects of health care.

There are currently two incentives to get the vaccine. The first is self-interest; the Pfizer vaccine is 95 percent effective in preventing the individual from getting sick from Covid (CDC, 2020). The second incentive is to achieve the 80-85 percent coverage that will enable the country to re-open, an example of externalities. A possible third incentive will be true if scientists can show that a person who is vaccinated cannot infect someone else, another example of externalities.

But there is another problem. Even though private and government health insurance will cover the cost of the vaccine (Schwartz et al., 2020), some people are reluctant to get vaccinated. They fear that the development and approval were rushed and are concerned about possible short-term and long-term side effects (Neergaard and Fingerhut, 2020). But in order for the vaccine to eradicate the virus, at least 80-85 percent of the population must be vaccinated (Jagannathan, 2020).

Pay People to Take the Vaccine?

The basic economic principle that people respond to incentives can help to solve this problem. Economist N. Gregory Mankiw describes a proposal to pay people to get vaccinated. "Immunology, meet economics. One of the first principles of economics—perhaps the most important—is that people respond to incentives. Applying this principle to the case at hand, Mr. Litan recommends that the government pay $1,000 to whoever gets the vaccine. With a large enough incentive, most Americans are likely to get vaccinated (Mankiw, 2020)." At first glance, it appears to be a clever and likely effective solution. But upon deeper examination, there are several concerns.

First, many people will get the vaccine because the incentive of being immune is sufficient, so paying them $1,000 is a waste of taxpayer money. Their reservation price is much lower (perhaps zero) than others who have concerns. These people, who would take the vaccine for free, would earn the largest consumer surplus from this payment. There is little incentive for anyone to admit they would get the vaccine without getting the $1,000.

More troubling, however, is that $1,000 will most likely not convince a millionaire to get the vaccine who does not otherwise want to, but it is most likely enough for someone who has not been employed for seven months. Making voluntary decisions is a hallmark of the market; one could make the case that the person who is unemployed is not making a free choice. This also shows how the pandemic has had an unequal effect on people by income level (see Part III).

In a response to Mankiw's article, George Loewenstein and Cynthia Cryder (2020) write that the incentive mechanism could "backfire." In a reference to *Tom Sawyer*, they found "when people aren't sure whether something is good or bad, the prospect of payment helps them decide, in the negative." (Loewenstein and Cryder, 2020). In other words, there must be something wrong with the vaccine if the government must persuade people to get it with what is essentially a bribe. "Paying people to be vaccinated might, similarly, lead them to infer that it is riskier than they would otherwise assume." (Loewenstein and Cryder, 2020).

There is yet another application of basic economics to the pandemic. In a market, people are assumed to make rational decisions, which depends on having accurate information. That certainly has not been the case since the beginning of the pandemic. Politicians and doctors contradicted accepted, legitimate science and told the public that masks don't work (or even, that you can get Covid because you are wearing a mask) and have touted doubtful or even dangerous treatments. There is significant misinformation about the vaccine as well (Factcheck.org, 2020).

"In addition to making the vaccine seem riskier, payments might also make people less likely to get vaccinated for the selfless goal of helping others." (Loewenstein and Cryder, 2020). There is a vast literature on what we can or should put a price on, what we can "commodify."[3] Though there is solid research that the vaccine is very effective in protecting the person who is vaccinated, there is no definitive evidence (yet) on whether it protects others (Jagannathan, 2020). If research ultimately shows that the Covid vaccine protects only the person who has the inoculation, then this externality does not apply, and there is no reason to consider altruism as in incentive to get the vaccine. But there is another application of externalities to the vaccine. Dr. Anthony Fauci says we need 80-85% of the population to be vaccinated in order to eradicate the virus (Jagannathan, 2020). In that sense, getting the vaccine benefits the individual directly and the common good indirectly. Paying someone to get the vaccine corrupts the altruistic reason to get it. [4]

Trader Joe's, Instacart, and Dollar General announced in January 2021 that they would pay employees to take the vaccination. The pay is typically under $100 and is viewed as compensation for time missed to get the vaccine. "'Our goal with the introduction of our new Vaccine Support Stipend is to ensure that, when the time comes, Instacart shoppers don't have to choose between earning income as an essential service provider or getting vaccinated,' (Instacart CEO) Mehta said" (Snider, 2021).

Epidemiologists have been consistent (after the early days of the pandemic) that masks help stop the spread of Covid (Schumaker, 2020). The president of the United States does not have authority to impose a national mask mandate (Subramaniam, 2020). During the campaign, then-candidate Biden said, "First, I'll go to every governor and urge them to mandate mask-wearing in their states. And if they refuse, I'll go to the mayors and county executives and get local masking requirements in place nationwide (Subramaniam, 2020)." Governors do have authority to issue mask mandates and 37 have imposed them, as of November 2020. (Schumaker, 2020).

More extensive mask wearing could also help the economy. According to an economic analysis of U.S. data that the Centers for Disease Control and Prevention highlighted, "Increasing universal masking by 15% could prevent the need for lockdowns and reduce associated losses of up to $1 trillion or about 5% of gross domestic product." (Schumaker, 2020).

As of December 2020, the federal government had purchased several hundred million doses of the vaccine (Health and Human Services, December 11 and December 23, 2020), which it will distribute to the states, another application of allocation of scarce resources. The economics principle that people respond to incentives may provide a way to increase mask mandates. With a nod to Jonathan Swift's *A Modest Proposal*, what if President Biden made distribution of the vaccine to each state contingent on the governor's instating a mask mandate? This may sound unethical, but it employs the concept of response to incentive to achieve the common good.

Pay College Students to Follow Covid Guidelines on Campus?

When college students returned to campus (if they did) for the Fall 2020 semester, there was considerable concern about whether they would follow the mitigation behavior that would be required. Psychologists who study adolescent behavior issued warnings over the summer of 2020.

Most types of risky behavior — reckless driving, criminal activity, fighting, unsafe sex and binge drinking, to name just a few — peak during the late teens and early 20s. Moreover, interventions designed to diminish risk-taking in this age group, such as attempts to squelch binge drinking on campus, have an underwhelming track record. There is little reason to think that the approaches proposed to mitigate transmission of the coronavirus among college students will fare any better (Steinberg, 2020).

In anticipation of this sort of behavior, colleges appealed to students' concern for the common good for compliance (Lederer and Stolow, 2020). In anticipation that this approach may not be successful, they also included penalties, some as harsh as suspension, for violating the rules. In the beginning of the Fall 2020 semester, students at Syracuse and Northwestern University were suspended for violating university COVID-19 protocols (Smith, 2020).

Not only was this remedy disruptive to the students' academic careers, it was costly, as schools were not willing to refund tuition (Smith, 2020). Perhaps more significant, this penalty was *reactive* to behavior that most likely had caused significant health and safety damage. The concept that people respond to incentives provides a *pro-active* alternative, one that could have prevented the behavior in the first place.

On campuses with regular Covid testing, offer a financial reward to students for testing negative. This could be accomplished in a number of ways—a reward for each negative test, an end of semester (larger) reward for consistently testing negative, or a mid- and end-of-semester reward. These types of programs could prevent spread and lower costs of outbreaks (Jayachandran, 2020). Rewards for healthy behavior are not uncommon; for example, companies offer financial rewards to employees who exercise regularly (Jayachandran, 2020).

Jumping the Vaccine Line

As of January 2021, only the federal government was able to purchase the vaccine from the manufacturers. (There is no indication so far that this will change in the coming months.) The federal government distributes the vaccines to states, which determine the order in which the vaccine is administered, based on need (health), risk (exposure), and essential status. The vaccine is not yet for sale to private doctors and citizens. (Nelson and Lau, 2020). "With the first doses in short supply, California has laid out a strict order of vaccinations based on need and risk: Health-care workers and nursing home residents, then essential workers and those with chronic health conditions, then, finally, everyone else." (Nelson and Lau, 2020); this system is consistent with CDC recommendations.[5] The vaccine is probably unique in the sense that it does not have a market price. No matter much how much an individual offers to pay, they cannot acquire the vaccine. That hasn't stopped some from trying.

In December 2020, New York State health officials investigated a Brooklyn clinic that allegedly obtained the vaccine fraudulently and administered it to patients, contrary to state guidelines (Sullivan et al., 2020). [6] Patients in concierge practices (also known as DPC, direct primary care) have "same-day appointments, longer exam times, home delivery of medications, and round-the-clock telephone and email access to your doctor." All this comes with a cost that ranges from $10,000 to $20,000 a year, on top of regular health insurance. (Levine, 2020). Doctors in these practices report that their patients are asking what they could possibly do (i.e., how much could they pay) to get the vaccine. "Physician Jeff Toll, who has admitting privileges at Cedars-Sinai Medical Center (Los Angeles), one of the first hospitals to stock the vaccine, recalled a patient asking 'If I donate $25,000 to Cedars, would that help me get in line?' Toll said no." (Nelson and Lau, 2020). But even so, when the vaccine is more widely available, these offices are in a better position to have the storage equipment necessary to keep the vaccine cold, something doctors in more ordinary practices do not (Nelson and Lau, 2020), which effectively privileges these patients over ones with more typical health insurance.

In contrast, the NBA appears to be taking the high road. In a December 2020 interview, Adam Silver, NBA Commissioner, said that the NBA would never "jump the line" for Covid vaccines and that the NBA would be willing to work on public service announcements to encourage vaccinations (Bontemps, 2020). First thoughts might be to applaud the NBA for following the rules in place for distributing the vaccine to over 300 million Americans and offering to help with messaging. But might there be other reasons? At the time of that statement, only the federal government could purchase the vaccine, so it's not clear how the NBA could have "jumped the line." And if they could, it most likely would have created a public relations nightmare (as opposed to their offer to help with public messaging, which conveys the opposite value). And perhaps most cynically, how would getting the vaccinations early affect the NBA? Players would not have to sit out games if they were sick or exposed, but otherwise, not much would change. It would still not be safe to have fans in the seats, and regular testing has so far proved effective in enabling regular play. All this raises another question—why were they willing to "jump the line" for Covid tests?

ESPN reports that the top NBA salary in the 2020-21 season was about $43 million to Stephen Curry (ESPN, 2020). The 40 highest paid players had an average salary that season over $27 million. The average NBA salary in the preceding season was $7.7 million (Huddleston, 2020). Instead of spending that money on the Orlando "bubble" and daily testing for players, why didn't the NBA use their wealth to get tests for schools or PPE for medical facilities? Perhaps because they wanted to have a season so that they could earn revenues. The market works.

Perhaps there is a case to be made for allowing people to buy their way to the front of the line in a way that would further the common good. "Have the wealthiest and most influential Americans donate large sums of money to get to the front of the vaccine line, and use that money to fund the broader effort to vaccinate people against COVID-19." (Levine, 2020).[7] Levine proposes five "tiers," beginning with a $100 million donation to be first in line through a fifth tier of $25,000 to get the vaccine within two months of availability (Levine, 2020). He envisions these people as "influencers" who would be very public about getting the vaccine, similar to the way they televised Elvis Presley receiving the polio vaccine. Under Levine's proposal, "$50 billion (would be raised) for the cause by vaccinating just 511,000 people" (Levine, 2020).

He argues that this would decrease uncertainty for business and thus help open the economy more quickly. He also claims that it is a non-political solution. "For conservatives, it is a free-market solution: People and businesses are making a choice on how they use their money. Liberals can view it as a wealth tax: People who can afford it pay for early access to a vaccine and, in doing so, pay for others to get vaccinated (Levine, 2020).

While intriguing, this proposal misses a few points. Many celebrities, including those in business like Jeff Bezos (Amazon), Bill Gates (Microsoft), and Mark Zuckerberg (Facebook), may be willing to be influencers without receiving anything in return. They may also be willing to donate to the cause without "compensation." And it's hard to consider anything that is voluntary as a "tax." If anything, this proposal makes a stronger case for increasing taxes on the wealthy so that the government can more easily achieve the common good. Former presidents Barack Obama, Bill Clinton, and George W. Bush have all said they would be willing to have their vaccinations televised, but "Obama and spokespersons for Bush and Clinton have said the former presidents would receive their vaccinations only within their priority groups" (St. Fleur, 2020).

Nobel Laureate Richard Thaler offers a different perspective on the market and the common good regarding distributing the vaccine. He agrees with CDC recommendations that the first group should be frontline healthcare workers and nursing home residents, and there is no place for the market at that point (Thaler, December, 2020). But when we reach the second group, which includes essential workers, people over 75, and people at higher risk because of underlying health conditions, he proposes allowing anyone to buy the vaccine through what he calls a "charity auction" (Thaler, December, 2020). Rich people and companies would be able to buy their way to the front of the line for a price (he does not suggest what that price would be). He calls this a "Robin Hood in action," because it would redistribute money from the wealthy to the poor. "This money could be used to help people who have suffered most in the pandemic: those who have lost their jobs and face evictions, whose health has been permanently impaired, who face grievous hardship of all kinds" (Thaler, December, 2020). A charity auction would also decrease the likelihood of a black market for vaccines. "As the bioethicist Arthur Caplan of New York University says: 'Anything that's seen as lifesaving, life-preserving and that's in short supply creates black markets'" (Thaler, December, 2020).

TRADE-OFFS: YOUR MONEY OR YOUR LIFE

Some may remember Jack Benny, a comedian in the mid-twentieth century who portrayed himself as being cheap. One well-known joke he told was when he was held up at gunpoint. The robber said, "Your money or your life?" When Benny did not answer right away, the robber repeated the question, and Benny replied, "I'm thinking it over." It is difficult to find a more succinct and compelling way to describe the options during the pandemic: keep the economy open and people will die, or save lives and shut down the economy, which would lead to unemployment and recession. Two horrible options, but this illustrates the basic economic concept of trade-offs; there is no way to have it all. The relevant question is how the benefits of saving lives compares with the economic cost of shutting down the economy.

We take risks every day —every time we get in a car, for example—and probably without thinking about it, we weigh the costs and benefits. We could eliminate deaths from traffic accidents if we outlawed cars, but most would agree that the costs of doing that are greater than the benefits. So, we have cars, but we also have speed limits, seat belts, air bags, and anti-lock brakes, the last three required in all cars by government regulation, which "saved over 600,000 lives between 1960 and 2012 (NHTSA, 2020)."

Measuring the Value of a Human Life

Most people are appalled by the idea of putting a dollar value on a human life.[8] They are typically surprised to learn that it is done on a daily basis. Courts routinely issue settlements for wrongful deaths based in part on lost income.[9] "…there are three types of damages that may be available to the survivors in a wrongful death lawsuit: (1) economic, (2) non-economic, and (3) punitive … (economic damages) … include the value of the financial contributions the victim would have made to the survivors if he or she didn't die, and include … loss of the victim's expected earnings" (Michon).

"In states that use the 'loss to dependents' measure, these damages are supposed to make dependents whole; roughly, they provide the support that dependents would have received if the victim had lived" (Posner and Sunstein, 2005, p. 3). Courts will award less (or no) economic damages to a homeless, unemployed person than to a CEO who earned millions a year.[10]

Value of a Statistical Life (VSL)

The government does not use that method; instead, it uses VSL, the value of a statistical life. VSL was developed by economist Kip Viscusi in the 1980s, based on earlier work during the Cold War by economist Tom Schelling. Schelling examined data on wages and risks of death associated with various jobs.

Using today's numbers, they basically find that on average workers earn about $1,000 a year more for taking on a one-in-10,000 chance of dying on the job… "In total we would be having to pay the workers $10 million for the one expected death that would occur to their group," Viscusi explained. Ten thousand workers each *paid $1,000 gets you $10 million. .... That's what is called the value of a statistical life, and it is the dollar value assigned to a theoretical human life — $10 million when you do this calculation today. (Ben-Achour, 2019).*

The OMB (Office of Management and Budget) currently uses $10 million per person, about 150% of average annual income, as the VSL (Fleurbaey, 2020). Technically, VSL is a measure of the value of risk, *not* the value of human life, despite any impressions otherwise (Ben-Achour, 2019). When deciding the costs and benefits of a new regulation, for example, the FDA (Food and Drug Administration) would calculate how many lives would be saved and multiply that figure by $10 million and compare the dollar value of lives saved with the cost of the regulation.[11] This is exactly how a regulation on labeling hazardous chemicals was approved in the 1980s (Ben Achour, 2019).

This methodology can be applied to the pandemic in order to provide a dollar value of potential lives saved. A Spring 2020 study by researchers at Columbia University determined that 54,000 lives would have been saved if lockdowns and stay-at-home orders had started at the beginning, instead of the middle, of March 2020 (Krugman, 2020). Using the VSL of $10 million per person, that is $540,000,000,000, about $500 billion.

In the first quarter of 2020, GDP fell by 5%, mostly from pandemic-related shutdowns in March. If researchers estimate that GDP would have decreased by 1% in the first two weeks of March if the economy had closed down then, that would be a decrease of about $210,000,000,000, or approximately $200 billion.[12] A simple application of cost benefit analysis indicates clearly that economically the country would have been better off—by about $300 billion—had we shut down at the beginning of March. Nobel Laureate Paul Krugman (2020) estimated the benefits at five times the cost in lost GDP (Krugman, 2020). One could quibble with the accuracy of the numbers and some of the assumptions, but given the orders of magnitude, any calculation would likely have come to the same conclusion—we would have been better off economically shutting down earlier in March 2020. A discomfort or even revulsion of the methodology seems to be unfounded. This replicates the methodology that the U.S. government uses on a regular basis to make decisions about regulations and laws—whether the benefit in lives saved is worth the cost of a particular action or regulation (Ben Achour, 2019).

Disparities among how different populations are affected by the virus might affect the cost benefit calculation. "Adults 65 and older account for 16% of the US population but 80% of COVID-19 deaths in the US." (Freed et al., 2020). This disparity might skew the benefit calculation downward, but the benefits still outweigh the costs by the same order of magnitude (Fleurbaey, 2020). Straightforward use of VSL ignores the disproportionate effect of the virus on people of color. The Kaiser

Family Foundation reports that per 100,000 people, there are 36 deaths from Covid among white people, 80 among Black people, and 46 among Hispanics (Artiga et al., 2020). Some researchers are using a "social well-being" approach in simulations of various mitigation policies. Their methodology "…allows the decision-maker to pick a key ethical parameter: the degree of priority granted to the worse-off. It will give more weight to health benefits if the victims of the virus are among the worse-off, and more weight to economic costs if the burden falls on the most disadvantaged." (Fleurbaey, 2020).

IMPLICATIONS FOR ECONOMIC INEQUALITY

While no one is immune from the effects of the coronavirus, low-income households, women, and people of color have been affected disproportionately (Calefati, Semuels, 2020). A stunning example of the disparities is the number of rich people in New York City who simply left the urban "hot spot" for their vacation homes at the beginning of the pandemic (Quealy, 2020).

Income Disparities

Starting at the beginning of the pandemic, daily life was safer for middle- and high-income households. They could drive in their own cars, arguably the safest mode of transportation, during the pandemic. Most households in that income level have credit cards with generous credit limits; consumers with excellent credit scores have an average credit card limit of $11,000 (Irby, 2020). The Federal Reserve reports that only 61% of households with income under $40,000 have a credit card, compared with 98% for a household with income above $100,000 (Board of Governors and the Federal Reserve System, 2020).

The ability to purchase a large amount of groceries in one trip, both because of the generous credit limit and having a car to transport it, allows people in higher income socio-economic groups to minimize trips to the grocery store, thus decreasing their risk of exposure. Low-income households with no credit card or lower credit limits are constrained by their cash flow or possibly SNAP benefits, which they receive only once a month. SNAP has limitations on what can be bought and prohibits online purchases, although this restriction was eliminated during the pandemic (USDA Food and Nutrition Service, 2020).

Low-income households are less likely to own a car (Bureau of Transportation Statistics, 2020). Dependence on public transportation has many negative effects. It limits the quantity of groceries a person can transport in one trip, so that they have greater exposure through multiple shopping trips than if they had a car. During the early weeks of the pandemic, public transportation in major cities was limited (Spivack, 2020), which made shopping more difficult. Travelling by public transportation with others increases exposure and risk, compared with travelling in one's own car.

Professionals were able to work from home (Calefati, 2020). Essential workers, by definition, worked in person. In addition to high-earning medical personnel, this group includes grocery clerks, nursing home aides, cleaning staff in hospitals and assisted living facilities. About 60% of people who said they work in "management, business, and financial operations" said they can work from home. But fewer than 10% of workers said they could do so in categories such as "services," "construction and extraction," "installation, maintenance and repair," "production," and "transportation and material moving" (Calefati, 2020).

A Pennsylvania study found that essential workers earned $30,000 or less (Calefati, 2020). A Bureau of Labor Statistics survey indicates there are educational and demographic disparities as well. "Thirty-seven percent of Asian Americans and 30% of whites said they could work remotely. But only 20% of African Americans and 16% of Hispanics said they had that ability. Almost 52% of those with a college education or higher said they could work from home, but only 4% of those with less than a high school diploma said they could (Calefati, 2020)." One study found that in California, "nearly 37% of workers with just a high school diploma have filed for (unemployment) benefits since March 15 (2020), compared with less than 6% of those with a bachelor's degree (Semuels, 2020)."

Gender and Racial Disparities

Although it is very difficult to work from home while watching young children, it is far easier to do so than if you actually have to go to work. With schools and day care centers closed in the early stages of the pandemic, essential workers faced a dilemma of how to do their jobs so they could provide for their families and simultaneously care for their children. They had to make sure that their children were properly supervised so that they could remain healthy and safe, as well as complete their schooling at home. It was problematic to ask grandparents for help, as they typically fall into what has been considered to be a high-risk group (CDC, December 13, 2020). Childcare responsibilities fell disproportionately on women.

There are a range of estimates of the extent of this phenomenon. "Data from the U.S. Census Bureau's Household Pulse Survey collected between April 23, 2020, and August 31, 2020, found that, on average, 10 percent of working mothers reported not working each week because they were providing care to a child who was not in school or child care." (Kashen, Glynn, and Novello, 2020).

Between August and September, 865,000 women dropped out of the labor force, according to a National Women's Law Center analysis of the Bureau of Labor Statistics September jobs report. In the same time period, just 216,000 men exited the workforce. Meanwhile, one in four women are considering reducing work hours, moving to part-time roles, switching to less demanding jobs, taking leaves of absence from work, or stepping away from the workforce altogether, according to an annual Women in the Workplace study published in September by McKinsey & Co. and Lean I (Vesoulis, 2020).

Early in the pandemic, there were massive layoffs in service industries like housekeeping and restaurants, where women are about 70% of employees (Vesoulis, 2020). Day care centers closed and laid off 250,000 workers (Vesoulis, 2020). This was a double-edged sword: It affected both the people who lost jobs and the working mothers who depended on day care so they could go to theirs. The workers who were laid off were eligible for unemployment benefits, including the additional $600 per week provided by the CARES Act (and $300 under the second Covid relief bill (Lobosco and Luhby, 2020).

A Brookings analysis (pre-Covid) found that "nearly half of all working women—46% or 28 million—worked in jobs paying low wages, with median earnings of only $10.93 per hour. The share of workers earning low wages is higher among Black women (54%) and Hispanic or Latina women (64%) than among white women (40%). This is in contrast to 37% of working men in low paying jobs" (Bateman and Ross, 2020).

It is critical to distinguish between people who were laid off from their jobs from those who left the labor force. Workers who left the labor force, as opposed to being laid off, were not eligible for any unemployment benefits. People who are not in the labor force are not included in the calculation of the official government unemployment rate. Thus, the official unemployment rates significantly understate the effect of the pandemic.

Earning More Not Working than Going to Work

Among many other provisions, the CARES Act, passed in late March 2020, included an extra $600 in weekly unemployment benefits above the typical benefits for those who lost their jobs during the coronavirus pandemic. These payments lasted through July 31, after which unemployment benefits were to revert to their normal payment amount, which varies by state (Adamczyk, 2020). For many workers, the additional $600 resulted in their earning more than they did when they were working (Horsley, 2020). Some objected to this outcome, claiming that people who earned more *not* working than at a job would have no incentive to search for a job (Iacurci, 2020). These individuals missed several points.

Workers had no choice; when the country went on lockdown in March 2020, non-essential businesses were forced to close, and non-essential workers were required to stay home. The unemployment rate soared to 14.4% in April 2020, surpassing the peak 10.6% unemployment rate set in January 2010, during the Great Recession (Kochhar, 2020). There were no jobs to find. The extra $600 was temporary; it expired in July, 2020 (Adamczyk, 2020).

The official unemployment rate, 6.7% in December 2020 (Bureau of Labor Statistics), does not give an accurate picture. “The unemployment rate among the highest-paid workers is around 5%, while the rate among low-wage employees is as high as 20%” (Ryssdal, 2021).

Perhaps the most significant point is from a social justice perspective. Why does adding $600 a week actually result in more income for someone than if they had been working? Consider the difference in income while working with income with unemployment benefits, including the additional $600 a week. Why is the income they would have earned in their jobs so low that an additional $600 a week for about 12 weeks (late March through late July) would actually increase their annual income? Someone working full-time at the federal minimum wage of $7.25, which has not increased since 2009, would earn about $3,600 in 12 weeks, or about just under $15,000 annually, which is below the poverty level for a family of four (U.S. Department of Health and Human Services, 2021).

Some speculate that the pandemic might have been the impetus for a November 2020 ballot measure in Florida that increased the state minimum wage to $15. The measure passed with more than 60% of the vote, more than either presidential candidate. It will be phased in over six years (Allen, 2020).

The extended unemployment benefits under the CARES Act and the second Covid Relief bill lasted a much shorter time in than in previous recessions. “… unemployment benefits lasted up to 99 weeks—almost two years—as part of the recovery effort in the last recession. In 2003, when the nation was also recovering from recession, maximum benefits were extended as long as 72 weeks, or almost a year and a half” (Porter, 2020). Regular unemployment benefits in the United States are less generous than any other OECD country, both in duration (six months typically) and amount paid as a percent of lost wages. “In Denmark or Portugal, by contrast, unemployment benefits replace around 80 percent of the lost wages of workers even two years after they lose their jobs. are much less generous in the United States than other countries” (Porter, 2020).

Losing a Job Means Losing Health Insurance for Many

Equally, or perhaps more significant, is that many who lost their jobs lost their health insurance as well. For many, that also meant that family members lost health insurance coverage. Of the 17.9 million newly unemployed February through June 2020, "7.7 million lost jobs with ESI (employer-sponsored health insurance), and these job losers had 6.9 million dependents who were covered by ESI. As a result, 14.6 million individuals in total either lost a job with ESI or were the covered dependent of a job loser with ESI." (Fronstin and Woodbury, 2020). About 50% of Americans receive their health care through their employer (KFF, 2019).

Workers who were laid off and lost their health insurance had several options. Some might be able to continue their employer-based health insurance through COBRA, they could purchase health insurance on the ACA exchange, or, if their incomes were sufficiently low, they could apply for Medicaid. All these options entail significant transactions costs, difficult any time but especially so during the pandemic when offices were either closed or minimally staffed. More significant, the first two options come at a substantial out-of-pocket cost. The average monthly premium for a benchmark plan under the ACA (the second lowest-cost silver plan) in 2020 is $388 for a 27-year-old enrollee and $1,520 for a family of four (Nania, 2019). Individuals below a certain income level may qualify for subsidies, which will bring down the cost (KFF, October, 2020). Then President Trump refused to re-open the window for open enrollment on the ACA exchange, creating an additional obstacle for laid off workers to obtain health insurance (Luhby, 2020).

Effect on Education

One of the extreme examples of the unequal effects of the pandemic occurred in schools, grades K-12. In early spring 2020, all schools closed, and education took place online. In fall 2020, private schools were more likely to re-open in person, while public schools were more likely to stay virtual or teach in a hybrid modality (Miller, 2020). The vast difference in resources accounted for this difference. For example, a private school in Honolulu has "an epidemiologist on staff and is installing thermal scanners in the hallways to take people's temperatures as they walk by…as well as an 80-acre campus that students can use to spread out. There were already two teachers for 25 children, so it will be easy to cut classes in half to meet public health requirements for small, consistent groups." (Miller, 2020). In suburban Philadelphia, "The Haverford School said it has spent 'seven figures' on measures intended to keep the virus from spreading through the all-boys campus, from improving air filtration to hiring additional cleaning staff" (Hanna and Graham, 2020).

In addition, the $13.5 billion in assistance to K-12 schools through the CARES Act was woefully inadequate. "An average district with 3,700 students and eight buildings would need to spend an additional $1.8 million on health and safety measures, a report estimated." (Miller, 2020)

Providing remote learning proved to be a challenge, because low-income families are less likely to have broadband internet access or devices, the so-called "digital divide." "Roughly one-third (35%) of households with children ages 6 to 17 and an annual income below $30,000 a year do not have a high-speed internet connection at home, compared with just 6% of such households earning $75,000 or more a year.... One-in-four teens in households with an annual income under $30,000 lacks access to a computer at home, compared with just 4% of those in households earning over $75,000, according to the 2018 survey." (Auxier and Anderson, 2020). Because it was unable to offer online education "equitably," Philadelphia initially opted for sending printed packets home instead of teaching online (Wooley, Sattiraju, and Moritz, 2020).

The disruption in teaching will likely have long-term, negative effects, and it is likely these effects will disproportionately affect low-income students and students of color. Pre-Covid research has already documented what is known as "summer slide." On average, students lose one month's worth of learning over the summer (Quinn and Polikoff, 2017). Lower-income students lose more than higher-income students, who have considerable resources over the summer (Quinn and Polikoff, 2017). Given the inequities in education during the pandemic and its duration, officials are concerned about the losses in learning.

New research has found that upon returning to school in Fall 2020, students will have fallen further behind than they would have if they had been in school under normal circumstance. "Racial and socioeconomic achievement gaps will most likely widen because of disparities in access to computers, home internet connections and direct instruction from teachers." (Goldstein, 2020). It is not difficult to imagine how an entire school year under COVID-19 restrictions will lead to even worse outcomes.

Food Insecurity

Students who are not attending school in person are missing meals. "Among low-income households with children who qualify for free or reduced-price school meals, only about 15% (of the 30 million who are eligible) have been getting those meals" (Turner, 2020). Many school districts switched to what they do in the summer; they have grab-and-go meals at schools for pick up. When virtual learning extended into the fall, the Department of Agriculture extended that policy (Turner, 2020). Once the lockdown was lifted, and many people returned to work, it became difficult to get to those locations to pick up the lunches. Officials in Tucson, Arizona and

Charlotte, North Carolina school districts reported that school lunch meals were down around 90% (Turner, 2020).

In Philadelphia, the school district provides free meals to all students because of the high poverty rate. The school district provided grab-and-go meals at various sites throughout the city. In March 2020, "(there were) 30,000 meals available for students to pick up each day for breakfast and lunch. The meals are available between 9 a.m. and noon for any child age 18 or under. On Monday, students picked up 2,000 brown bags." (Vargas and Hanna, 2020).

The decrease in the number of school-aged children receiving free meals at school partially explains the record high number of child food insecurity. Other factors include parents who were laid off or chose to stay home from work to take care of children.

In June 2020, around 16 percent of households with children reported that their children were not eating enough over the last week due to a lack of resources. While the overall rate is the highest on record, Black and Hispanic children are experiencing food insecurity at even higher and extremely alarming rates. About three in ten Black households with children and one in four Hispanic households with children did not have sufficient food due to a lack of resources in June 2020, while white households with children reported a child food insecurity rate just under 10 percent. (Bauer, 2020).

CONCLUSION

The coronavirus pandemic provides many applications of basic economic theory and can help inform policy decisions. The economic concept of responding to incentives is instructive to determine ways to allocate the vaccine and how to persuade college students to follow campus Covid protocol. Using the value of a statistical life, cost benefit analysis can be used to measure the trade-offs between saving lives and lockdowns. A deeper understanding of the how the pandemic has disproportionately affected certain sectors of the economy can guide lawmakers to more just Covid relief measures as well as structural changes to the economy, including raising the federal minimum wage.

REFERENCES

Adamczyk, A. (2020, August 28). *It's been a month since the extra $600 per week in enhanced unemployment benefits expired. Here's where things stand now.* Retrieved January 1, 2021, from https://www.cnbc.com/2020/08/28/its-been-a-month-since-enhanced-unemployment-benefits-ended.html

Allen, G. (2020, November 11). *Floridians Vote To Increase State's Minimum Wage To $15 Per Hour*. Retrieved January 1, 2021, from https://www.npr.org/2020/11/11/933937204/floridians-vote-to-increase-states-minimum-wage-to-15-per-hour

Artiga, S., Corallo, B., & Pham, O. (2020, August 17). *Racial Disparities in COVID-19: Key Findings from Available Data and Analysis - Issue Brief.* https://www.kff.org/report-section/racial-disparities-in-COVID-19-key-findings-from-available-data-and-analysis-issue-brief/

Auxier, B., & Anderson, M. (2020, July 27). *As schools close due to the coronavirus, some U.S. students face a digital 'homework gap'.* https://www.pewresearch.org/fact-tank/2020/03/16/as-schools-close-due-to-the-coronavirus-some-u-s-students-face-a-digital-homework-gap/

Bateman, N., & Ross, M. (2021, January 6). *Why has COVID-19 been especially harmful for working women?* Brookings. https://www.brookings.edu/essay/why-has-COVID-19-been-especially-harmful-for-working-women/

Bauer, L. (2020). *About 14 million children in the US are not getting enough to eat.* [web log]. https://www.brookings.edu/blog/up-front/2020/07/09/about-14-million-children-in-the-us-are-not-getting-enough-to-eat/

Ben Achour, S. (2019). *How to value a life, statistically speaking*. Marketplace. https://www.marketplace.org/2019/03/20/how-value-life/popout/

Board of Governors of the Federal Reserve System. (2020). *Report on the Economic Well-Being of U.S. Households in 2018-May 2019.* Board of Governors of the Federal Reserve System. https://www.federalreserve.gov/publications/2019-economic-well-being-of-us-households-in-2018-banking-and-credit.htm

Bontemps, T. (2020, December 21). *NBA commissioner Adam Silver says league won't 'jump the line' to get vaccines*. ESPN. https://www.espn.com/nba/story/_/id/30573657/nba-commissioner-adam-silver-says-league-jump-line-get-vaccines

Bontemps, T., & Lowe, Z. (2020, June 14). *NBA to test players and staff for coronavirus every other day before going to Orlando*. ESPN. https://www.espn.com/nba/story/_/id/29309011/nba-test-players-staff-coronavirus-every-other-day-going-orlando

Bureau of Labor Statistics. (2021, January 8). *The Employment Situation-December 2020.* https://www.bls.gov/news.release/pdf/empsit.pdf

Bureau of Transportation Statistics. (2020, May 17). *Household, Individual, and Vehicle Characteristics*. Household, Individual, and Vehicle Characteristics | Bureau of Transportation Statistics. https://www.bts.gov/archive/publications/highlights_of_the_2001_national_household_travel_survey/section_01

Calefati, J. (2020, April 21). Still going in to work in Pennsylvania amid the coronavirus? Chances are, you're a low-wage worker, data show. *The Philadelphia Enquirer*. https://www.inquirer.com/politics/essential-grocery-work-home-pennsylvania-true-false-20200421.html

Dubner, S. (2016, August 8). *Who Decides How Much a Life Is Worth? (Ep. 344).* Freakonomics. https://freakonomics.com/podcast/kenneth-feinberg/

FactCheck.org. (2020, December 22). *A Guide to Our Coronavirus Coverage*. https://www.factcheck.org/a-guide-to-our-coronavirus-coverage/

Feinberg, K. (2008, May 25). *What Is the Value of a Human Life?* NPR. https://www.npr.org/templates/story/story.php?storyId=90760725

Fleurbaey, M. (2020). *Essay: Should We Save Lives—or Save the Economy?* Princeton University. https://paw.princeton.edu/article/essay-should-we-save-lives-or-save-economy

Freed, M., Cubanski, J., Neuman, T., Kates, J., & Michau, J. (2020). *What Share of People Who Have Died of COVID-19 Are 65 and Older – and How Does It Vary by State?* Kaiser Family Foundation. https://www.kff.org/coronavirus-COVID-19/issue-brief/what-share-of-people-who-have-died-of-COVID-19-are-65-and-older-and-how-does-it-vary-by-state/

Fronstin, P., & Woodbury, S. (2020, October 7). *How Many Americans Have Lost Jobs with Employer Health Coverage During the Pandemic?* Commonwealth Fund. https://www.commonwealthfund.org/publications/issue-briefs/2020/oct/how-many-lost-jobs-employer-coverage-pandemic

Garcia, C., & Smith, S. V. (2020, September 8). *Egg Prices Skyrocket During The Pandemic*. NPR. https://www.npr.org/2020/09/08/910788715/egg-prices-skyrocket-during-the-pandemic

Goldstein, D. (2020, June 10). Research Shows Students Falling Months Behind During Virus Disruptions. *The New York Times*. https://www.nytimes.com/2020/06/05/us/coronavirus-education-lost-learning.html

Grasso, J. (2020, June 14). *NBA Players Will Test for COVID-19 'Every Other Day' Before Orlando*. Sports Illustrated Philadelphia 76ers News, Analysis and More. https://www.si.com/nba/76ers/news/nba-players-test-COVID-19-every-day-orlando

Hanna, M., & Graham, K. A. (2020, August 18). *Philly-area private schools press ahead on in-person openings: 'Everybody's looking for the best option'*. https://www.inquirer.com. https://www.inquirer.com/education/pennsylvania-archdiocese-philadelphia-private-schools-reopening-20200816.html

Horsley, S. (2020, May 26). *For Many, $600 Jobless Benefit Makes It Hard To Return To Work*. NPR. https://www.npr.org/2020/05/26/861906616/when-returning-to-your-job-means-a-cut-in-pay

Huddleston, T. (2019, October 22). *These are the highest paid players in the NBA right now*. CNBC. https://www.cnbc.com/2019/10/22/highest-paid-players-in-the-nba-right-now.html

Iacurci, G. (2020, August 3). *The $600 unemployment boost has ended. What's next?* CNBC. https://www.cnbc.com/2020/07/31/the-600-unemployment-boost-has-ended-whats-next.html

Irby, L. T. (2020, July 21). *Here Is a Look at What a Good Credit Limit Is on a First Credit Card*. The Balance. https://www.thebalance.com/what-s-a-good-credit-limit-on-a-first-credit-card-960003

Jagannathan, M. (2020, December 23). *How many people have to get vaccinated against COVID-19 to reach herd immunity? 'The faster we do it, the faster we get back to life.'* MarketWatch. https://www.marketwatch.com/story/how-many-people-have-to-get-vaccinated-against-COVID-19-to-reach-herd-immunity-the-faster-we-do-it-the-faster-we-get-back-to-life-11608740335

Jayachandran, S. (2020, December 29). Financial Rewards for College Students Could Help Curb the Pandemic. *The New York Times*. https://www.nytimes.com/2020/12/29/business/rewards-college-students-coronavirus.html

K. (2021, January 14). *Economic recovery: one step forward, several steps back.* Marketplace. https://www.marketplace.org/shows/marketplace/economic-recovery-one-step-forward-several-steps-back/

Kashen, J., Glynn, S. J., & Novello, A. (2020, October 30). *How COVID-19 Sent Women's Workforce Progress Backward.* Center for American Progress. https://www.americanprogress.org/article/covid-19-sent-womens-workforce-progress-backward/

Kochhar, R. (2020, August 26). *Unemployment rose higher in three months of COVID-19 than it did in two years of the Great Recession.* Retrieved January 1, 2021, from https://www.pewresearch.org/fact-tank/2020/06/11/unemployment-rose-higher-in-three-months-of-COVID-19-than-it-did-in-two-years-of-the-great-recession/

Krugman, P. (2020, June 01). *On the economics of not dying.* Retrieved January 1, 2021, from https://www.palmbeachpost.com/story/opinion/columns/more-voices/2020/06/01/paul-krugman-on-economics-of-not-dying/41744823/

Lederer, A., & Stolow, J. (2020, September 18). *Don't Rely on Student Contracts to Safeguard Your Campus. Student contracts won't do enough to encourage safe behaviors during the pandemic (opinion).* https://www.insidehighered.com/views/2020/09/18/student-contracts-wont-do-enough-encourage-safe-behaviors-during-pandemic-opinion

Levine, A. (2020, December 21). *Let the ultra-rich and influential skip the line for COVID-19 vaccines? Hear me out.* STAT. https://www.statnews.com/2020/12/22/let-the-ultra-rich-and-influential-skip-the-line-for-COVID-19-vaccines-hear-me-out/

Lobosco, K., & Luhby, T. (2020, December 28). *Here's what's in the second stimulus package.* CNN. https://www.cnn.com/2020/12/20/politics/second-covid-stimulus-package-details/index.html

Loewenstein, G., & Cryder, C. (2020, December 14). Why Paying People to Be Vaccinated Could Backfire. *The New York Times.* https://www.nytimes.com/2020/12/14/upshot/covid-vaccine-payment.html

Luhby, T. (2020, April 1). *Trump administration won't reopen Obamacare enrollment for uninsured.* CNN. https://www.cnn.com/2020/03/31/politics/affordable-care-act-obamacare-open-enrollment-trump/index.html

Mankiw, N. G. (2020, September 9). Pay People to Get Vaccinated. *The New York Times.* https://www.nytimes.com/2020/09/09/business/pay-people-vaccine-coronavirus.html

Michon, K. (2013, October 3). *Damages in a Wrongful Death Lawsuit*. www.nolo.com. https://www.nolo.com/legal-encyclopedia/wrongful-death-claims-overview-30141-2.html

Miller, C. C. (2020, August 4). In the Same Towns, Private Schools Are Reopening While Public Schools Are Not. *The New York Times*. https://www.nytimes.com/2020/07/16/upshot/coronavirus-school-reopening-private-public-gap.html

Nania, R. (2019, October 22). *Affordable Care Act Costs, Plans for 2020 Announced*. AARP. https://www.aarp.org/health/health-insurance/info-2019/aca-plans-premium-rates-announced.html

Neergaard, L., & Fingerhut, H. (2020, December 9). *AP-NORC poll: Only half in US want shots as vaccine nears*. AP News. https://apnews.com/article/ap-norc-poll-us-half-want-vaccine-shots-4d98dbfc0a64d60d52ac84c3065dac55

Nelson, L., & Lau, M. (2020, December 18). The wealthy scramble for COVID-19 vaccines: 'If I donate $25,000 ... would that help me?' *Los Angeles Times*. https://www.latimes.com/california/story/2020-12-18/wealthy-patients-scramble-COVID-19-vaccine

Nguyen, T. (2020, April 3). Toilet paper is disappearing from shelves - again. *Vox*. Retrieved January 15, 2021, from https://www.vox.com/the-goods/2020/4/3/21206942/toilet-paper-coronavirus-shortage-supply-chain

Piper, Y. (2021, January 6). Pa. lags nation in people tested per day, is nowhere near level needed to suppress the virus. *Pittsburgh Post-Gazaette*. Retrieved January 15, 2021, from https://www.post-gazette.com/news/health/2021/01/06/Pennsylvania-lags-nation-people-tested-per-day-COVID-19-falls-short-suppression-testing-pandemic-spread/stories/202101060116

Porter, E. (2020, December 14). What Happens to the Unemployed When the Checks Run Out? *The New York Times*. https://www.nytimes.com/2020/12/14/business/economy/unemployment-benefits-economy.html

Posner, E.A., & Sunstei, C.R. (2005, Spring). Dollars and Death. *The University of Chicago Law Review. University of Chicago. Law School*, 537.

Quealy, K. (2020, May 15). The Richest Neighborhoods Emptied Out Most as Coronavirus Hit New York City. *The New York Times*. https://www.nytimes.com/interactive/2020/05/15/upshot/who-left-new-york-coronavirus.html

Quinn, D. M., & Polikoff, M. (2017, September 14). *Summer learning loss: What is it, and what can we do about it?* Brookings. https://www.brookings.edu/research/summer-learning-loss-what-is-it-and-what-can-we-do-about-it/

Sandel, M. J. (2012). *What Money Can't Buy: The Moral Limits of Markets*. Farar, Straus and Giroux.

Schumaker, E. (2020, November 19). *Which States Have Mask Mandates: Map*. Retrieved January 1, 2021, from https://abcnews.go.com/Health/states-mask-mandates-map/story?id=74168504

Schwartz, K., Freed, M., Cubanski, J., Dolan, R., Pollitz, K., Michau, J., … Neuman, T. (2020, November 18). *Vaccine Coverage, Pricing, and Reimbursement in the U.S.* KFF. https://www.kff.org/coronavirus-COVID-19/issue-brief/vaccine-coverage-pricing-and-reimbursement-in-the-u-s/

Semuels, A. (2020, May 7). *Life for the Millions of Americans Facing Financial Ruin*. Retrieved January 12, 2021, from https://time.com/5833008/us-unemployment-coronavirus/

Silberner, J. (2020, December 12). *What You Need To Know As The First COVID-19 Vaccines Head Your Way*. NPR. https://www.npr.org/sections/health-shots/2020/12/12/945288710/what-you-need-to-know-as-the-first-COVID-19-vaccine-heads-your-way

Smith, T. (2020, September 17). *Students Accused Of Breaking College COVID-19 Rules Fight Their Punishments*. NPR. https://www.npr.org/2020/09/17/914046958/students-accused-of-breaking-college-COVID-19-rules-fight-their-punishments

Snider, M. (2021, January 14). Coronavirus vaccine incentive: Trader Joe's, Instacart and Dollar General to pay workers to get vaccinated. *USA Today*. https://www.usatoday.com/story/money/business/2021/01/14/covid-vaccine-dollar-general-instacart-pay-employees-getting-vaccine/4160708001/

Spivack, C. (2020, May 21). *Here's how the coronavirus pandemic is affecting public transit*. Curbed NY. https://ny.curbed.com/2020/3/24/21192454/coronavirus-nyc-transportation-subway-citi-bike-COVID-19

St. Fleur, N. (2020, December 14). *Can celebrities spur acceptance of the COVID-19 vaccine?* STAT. https://www.statnews.com/2020/12/14/the-polio-vaccine-had-elvis-can-celebrities-similarly-spur-acceptance-of-the-COVID-19-vaccine/

Steinberg, L. (2020, June 15). Expecting Students to Play It Safe if Colleges Reopen Is a Fantasy. *The New York Times.* https://www.nytimes.com/2020/06/15/opinion/coronavirus-college-safe.html

Subramaniam, T. (2020, November 1). *Fact Check: Can the President enact a nationwide mask mandate?* CNN. https://www.cnn.com/2020/11/01/politics/mask-mandate-fact-check/index.html

Swift, J. (1729). *A Modest Proposal.* https://www.gutenberg.org/files/1080/1080-h/1080-h.htm

Thaler, R. (2020, May 20). The Law of Supply and Demand Isn't Fair. *The New York Times.* https://www.nytimes.com/2020/05/20/business/supply-and-demand-isnt-fair.html

Thaler, R. (2020, December 9). Getting Everyone Vaccinated, With 'Nudges' and Charity Auctions. *The New York Times.* https://www.nytimes.com/2020/12/09/business/coronavirus-vaccination-auctions-celebrities.html

Thompson, D. (2020, April 27). There Aren't Enough Coronavirus Test Kits to Safely Reopen America, Experts Warn. *U.S. News & World Report.* https://www.usnews.com/news/health-news/articles/2020-04-27/there-arent-enough-coronavirus-test-kits-to-safely-reopen-america-experts-warn

Turner, C. (2020, September 8). *'Children Are Going Hungry': Why Schools Are Struggling To Feed Students.* NPR. https://www.npr.org/2020/09/08/908442609/children-are-going-hungry-why-schools-are-struggling-to-feed-students

U.S. Department of Health and Human Services. (2021, January 8). *Poverty Guidelines.* ASPE. https://aspe.hhs.gov/poverty-guidelines

USDA Food and Nutrition Service. (2020). *SNAP COVID-19 Waivers.* USDA. https://www.fns.usda.gov/programs/fns-disaster-assistance/fns-responds-COVID-19/snap-COVID-19-waivers

Vargas, C., & Hanna, M. (2020, March 24). *Free breakfast and lunch begins, but not many students in North Philly bite.* https://www.inquirer.com. https://www.inquirer.com/health/coronavirus/coronavirus-philadelphia-schools-free-lunches-grab-and-go-20200316.html

Vesoulis, A. (2020, October 17). Women's COVID-Fueled Exodus From the Workforce Hurts Us All. *Time.* https://time.com/5900583/women-workforce-economy-covid/

Vigdor, N. (2020, April 23). Tennessee Brothers Who Hoarded Hand Sanitizer Settle to Avoid Price-Gouging Fine. *The New York Times*. https://www.nytimes.com/2020/04/22/us/hand-sanitizer-matt-colvin-noah-coronavirus.html

Wooley, S., Sattiraju, N., & Moritz, S. (2020, March 26). *U.S. Schools Trying to Teach Online Highlight a Digital Divide*. Bloomberg. https://www.bloomberg.com/news/articles/2020-03-26/COVID-19-school-closures-reveal-disparity-in-access-to-internet

ENDNOTES

1. Guidelines and procedures for administering the vaccine change frequently. Information here is accurate as of January 2021.
2. WHO and other health organizations do not have a definitive number for herd immunity, but Dr. Anthony Fauci gave this 80-85percent percent figure in late December 2020. See Jagannathan for details.
3. See Sandel for an excellent discussion of commodification.
4. See Sandel for an excellent discussion of how markets crowd out morals.
5. CDC's Advisory Committee on Immunization Practices (ACIP) released an interim recommendation on December 1 for the highest priority group ("Phase 1a") to include health care workers (HCWs) and long-term care (LTC) residents; we estimate that this populations together represents about 17.6 million people. ACIP also provided further guidance regarding sub-prioritization within these groups. While ACIP has yet to finalize recommendations on subsequent prioritization (expected soon), according to presentations and materials provided in recent ACIP meetings, the committee is likely to recommend that (non-health care) essential workers be the next priority group ("Phase 1b"), followed by persons age 65 and older and those with conditions that place them at high risk for severe illness from COVID-19 ("Phase 1c"). These groups are much larger, which will likely make the next stages of prioritization much more difficult given that supply will still be limited (according to ACIP, there are an estimated 87 million essential workers, 53+ million seniors and more than 100 million individuals with high-risk medical conditions). https://www.kff.org/policy-watch/how-are-states-prioritizing-who-will-get-the-COVID-19-vaccine-first/

6 My thanks to Dr. Alison Bateman-House, Grossman School of Medicine, NYU Langone Health, for suggesting this reference.

7 My thanks to Dr. Alison Bateman-House, Grossman School of Medicine, NYU Langone Health, for suggesting this reference.

8 See Dubner for interviews with Ken Feinberg, the attorney charged with deciding compensation for victims of 9/11, and Kip Viscusi. Also see Feinberg for his fervent reflection of his decisions on compensation for victims of 9/11.

9 I am grateful to my son, Dr. Sam Fox Krauss, for a helpful tutorial on tort law as well as for the Michon and Posner and Sunstein references.

10 See Table 1 in Posner and Sunstein for examples of examples of tort values of life.

11 See Table 2 in Posner and Sunstein for examples of Agency Values of Life.

12 Assuming a GDP of about $21 trillion. https://www.bea.gov/news/2020/gross-domestic-product-fourth-quarter-and-year-2019-advance-estimate#:~:text=Current%2Ddollar%20GDP%20increased%204.1,table%201%20and%20table%203).

Chapter 3
Global Health Crisis:
The Microeconomic and Socio-Dynamic Implications of COVID-19 Pandemic in Sub-Saharan Africa

Okanlade Adesokan Lawal-Adebowale
https://orcid.org/0000-0003-3418-4250
Federal University of Agriculture, Abeokuta, Nigeria

ABSTRACT

The emergence and spread of severe acute respiratory syndrome corona virus 2 (SARS-CoV-2) with its attendant coronavirus disease in late 2019 (COVID-19) have brought untold social and economic hardships on the global society but with severe impacts on the sub-Saharan African households. The social and economic impacts were severe given that lifestyle in Africa is largely characterised by poor infrastructure development and social amenities. This situation increased food insecurity arising from complete loss or temporary halt of means of livelihood of the continent's households. Alongside this is loss of social security with resultant psychological stress and anxieties. This notwithstanding, developed resilience and social protection support have strengthened the African households to cope and possibly recover from the negative impacts of the COVID-19 pandemic.

DOI: 10.4018/978-1-7998-6900-9.ch003

INTRODUCTION

Healthy living is an important livelihood asset of high value to every individual and the larger human society; because it underscores the active engagement of any individual or group of individuals in any social and economic endeavor. It is a non-material wealth that is acquired and maintained through the cultivation of behaviors that guarantees the mental soundness and physical fitness of individuals at all times. According to the Public Health Agency of Canada – PHAC (n.d.), healthy living, concerning individuals, is the practice of health-enhancing behaviors that build physical, mental, and spiritual capacity to make choices or actively engaged in social and economic functions. By extension, healthy living by individuals would reflect a healthy society. Hence, healthy living concerning the larger society refers to practices by the population groups that are consistent with supporting, improving, maintaining and/or enhancing good health conditions. Such health supporting practices or behaviors primarily center on hygiene practices, daily and regular consumption of good and nutritious food, and physical activities. In Africa, where access to good and nutritious food remains a challenge, particularly among the poor households (FAO, 1998; Sasson, 2012; Dodo, 2020; FAO, 2020), which constitutes the largest population of the content, hygiene practice is well recognized and promoted through cultural communication and much more in the school system. In songs and folklores is an emphasis on the need for daily and regular bathing, laundry of clothes, sweeping of the environment, and good handling of food for safe consumption. Further to this are the dictums – health is wealth; cleanliness is next to godliness, and hygiene practices override all forms of illnesses. Based on this many efforts are made to ensure hygiene practice and healthy living in Africa, especially among the elites and urban dwellers.

This notwithstanding, ill-health seems inevitable among the human society as individuals sometimes or occasionally contend with one form of disease or the other. A disease is generally caused by a variety of pathogenic organics or disease-causing organisms, which exist in five groups – viruses, bacteria, fungi, protozoa, and helminths. These pathogens pervade man's environment and as such exist in the air, water, soil, food, surfaces, even in humans and other living organisms that may serve as hosts. In essence, humans could readily and unknowingly get in contact with the pathogens thereby becoming pre-dispose to infectious diseases. The pathogens however need to gain entry into the human body and establish a site of infection for disease to occur (Janeway Jr et al., 2001). The pathogens which may be intracellular or extracellular, depending on their mechanism of replications, could gain entry into the body through the epithelial surface, which may be the skin or internal mucosal surfaces of the respiratory, gastrointestinal, and urogenital tracts, eyes, mouth wound, or bite that breach the skin barrier (The National Academies, n.d.). Adhering to the epithelial surface, the pathogens penetrate the body tissues for replications and secretion of toxins that may spread to other parts of the body system and as such begin to cause deterioration of the body cells with significant signs as symptoms of a particular disease. In essence, different pathogens or infectious organisms cause markedly different diseases with definite symptoms by which the diverse damaged tissues are manifested. In today's world, there are arrays of diseases impinging on the health status of human society with consequential health and socioeconomic implications.

INFECTIOUS DISEASES AND MECHANISMS OF TRANSMISSION

Although there exists several neglected tropical diseases in human's society, attention has largely been given to the more pronounced or death-dealing diseases, among which are tuberculosis, whooping cough, human immunodeficiency virus/acquired immunodeficiency syndrome (HIV/AIDS), flu (influenza), hepatitis, human papillomavirus, measles, norovirus, Zika, Ebola, and more recently novel coronavirus, etc. Diseases could either be communicable or non-communicable. The communicable ones could however be contacted or transmitted through various means, generally classified as direct or indirect contacts. As indicated by Higuera (2017), direct contact could be by person-to-person, the spray of droplets; while indirect contact takes the form of airborne transmission, contaminated objects, food and drinking water, animal-to-person contact, insect bites, animal and environment reservoirs. The extent to which a particular disease affects humans depends on its virulence and the strength of an individual's immunity to the disease. But when infected by any disease, treatment becomes essential for recovery and maintenance of health status. This is however usually at great cost to individuals or groups. Consequently, conscientious efforts are made by individuals, households, communities, and/or nations to prevent disease infestation rather than treatment. There could however be an emergence of a contagious and life-threatening disease, even with no immediate vaccine for prevention or drugs for treatment. The outbreak of such disease could greatly inflict untold social and economic hardships on households in the community with multiplier effects on the national economy. The reality of this scenario is the emergence of a novel coronavirus disease (COVID-19) in November 2019, in Wuhan, China from where it spreads to every country of the world.

COVID-19 is a respiratory-related viral disease or illness caused by severe acute respiratory syndrome coronavirus 2 (SARS-CoV-2), commonly referred to as a novel coronavirus (Cennimo, 2020; Nicola, et al., 2020). The disease, with symptoms such as fever, cough, and shortness of breath, could be transmitted through direct contact with respiratory droplets of an infected person, generated through coughing and sneezing, touching of surfaces contaminated with the virus, and getting into the body by touching the eyes, mouth, and nose with the hand contaminated by the virus (UNICEF, 2020). In more severe cases, the infection could result in pneumonia or breathing difficulty. The disease could though affect anybody, older people and those with chronic medical conditions, such as diabetes, and heart disease, are more at risk of developing severe symptoms. Due to the newness of the virus, the disease has no vaccine at the moment, and as such prevention is advocated to stay safe against the disease. The public health measures as preventive actions include staying at home, covering of mouth and nose with flexed elbow or tissue when coughing or sneezing, regular washing of hands with soap and running water, cleaning of frequently touched surfaces and objects, avoiding crowded places, and maintain social distancing.

COVID-19: THE GLOBAL PANDEMIC AND HEALTH CRISIS

Based on the virulence and death-dealing nature of COVID-19, the disease did not only lead to loss of lives around the world, but also the shut down of the global economy and social engagement (UNDP, 2020). The outbreak of the disease, which began in Wuhan, China, was officially communicated to the World Health Organisation (WHO) on December 30, 2019. The global health agency thus began monitoring the cases of infection and the resultant deaths from December 31, 2020. And due to the steady rise in cases of infections and deaths across the countries of the world, WHO declared the disease a global health emergency of international concern on January 30, 2020; and by March 11, 2020, it was declared a global pandemic (UNICEF, 2020; Sohrabir et al., 2020). According to the European Centre for Disease Prevention and Control – ECDC (2020), the global cases of COVID-19, as of December 12, 2020, were 70.3 million and 1. 6 million deaths. In Africa were 2.3 million cases and 55, 646 deaths; 16.6 million cases and 287, 978 deaths in Asia; 30.3million cases and 778, 696 deaths in America; and 20.9 million cases; 472, 520 deaths in Europe, 53, 394 cases and 1, 153 deaths in Oceania.

Based on the resultant deaths and mechanisms of the disease transmission, the need to stem the tide of its sporadic spread necessitated the enactment and imposition of lockdown by the governments of different countries whereby individuals and families are expected to stay indoors until the situation improves. Consequently, businesses, schools, recreation and event centers, banks and financial institutions, air travel and public transportation, and several other social and economic hubs were closed down, except for health facilities and foods sources, termed essential units or essential workers (UNESCO, 2020; Sohrabir et al., 2020). Implications of the lockdown is the disruption of social and economic balance, whereby tens of millions of people are put at the risk of falling into extreme poverty as a result of loss of jobs and becoming malnourished due to lack of adequate food supply. As further pointed out by WHO (2020a), millions of enterprises face an existential threat, putting close to half of the world's global workforce at the risk of losing their means of livelihood. Thus, the situation is beginning to result in an economic meltdown across the globe, with stronger impacts on the developing countries, especially in the sub-Saharan Africa countries.

COVID-19: THE INROAD TO AFRICA AND COMMUNITY TRANSMISSION

Dynamisms of human society and the drive for the attainment of improved social and economic development underscore frequent mobility across the globe and doing so swiftly with an improved system of transportation (Glaesser et al, 2017). According to Lew (2018), new technologies are moving products, ideas, and people across the planet in shorter times than one could ever be conceived in the past, leading to rising economic and cultural globalization (Guy, 2016). This certainly takes place alongside anti-globalization issues, one of which is the spread of diseases. Trending in today's global society is widespread of COVID-19 with the virus getting into Africa through travelers from hotspot areas in Asia, Europe, and the United States. The first case of the virus in Africa was recorded on February 14, 2020, in Egypt, with the second case in Algeria on February 17 (WHO, 2020b; c). On February 27, 2020, the third case in Africa, or the first case in sub-Saharan Africa, was confirmed in Nigeria; brought into the country by an Italian citizen who flew into Lagos from Milan (WHO, 2020d). The virus has since spread to other 51 countries in the continent with varying degrees of confirmed cases, deaths, and recoveries (Africa News, 2020). As of December 13, 2020, confirmed cases across 55 African countries was 2.4million, with 56, 009 deaths and 2million recoveries (allAfrica, 2020). Examination of cases in each of the countries (Appendix I) shows that five countries, namely, South Africa (852,965), Morocco (397,597), Egypt (121,089), Ethiopia (116, 297), and Tunisia (110,393), had cases of COVID-19 in hundreds of thousands, 21 countries had the cases in tens of thousands, 22 countries had the cases in a unit of thousands with the remaining 7 countries having the cases in hundreds. Computation of proportionate rate of recovery and deaths from the cases (Appendix I) shows that recovery rate across the countries ranged between 98.5 and 36.0percent, with death rate ranging between 0 and 6.0percent (Figure 1).

Figure 1. Percentages of recovery and death rates of confirmed Covid-19 cases in Africa
Source: *Data sourced from allAfrica/Africa CDC*

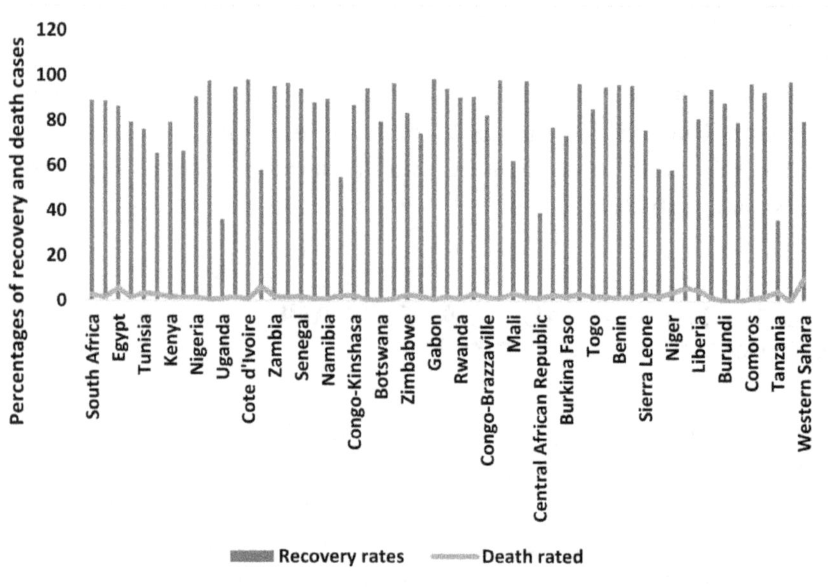

Based on the high rate of recovery and comparatively low rate of death cases in Africa, it suggests that most of the infected persons are possibly younger with high immunity; and inhibition of SARS-CoV-2 viability by sub-Saharan Africa's high temperature, which is in the range of 38°C and above. Association of lower cases of death with a large number of the younger population in Africa could be corroborated with WHO (2020e); Wyper et al. (2020) indication that elderly people – 60years and above, and those with critical health conditions – like lung or heart disease, diabetes, and low immune system, are more vulnerable to COVID-19. The temperature-related submission is based on Chan et al., (2011) indication that viability of the virus is lost at a higher temperature range of 38°C and 95percent relative humidity. Further to this is Riddell et al (2020) indication that survivability of the infectious SARS-CoV-2 is drastically reduced at 40°C within 24hours. Wu et al. (20020) thus stress that with every rise in temperature and humidity, COVID-19 becomes partially suppressed. The recovery potentials may though have to do with the strength of immunity and blood group of the infected persons (Ziet et al., 2020; Latz et al., 2020), younger individuals are less likely to have severe COVID-19 symptoms and could recover faster from SARS-CoV-2 infection than the older ones (Voinsky, et al., 2020; Das & Gopalan, 2020).

This notwithstanding, cases of infections are on the increase day-by-day, affecting all age groups with serious socioeconomic implications across the African countries. With the daunting financial cost of caring for rising cases of infection, which may be up to US$8.1 or US$15.8 trillion globally (World Economic Forum – WEF, 2020), the need for containment of the virus become essential, particularly for the protection of the vulnerable groups (Kuy, et al., 2020) and recovery of the societal social and economic balances.

COVID-19 CONTAINMENT: THE LOCKDOWN AND STIPULATION OF STAY SAFE PROTOCOL IN AFRICA

In the wake of the demeaning and inflicted social and economic hardships ingrained in the societal fabrics by the sporadic spread of COVID-19 containment actions were taken by the African political leaders, alongside the taken actions by the hotspot countries of Asia, Europe, and America. The foremost actions are the imposition of lockdown, whereby citizens across the countries were expected to stay indoors; and strengthening of the health system to care for infected individuals. The lockdown includes the closure of borders, travel restrictions, and bans on social and religious gatherings (Frimpong et al., 2020). The strength of the health system for medical provision was underscored by the given technical guidance and financial supports to African countries by WHO-Africa and the Africa Centre for Disease Control (Africa CDC) in preparation for the anticipated COVID-19 spread which eventually got into Africa less than two months after its emergence in China (Ihekweazu & Agogo, 2020) and after the first case outside China was reported in the Republic of Korea (Das & Gopalan, 2020). With the given supports, the countries were able to strengthen their national public health institutes, rapidly scale up their testing and diagnostic capacity, entrench capacity for real-time surveillance and contact tracing, with good coordinating mechanisms.

The state of preparation did not in any way imply a perfect preparedness as over ten countries in sub-Saharan Africa had no ventilators, lacked space for isolation of critical cases, and had fewer experts to manage the critical patient with complex respiratory needs (Maclean & Mark, 2020). In reality, most countries in the sub-region have only leveraged the existing health capacities that were originally built to handle the previous outbreaks of viral and other related respiratory diseases, namely Ebola, HIV, influenza, in the sub-region (WHO, 2020f). On this note was deployment of integrated disease surveillance and response framework – that has been in place over the two decades for surveillance of cases like influenza and severe acute respiratory illnesses; and the molecular laboratory diagnostic capacity – originally put in place for testing related diseases like drug-resistant tuberculosis,

Lassa fever and HIV (Ihekweazu & Agogo, 2020). This is more pronounced in West African countries such as Sierra Leone, Guinea, Liberia, and Nigeria, which had experienced the outbreak of Ebola in 2014. With this, the local health systems have accumulated useful experiences in monitoring and containing infectious diseases, and in communicating effective response strategies to the local populations (Booth & Stern, 2020). Coupled with the given technical support by WHO and Africa CDC, and training of 12, 500 health workers on pandemic readiness, most of the African countries were better prepared for the anticipated SARS-CoV-2 transmission (WHO, 2020e, f).

Alongside the imposed lockdown and health service provisions as response mechanisms for containment of the community spread of the coronavirus was the enactment of 'stay safe' protocol that is daily and frequently communicated to the public for awareness and adherence. The protocol, include regular washing of the hands with soap and running water, cleaning of hands and frequently touched surfaces with a sanitizer, covering of the mouth and nose with tissue paper when coughing and sneezing or doing so in the flex of the elbow, avoidance of hand touching of the eyes and mouth, restriction of travels or needless movement within communities, and refusal of visitors. Other protocols include all-time use of face masks, staying away from crowded places, and maintenance of social distancing of, at least, 2 meters away from another person. To ensure compliance with the safety protocol, task forces were deployed across sub-Saharan Africa to restrict the movement of people and ensure all-time use of face masks whenever there is a relaxation of the lockdown for people to move and source for food. In the same vein were surveillance-task-forces across the continent to monitor cases of infections and trace the previously made contacts by an infected person. On identification of cases, all positive test cases are referred to isolation centers to be quarantined for 14 days in the first instance as a way to contain community transmission. In recovery, such ones are released to rejoin their families. To create awareness and reinforce the safe protocol information on the public, arrays of media were deployed for reaching out to the public.

COVID-19 AND THE MEDIA: SPECULATIONS, MISREPRESENTATIONS, MISLEADING AND APPROPRIATE INFORMATION DISSEMINATION

In the wake of the widespread COVID-19 is the emergence of varying information about the causes and health implications of the disease in the media. At the forefront of the arrays of emerging information on COVID-19 is social media, which is widely accessible to quite a lot of people for information exchange. With the media, the spreading COVID-19 information emerges from all sorts of people, ranging from notable and political figures, through health personnel and research scientists, to the least person in the society, with such ones disseminating varying information on reality, health risks of the viral disease, and possible preventive or treatment methods. Many of the information, describes as 'infodemic' by WHO (2020g), turned out to be speculations, disinformation, misinformation, and misleading information. Trending in Africa, as retrieved from some of the social media, are information that: 'coronavirus was cultured as a biological weapon to reduce the ever-growing global human populations, especially in Africa'; 'coronavirus was caused by consumption of raw reptiles and uncooked animal intestines by the Chinese', even with accompanying videos to support the assumption on such consumptions. On another note, there was widespread of videos on the social media showing the effect of SARS-CoV-2 to be profuse convulsion and instant death of infected persons across China. Although, the convulsing and dead dropping of infected persons in the videos could not be officially confirmed, the scenes in the video clips created a great deal of anxiety among those that watched the footage.

On another note were utterances by political leaders in and outside Africa that either downplay or misrepresent the reality of the viral disease. In Africa was the use of religious rhetoric, by the likes the former President of Burundi, Pierre Nkurunziza, proclaiming that 'God has cleared coronavirus from Burundi's sky' and the President of Tanzania, John Magufuli, doubting the efficacy of COVID-19 tests and declaring that 'the country is coronavirus free and thanks to prayers by citizens' (Frimpong et al., 2020). Away from Africa are political leaders like the Presidents of Brazil (Jair Bolsonaro) and United States (Donald Trump) trivializing the risks of COVID-19 and equating the diseases with seasonal influenza, questioning the effectiveness of mitigation and control measures like the use of masks, and promoting unproven treatments like the use of hydroxychloroquine (Galvao, 2020). From medical personnel and individuals in Africa is the free flow of information like frequent drinking of water, taking of gin alcohol, warm water, and concoction of onions, garlic, and ginger, and steam bathing as preventing and curative measures of the coronavirus disease. The traditional herbal medicine is not left off the festering COVID-19 information as many of them laid claim to discovery of curative breakthrough for the disease.

The pervading misinformation and misrepresentations of COVID-19 in the social media platforms have greatly facilitated an information environment that heightens the uncertainty about the novel coronavirus and as such stimulates, not only a widespread confusion about the disease among the public but also plagued the public's affective response to the containment protocol of the disease (Simpson & Conner, 2020). Misinformation, as an element of media, influences and undermines individual responses to COVID-19 protocol, especially when it comes to a perceived credible source (Barua, et al., 2020). The consequential effect of the COVID-19 misinformation was an overdose of chloroquine by an entire family in Nigeria on getting to know from the social media that the pharmaceutical drug is a COVID-19 preventive and/or curative measure (Omigbodun & Abdulmalik, 2020). Alongside this are inflictions of psychological traumas and health anxieties on the generality of human society (Serafini et al, 2020). The psychological problems though emerged progressively (Cao, et al., 2020), the greatest effects are on children, older people, and those with underlying health conditions (Kontoangelos et al., 2020; Akat & Karanta, 2020); with the anxieties that they may eventually get and as such died of the disease within the shortest period of infection. As indicated by Mendenhall and Kim (2020), many such individuals with perceived risk of COVID-19 exhibited depressive symptoms as a result of the avalanche of the disease-based misinformation

Notwithstanding the perverseness of misleading and misinformation on COVID-19 in social media, media integration for appropriate information dissemination on the disease remains crucial to reconstructing the misinformation and undoing its damaging effects on human society. In other words, successful containment of community spread of the COVID-19 largely depends on the availability of the right information to the public, which of course, could only get to them through the mutually accessible media between them and the sources of the information. Consequently, media such as radio, television, internet/online channel, mobile phone message applications, postal and handbills, banners and billboards, and social media, were tactically and conscientiously deployed by governments, and other non-governmental agencies, individuals, and private companies for communication of appropriate information on COVID-19. In Africa, media such as radio television, and national health services' official websites were tactically deployed by the governments for regular broadcast and web-posting of the daily cases of infections and recoveries.

On the same note, related information on the disease is largely packaged in mutually acceptable or local languages, and frequently communicated daily for a clear and in-depth understanding of all that should be known about COVID-19 by everyone across the continent. The messages are thus presented in fourms of talks, jingles, songs, cartoons, expert discussions on radio and television. In addition to this is the provision of free toll numbers for communication with health agencies on issues relating to COVID-19 across the countries of the continent (Mviena, et al., 2020; Dessalegn & Frissa, 2020). Based on this, nearly everyone, if not all, across the continent is well aware of the COVID-19 and abreast of all other information that has to do with the disease. The media have thus played significant roles, not only in creating awareness of the causes, mode of transmission, symptoms, and actions to be taken in case of symptoms manifestation by anyone in a family or the neighborhoods, but also proved to be of great value in the attempt to contain the community spread of the coronavirus and strengthening of psychological wellbeing of the African residents. While the media may have proven to be of great value in containing the community spread of the COVID-19 across the African countries, the emergence and initial transmission of the disease have in one way or the other hampered the social and economic lives of the people, with many implications, across the continent.

MICROECONOMIC EFFECTS OF COVID-19 LOCKDOWN ON HOUSEHOLDS' IN AFRICA

Traditionally, human society shares several biological characteristics, among which are respiration, feeding, and mobility. While respiration is essential to sustaining life, food consumption aided life and ensures physical fitness, soundness of mind, and psychological wellbeing. Complementing the two characteristics is the ability to move from one place to the other in search of food and/or to escape danger. The freedom to exercise this biological characteristic however became restricted as a result of the imposition of lockdown on all social and economic engagement by the government of the different countries across the world. Having to stay indoors indefinitely was not only strange to the generality of human society but inflicted hardship on all, especially poor or low-income earners, basically because their means of livelihood have become stalled. In Africa are the following microeconomic implications of the lockdown.

Loss of International-Based Businesses: In Africa, the majority of the human populace are largely employed in the informal sector as traders, street vendors, subsistence farming, transporters, barbers, handcraft and fabricators, carpentry, sand and stone miners, auto mechanics, etc. for daily income. Also in the sector are quite several merchandisers trading on imported products from the developed countries and have such products distributed for marketing in the Africa countries. The lockdown has however led to the closure of the manufacturing companies abroad and as well the airports thereby making it impossible for the merchandisers to get supplies for distribution to the teeming retail dealers of the products. The resultant effect of this is primarily loss of means of livelihood to both the importers and small-scale dealers of the goods. Given this, Booth and Stern (2020) stress that the informal sector in Africa, which constitute about 72percent of the total employment, with the contribution of about 41percent Gross Domestic Product (GDP) to economies of the region (Chilufya, 2020), is severely impacted on by the lockdown; threatening the continent's precarious economic position and basic living standards.

Loss of Revenue and Remittances from Abroad: Inability of the economic system to properly function due to the lockdown across the continent, not only impinged on workers' or businesses' incomes, but also governments' revenues (Ataguba, 2020). Since cash flow could not be stimulated through the normal buying and selling transactions in the informal sector, taxes and tariffs could not be levied and collected by governments' agencies across the continent of Africa, and even elsewhere around the world. On another note is the loss of remittances from Europe and America to Africa. The remittances, which comprise more than 5percent of the GDP in 15 African countries, dramatically declined between 19.7 to 21percent as a result of severe job losses by Africans in the diaspora due to the lockdown (World Bank, 2020; Aidi et al., 2020). This represents a loss of a crucial financial lifeline for many vulnerable households across the continent of Africa.

Loss of Jobs and Income an the Local Informal Businesses: At the local level, restriction of movement as a result of the lockdown equally made it extremely difficult for people in the informal sector to get engaged in any economic activities as their business outlets, such as shops, stores, markets, and workshops, were all closed down. This implies that most of those employed in the informal sector could not earn any income with which to care for essential needs of life during the lockdown. This submission is buttressed by Michler and Kilic's (2020) indication that an estimated 258million individuals, constituting 80percent of the populations across Ethiopia, Malawi, Nigeria, and Uganda, were shut out of the opportunity to operate their business for income generation due to the lockdown. The resultant effect of this is the financial strain of families' abilities to meet their essential needs of life (Ataguba, 2020). These daunting effects became obvious in most communities across the continent as purchases of essential commodities, such as food and pharmaceutical drugs in the neighborhoods, were largely on credit or part payment during the lockdown to pay offsetting the costs later. A similar observation by Michler and Kilic (2020) revealed that an estimated 20 percent to 25 percent of households across the four African countries were unable to purchase essential commodities. In South Africa, Arndt et al., (2020) indicated that the reduction of hours worked ranged between 26 and 40, coupled with a 40percent decline in the use of capital. Consequently, food insecurity became a contentious issue among African households during the lockdown. The rural areas are not left of the economic losses as Buonsenso et al (2020) reported that most people across villages is in Sierra Leone lost their jobs as a result of the lockdown.

Disruption of Food Supply System: To ensure ready availability of food during the lockdown, farmers, regarded as essential service workers, were granted the opportunity to go to farms for farm enterprise production, though with strict observation of the COVID-19 protocol. The farming activities were however marred by the COVID-19 lockdown as farmers could not access agro-inputs, particularly seeds, fertilizer, and agrochemicals basically because markets, where such inputs are to be accessed, were under lock. With the coincidence of the COVID-19 outbreak and the imposition of the lockdown between February and March, which are months that farming activities often begin in sub-Saharan Africa, food production could not commence as expected in most of the sub-region. In addition, it was extremely difficult to have the harvested food crops from the previous season's production transported to the markets due to lack of transportation. This difficulty was engendered by a lack of access roads to farms and the rare availability of vehicles plying the rural areas. Consequently, the agri-food system GDP in the continent thus fell by 11 percent or by US$1.6billion (Andam et al., 2020). The resultant effects of this include shortage of food supply with its attendant increase in the prices of food due to an increase in demand by the teeming populations across the continent.

Sharp Increase in Food Prices and Household's Food Expenditure: In the wake of COVID-19 lockdown, the need for ensuring food availability while indoors led to panic buying and stockpiling of food. This rush thus led to a sharp increase in food prices by 14 to 18 percent in South Africa (Bassier et al., 2020), by 14.9 percent to 15.2 percent in Nigeria (Adegboye, 2020), and in Zimbabwe, South Sudan, and Sudan, the prices continue to increase substantially (Blanke, 2020). Notwithstanding the increase in food prices, the essentiality of this commodity made the demand for food remains on the increase, with the consequential exponential increase in households' expenditure on food, during the lockdowns (Reinsdorf et al., 2020; Blanke, 2020). In Nigeria, 56 percent of the total household expenditure was on food leading to impoverishment of the of the larger proportion of the citizens and a 9 percent increase in the national poverty rate (Andam et al., 2020).

SOCIO-DYNAMIC EFFECTS OF COVID-19 LOCKDOWN ON HOUSEHOLDS IN AFRICA

Against the traditional social and economic interactions that characterize the daily activities of nearly everyone in Africa is the imposed stay-at-home orders by the African governments in an attempt to flatten the COVID-19 curve across the region. Implications of the policy action include compulsorily staying indoors with the consequential hindrance of public physical interactions and restriction of movement from one place to the other. This raises concerns about individuals and families' social safety nets to have their incomes and livelihoods protected, access essential goods and services, social support availability, and psychological wellbeing (Tull et al., 2020; Marroquin et al., 2020). These concerns became manifested in various dimensions as the days of the lockdown progresses, which include:

The Challenge of Food Insecurity: The very first concern of the possible effects of COVID-19 lockdowns across Africa is steady food access, especially among the daily income earners. In Nigeria for instance, the need for households to stock up food resources before the commencement of the lockdown in March could not be adequately fulfilled due to lack of the financial base to do so. With this situation and uncertainty of how long the lockdown would be, most people were apprehensive of becoming starved and possibly dying of hunger rather than that of COVID-19. Reporting the impact of the COVID-19 stay-at-home orders on the African citizens, Bodwig et al., (2020) observed rumblings of discontent by households as they were hit hard by the government imposed lockdown, putting their livelihoods at risk due to disruption of their economies and sources of income generation. During the lockdown, apprehension of food insecurity become manifested as households could not adequately meet their food needs. In Kenya and Uganda, the proportion of food insecurity increased by 38 percent and 44 percent respectively (Kansiime et al., 2020). To cope with this situation, most people looked onto the government for the supply of food and/or cash gifts as a palliative to cushion the effects of the hardship imposed by the lockdown.

Apprehension of Hospital-Based Covid-19 Infection and Stigmatization: Because of the anxiety created by the available information on the mechanisms of COVID-19 transmission and its purported virulence, those with health issues became apprehensive of taking medical help in the hospitals, especially the public health facilities, for fear of getting infected in the place and/or being declared coronavirus positive. This is based on the fact that most people dreaded the viral disease a lot, largely because of being placed in isolation if infected, and maybe stigmatized by avoidance in the community. The stigmatization experienced played out in South Africa where a COVID-19 survivor had her son and place of resident labeled 'corona kid' and 'corona house' respectively (Owings, 2020). Consequently, people generally resort to self-treatment using herbs or beaconing on medical personnel in private hospitals for health services. In addition, quite several people began applying recommended treatment or preventive measures, such as steam bathing, the regular dosage of a concoction of ginger, onions, and garlic, and local herbs, as obtained from the social media or recommended by close associates.

Impairment of Association, Socialization and Recreation: The stay-at-home orders ordinarily disrupted all forms of physical contacts and as such, the traditional association at physical spots for recreation and socialization were halted. Consequently, people greatly missed out on partying, merry-making at joints and bars, and on celebrations and festivities. This situation is somehow difficult to bear in Africa where ceremonies are highly prized and as such, quite several people violated the social distancing component of the COVID-19 protocol. In Nigeria, some celebrities were arrested for hosting parties in violation of the lockdown rule. Similarly, a popular cleric was arrested in Niger for attending a traditional ceremony (Control Risks, 2020). The uneasiness of the lockdown was also felt by children as many had to trouble their parents for not being able to attend schools where they ordinarily socialize. A survey of the impact of the COVID-19 lockdown on children's education across the African countries by the Human Rights Watch – HRW (2020) revealed feelings of anxieties, depressions, and psychological stress from their expressions. From Kenya were expressions such as: "I tend to think a lot about school and my friends", and 'It is stressful too when I have to study all alone". From Cameroon comes the expression by a student that: "Especially as a teenager … I was completely struggling for a whole two weeks, like crying every day. … was like a big thing for me, starting to think that life was meaningless".

Community Crimes and Social Unrest: Life in Africa is generally characterized by poor living conditions with quite several people living below the poverty line. Among the poor are individuals without any form of employment but living on what might come their way as they socialize in the informal economic sector. This set of people are hard-hit by the lockdown as they had no one to interact with for income and to meet their daily food needs. Consequently, such individuals, as observed in some parts of Nigeria, resorted to community crime by looting food stores and breaking into houses to rob households of money and food items for self-satisfaction. This development not only heightens the already inflicted anxieties on people by the waves of COVID-19 but also amplifies their worries of insecurity and its attendant psychological traumas. In another development is the reportage of a clash between the Senegalese security forces and dozens of people who defied the stay-at-home orders to attend traditional ceremonies (Control Risks, 2020). Similarly is religious-cum-COVID-19 lockdown riot on account of the closedown of mosques and arrest of a popular cleric for defying the lockdown. In Kenya, Ethiopia and Uganda were violent mobs against foreign nationals perceived to be propagating COVID-19 across the respective countries.

Increased Rate of Food Consumption: In as much as feeding is essential to life sustenance and healthy living, food reserves may be quickly depleted with an increased rate of consumption and less opportunity to replenish the food stall. This situation played out among households across Africa in the wake of the COVID-19 lockdown. Against the traditional practice of daily taking of one or two meals at home, the prolonged state-at-home orders greatly induced an increased rate of food consumption among the households, especially in households with two or more under-aged children. With little or no opportunity to promptly replenish the food stall, stored food that would generally last a household for a month, barely last two or three weeks. While some households with savings could not be out to source for more food, many of the daily income earners found it difficult to replenish and as such had to resort to credit buying or relying on food support from other well-to-do individuals. With more spending on food than normal and less opportunity to generate additional income, most households are becoming impoverished and as such would need more social safety net support to save the continent from generating the 'new poor' in the social system.

Impact of Lockdown on Family Relationships: One of the advantages of the imposed stay-at-home orders is the togetherness of family members as they had more time together for the duration of the lockdown. In essence, time was spent together at meals and recreations by families; couples or fathers and mothers had time for affection for each other, and between parents and children. With the closedown of schools and day-care centers, parents became solely responsible for the care of the children, and the difficulty of striking a work-family balance, especially among the working couples, has become achieved among families during the COVID-19 lockdown (Fisher et al., 2020). Although the lockdown has pushed the existing conflicts among some families to the surface, it proved to be an opportunity to redress the contending issues among them thereby strengthening the bonds of their relationships and cohesiveness.

Innovative Schooling: The traditional system of schooling in sub-Saharan Africa is by physical interactions between teachers and students/pupils in classroom settings. With the lockdown running till August 2020, electronic schooling was deployed to keep the students/pupils busy academically between May and July 2020. In Nigeria for instance, while the state governments deployed the public radio and television stations for daily instructional delivery, the private schools integrated WhatsApp for the teaching of the students. Critical assessment of these electronic methods revealed that instructional delivery by radio and television was by oral delivery accompanied with screenwriting for the students. Similarly, teaching on WhatsApp was by audio recordings of lessons to be taught, uploaded with the lesson notes for the students to listen to, and copied as personal notes. While the two approaches of instructional delivery for learning kept the students busy academically, it was invariably impossible for any students to interact directly with the teachers for feedback or regain lost parts or the whole of the lessons delivered through the radio and television broadcast, possibly due to power outage. WhatsApp integration however enabled the students to revisit the accessed lesson notes and the audio recordings for explanations; given assignments could be done and submitted via the WhatsApp platforms as may be instructed by their teachers.

HOUSEHOLDS' RESILIENCE, SOCIAL PROTECTION SUPPORT, AND RECOVERY FROM IMPACTS OF COVID-19 PANDEMIC

Lifestyle in Africa is though generally characterized by poor living conditions, an outbreak of COVID-19, and its attendant stay-at-home orders further brought untold social and economic hardships on millions of people across the continent. In the region, where about 8 out of 10 people earn their daily living from informal employment (Bodwig et al., 2020), impacts of the imposed lockdown have been more daunting, plunging the majority of the households or citizens into intensified poor living conditions, exacerbating food insecurity and excruciating health challenges. This calls for a great deal of social protection support for most households across the continent, which could be from governments and individuals. In response to this were organizations of palliative measures in terms of food distribution and cash transfers by government and individuals to the needy individuals and households across the continent. In Mauritania, Kenya, and Ethiopia, there was the direct distribution of food support by the government to households (Bodwig et al., 2020). In countries like Togo, Burkina Faso, and South Africa, there was the transfer of cash to the bank and mobile accounts of holders to cushion the financial needs of households in the countries (Grun, et al., 2020; Arndt et al., 2020).

Supporting the governments on social protection support in Africa are philanthropies, private organizations, and multilateral organizations. In Nigeria, there were donations in cash and kinds by philanthropies and private companies to the government for the care of the needy in the country. In addition to this was support by Private Sector Coalition Against COVID-19 (CACOVID), comprising more than 50 partner organizations, to the Nigerian government with the sole aim of combating COVID-19 in the country. As of June 2020, the coalition has mobilized more than US$72million as donation. In addition to this were donations of food items in the worth of N23billion (US$47.9million @ N480 to $1), with CA-COVID labels, for onward distribution as a palliative to the needy and vulnerable, put at 1.7 million families or 10million people across the 774 Local Government Areas in the country, during the lockdown (Bassey, 2020). The multilateral aid agencies, such as European Union (EU) and United Nations (UN), supported the Nigerian government with a grant of €50million and a donation of 50 A30 ventilators and personal protective supplies in the worth of US$2.2million, respectively (Eribo, 2020). The UN Women also supported the government with a donation of US$100, 000 for the purchase and distribution of palliatives to the most vulnerable women across 14 states in the country.

Notwithstanding the given social protection support, the need for food is ever on the increase and as such, households had to ration what is available to them for sustenance. To cope with this situation, most households have foregone all other purchases by reserving their savings mainly for food, and in rare cases for medicine, which are considered essential needs. On another note, family members, particularly parents had to skip some meals or eat less for the children to be satisfied, as they eat more often than adults. As expressed by Buheji (2020), the resilience put up by families during hardships could help to create an equilibrium that supports the attainment of balance, harmony, and recovery from the COVID-19 challenging effects. Further help to cope with the impact of the lockdown was intermittent relaxation of the lockdown which made it possible for people to source food in the markets. This is however under the strict observation of the COVID-19 protocol (Moseley & Battersby, 2020).

Psychological protection also plays significant role in coping with the effects of the COVID-19 lockdown among African households. This was affected by regular calls on friends and relatives to cheer up one another and to know whether they are staying safe. In addition to this, were reminders on the need for careful observation of the stay safe protocol and suggestions on actions to be taken as a way to cope with the lockdown. This made it possible for several people to curtail negative thinking thereby boosting their self-esteem. Households' engagement in value-driven activities, acknowledgment, and acceptance of the reality of the lockdown, and its attendant negative experiences, were of value in coping with the anxiety of the lockdown (Polizzi & Lynn, 2020). Individuals equally took solace in religious or philosophical beliefs to cope with the COVID-19 harsh condition as this forms part of the human psyche, healthcare, and wellbeing (Roman et al., 2020).

CONCLUSION AND POLICY RECOMMENDATIONS

The least expected event with daunting effects on the global human society is the outbreak of the COVID-19 pandemic in late 2019. The yet to be fully understood viral disease began in the city of Wuhan in China and spread to the most distant parts of the earth through human-to-human transmissions. The death-dealing effect of the disease is though more pronounced among older people and those with critical health conditions, the social and economic impacts are harshly felt by all strata of the human society as a result of the stay-at-home orders imposed by governments of the different countries. The resultant shutdown of the global economy due to peoples' inability to move about for engagement in social and economic activities has invariably resulted in the infliction of hardships on the global human society, but with severe impacts in Africa. Although transmission and death cases from the COVID-19 pandemic were relatively low in Africa, the impinged social and economic hardships in the continent are enormous and these ranged through complete loss or temporary halt of means of livelihood, heightened food, and nutrition insecurity, increased poverty condition and emergence of new poor, and excruciating health challenges. This suggests that any social policy that restricts social interactions among the human populace will greatly impinge hardships on their wellbeing, and may in turn result in various social vices that may heighten the existing anxieties in human society. While the contemporary generations may have developed social strategies to cope with the restriction effects, social protection supports by government and non-government organizations become essential to enhance the living condition of Africans. As an outcome of this write-up, the following recommendations are conceived as policy actions to guide sustainable livelihood amidst pandemic in Africa:

1. The present community spread of COVID-19 in Africa should be stemmed by strengthening the regular information dissemination on the reality, virulence, mode of transmission and preventive actions to be taken against the disease using the mutually accessible media to all strata of the African societies
2. Total lockdown should as much as possible be prevented to enable the citizens to maintain and sustain their means of livelihoods, but under the strict guidance of the 'stay safe' protocol, if possible by the enforcement
3. The mass media should as well be integrated for communication of experiences by survivors of coronavirus as a way to alleviate the public's apprehension of the wrong notions about the diseases
4. Social protection support should be well arranged and coordinated for reaching out to the needy and vulnerable groups across the African countries
5. The psychological well-being of citizens should be strengthened by encouraging them to rather contemplate and generate positive feelings and tolerance towards selves and others
6. People should be motivated to be engaged in value-driven activities and marshaling social support to improve their stressful living condition
7. Social connectedness to communities or faith-based organizations, healthcare providers should be strengthened to nurture the much-needed resilience to cope with the lingering health crisis

REFERENCES

Adegboye, F. S. (2020). Food prices in Nigeria have shot through the roof. But is the pandemic to blame? *The Conservation*. https://theconservation.com/food-prices-in

Africa News. (2020). *Africa COVID-19 stats: 874, 036cases; 18,498 deaths; 524, 577 recoveries*. https://www.africanews.com

Aidi, W., Fatai, R., & Karingi, S. (2020). COVID-19 and migrant remittances: Supporting this essential lifeline under threat. *Brookings: Africa in Focus*. https://www.brookings.edu/blog/africa-in-focus/2020/10/26/COVID-19-and-migrnt-remittances-supporting-this-essential-lifeline-under-thereat

Akat, M., & Karanta, K. (2020). Psychological effects of COVID-19 pandemic on society and its reflections on education. *Turkish Studies*, *15*(14), 1–13. https://dx.do.org/10.7827/TurskishTudies.44336

All Africa. (2020). *Africa: Over 2milliom COVID-19 recoveries across the continent*. https://allafrica.com/stories/202012130022.html

Andam, K., Edeh, H., Oboh, V., Pauw, K., & Thurlow, J. (2020). Impacts of COVID-19 on food system and poverty in Nigeria. *Advances in Food Security and Sustainability*, *15*, 145–173. doi:10.1016/bs.af2s.2020.09.002

Arndt, C., Davies, R., Babriel, S., Harris, L., Makrelove, K., Robinson, S., ... Anderson, L. (2020). COVID-19 lockdowns, income distribution, and food security: An analysis for South Africa. *Global Food Security*, *26*, 100410. doi:10.1016/j.gfs.2020.100410 PMID:32834955

Ataguba, J. E. (2020). COVID-19 pandemic, a war to be worn: Understanding its economic implications for Africa. *Applied Health Economics and Health Policy*, *18*(3), 325–328. doi:10.100740258-020-00580-x PMID:32249362

Barua, Z., Barua, S., Aktar, S., Kabir, N., & Li, M. (2020). Effects of misinformation on COVID-19 individual responses and recommendations for resilience of disastrous information consequences of misinformation. *Progress in Disaster Science*, *8*, 100119. doi:10.1016/j.pdisas.2020.100119 PMID:34173443

Bassey, J. (2020). CACOVID launches 23bn food palliative for 1.7m households. *Business Day*. https://businessday.ng/coronavirus/article/cacovid-launches-n23bn-food-palliative-for-1-7m-households/

Bassier, I., Joala, R., & Vilankazi, T. (2020). South Africa needs better food price controls to shield poor people from COVID-19 fallout. *The Conservation*. https://theconservation.com/south-africa-needs-better-food-price-controls-to-shield-poor-people-from-COVID-19-fallout-143288

Blanke, J. (2020). Economic impact of COVID-19: Protecting Africa's food systems from farm to fork. *Brookings: Africa in Focus*. https://www.brookings.edu/blog/africa-in-focus/2020/06/economic-impact-of-COVID-19-protecting-africas-food-systems-from-farm-to-fork

Bodwig, C., Gentilini, U., Usman, Z., & Williams, P. (2020). *COVID-19 in Africa: How can social safety nets help mitigate the social and economic impacts?* World Bank Blogs. https://blogs.worldbank.org/african/COVID-19-africa-how-can-social-safety-nets-help-mitigate-social-and-economic-impacts

Booth, A., & Stern, O. (2020). Social and economic impacts of COVID-19 across sub-Saharan Africa. *Kroll.* https://www.kroll.com/en/insights/publications/africa/social-economic-impact-COVID-19-sub-saharan-africa

Buheji, M. (2020). Psychological resilience and poor communities coping with COVID-19 pandemic. *International Journal of Psychology and Behavioral Sciences, 10*(4), 100–108. doi:10.5923/j.ijpbs.20201004.03

Buonsenso, D., Cinicola, B., Rafaelli, F., Sollena, P., & Iodice, F. (2020). Social consequences of COVID-19 in a low resource setting in Sierra Leone, West Africa. *International Journal of Infectious Diseases, 97*, 23–26. doi:10.1016/j.ijid.2020.05.104 PMID:32497794

Cao, W., Fang, Z., Hou, G., Han, M., Xu, A., Dong, J., & Zheng, J. (2020). The psychological impact of the COVID-19 epidemic on college students in China. *Psychiatry Research, 287*, 112934. doi:10.1016/j.psychres.2020.112934 PMID:32229390

Cennimo, D. J. (n.d.). Coronavirus disease 2019 (COVID-19). *Medscape.* https://emedicine.medscape.com/article/2500114-overview#

Chan, K. H., Peiris, J. S., Lam, S. Y., Poon, L. L., Yuen, K. Y., & Seto, W. H. (2011). The effects of temperature and relative humidity on the viability of the SARS coronavirus. *Advances in Virology, 2011*, 1–7. Advance online publication. doi:10.1155/2011/734690 PMID:22312351

Chilufya, C. (2020). *The African economy is "infected": The economic impacts of COVID-19 is worsening poverty in Africa.* Xavier. https://xavier.network/news/the-african-economy-is-infected-the-economic-impacts-of-COVID-19-is-worsening-poverty-in-africa

Control Risks. (2020). *Sub-Saharan Africa: COVID-19 mitigation measures.* https://www.controrisk.com/COVID-19-mitigation-measures-across-sub-saharan-africa

Crowder, L. V., Lindley, W., Trulove, W., Ilboudo, J. P., & Castello, R. D. (1998). *Knowledge and information for food security in Africa: From traditional media to the internet.* Food and Agriculture Organisation. https://www.fao.org/3/w9290e/w9290e00.htm

Das, A. K., & Gopalan, S. A. (2020). Epidemiology of COVID-19 and predictors of recovery in the Republic of Korea. *Pulmonary Medicine, 2020*, 1–6. Advance online publication. doi:10.1155/2020/7291698 PMID:32774918

Dessalegn, B.-W. S., & Frissa, S. (2020). *Combating the mental health impact of COVID-19 in SubSaharan Africa*. ASSET. https://healthasset.org/combatting-the-mental-health-impact-of-COVID-19-sub-saharan-africa/

Dodo, M. K. (2002). *Understanding Africa's food security challenges*. doi:10.5772/intechopen.91773

ECDC. (2020). *COVID-19 situation update worldwide as of 12 December 2020*. European Centre for Disease Prevention and Control. https://www.ecdc.europea.eu/en/gographical-distribution-2019-ncocov-cases

Eribo, S. (2020). *In Nigeria, philanthropy's COVID-19 response raises questions*. Alliance for Philanthropy and Social Investment Worldwide. https://www.alliancemagazine.org/blog/nigeria-philantropy-COVID-19-response-raises-questions/

FAO. (2020). Africa: Regional overview of food security and nutrition. Food and Agriculture Organisation.

Fisher, J., Languilaire, J.-C., Lawthom, R., Nieuwenhuis, R., Petts, R. J., Runswick-Cole, K., & Yerkes, M. A. (2020). Community, work, and family in times of COVID-19. *Community Work & Family*, *23*(3), 247–252. Advance online publication. doi:10.1080/13668803.2020.1756568

Frimpong, O. B., Bihuzo, R. M., & Commodore, R. (2020). *The COVID-19 pandemic in Africa: Impact, responses, and lessons from Ghana, the Democratic Republic of the Congo and Rwanda*. https://www.wilsoncenter.org/publication/COVID-19-afroica-impact-responses-and-lessons-ghana-democratic-republic-congo

Galvao, J. (2020). COVID-19: The deadly threat of misinformation. *The Lancet. Infectious Diseases*. Advance online publication. doi:10.1016/S1473-3099(20)30721-0 PMID:33031753

Glaesser, D., Kester, J., Paulos, H., Alizadeh, A., & Valentin, B. (2017). Global travel pattern: An overview. *Journal of Travel Medicine*, *24*(4). Advance online publication. doi:10.1093/jtm/tax007 PMID:28637267

Grun, R., Semali, A., & Vandeninden, F. (2020). *The virus that spurred Burkina Faso and African nations to scale up its social safety nets*. World Bank Blogs. https://blogs.worldbank.org/nasikiliza/virus-spurred-burkina-faso-and-safrican-nations-scale-its-social-safety-nets

Guy, J. S. (2018). Beyond global modernity, global consciousness and global governmentality: The symmetrical anthropology of globalisation. *European Journal of Social Theory*, *19*(4), 451–467. doi:10.1177/1368431016655066

Higuera, V. (2017). *How are diseases transmitted?* Healthline. https://www.healthline.com/health/disease-transmission

HRW. (2020). Impact of COVID-19 on children's education in Africa. *The Human Rights Watch*. https://www.hrw.org/news/2020/08/26/imact-COVID-19-childrens-education-africa

Ihekweazu, C., & Agogo, E. (2020). Africa's response to COVID-19. *BMC Medicine*, *18*(151), 151. Advance online publication. doi:10.118612916-020-01622-w PMID:32438912

Janeway, C. A. Jr, Travers, P., Walkport, M., & Shlomchik, M. J. (2001). *Immunobiology* (5th ed.). Garland Science.

Kansiime, M. K., Tambo, J. A., Mugambi, I., Bundi, M., Kara, A., & Owuor, C. (2020). COVID-19 implications on household income and food security in Kenya and Uganda: Findings from a rapid assessment. *World Development*, *137*, 105199. doi:10.1016/j.worlddev.2020.105199 PMID:32982018

Kontoangelos, K., Economou, M., & Papageorgiou, C. (2020). Mental health effects of COVID-19 pandemia: A review of clinical and psychological traits. *Psychological Investigation*, *17*(6), 491–505. doi:10.30773/pi.2020.0161 PMID:32570296

Kuy, S. R., Tsai, R., Bhatt, J., Chu, Q. D., Ghandi, P., Gupta, R., ... Correa, R. (2020). Focusing on vulnerable populations during COVID-19. Note to the Editor. *Academic Medicine*, *95*(11), e2–e3. Advance online publication. doi:10.1097/ACM.0000000000003571 PMID:32639264

Latz, C. A., DeCarlo, C., Boitano, L., Png, C. Y. M., Patell, R., Conrad, M. F., Eagleton, M., & Dua, A. (2020). Blood type and outcomes in patients with COVID-19. *Annals of Hematology*, *99*(9), 1–6. doi:10.100700277-020-04169-1 PMID:32656591

Lew, A. A. (2018). Why travel? – Travel, tourism and global consciousness. *Tourism Geographies*, *20*(4), 742–749. doi:10.1080/14616688.2018.1490343

Maclean, R., & Mark, S. (2020). 10 African countries have no ventilators: That's only part of the problem. *The New York Times*. https://www.nytimes.com/2020/04/18/world/africa/ africa-coronavirus-ventillators.html

Marroquin, B., Vine, V., & Morgan, R. (2020). Mental health during the COVID-19 pandemic: Effects of stay-at-home policies, social distancing behaviours, and social resources. *Psychiatry Research*, *293*, 113419. doi:10.1016/j.psychres.2020.113419 PMID:32861098

Mendenhall, E., & Kim, A. W. (2020). People in Soweto told us about their fears in the first weeks of South Africa's lockdown. *The Conservation*. https://theconservation.com/people-in-soweto-told-us-about-their-fears-in-the-first-weeks- of-south-africa-lockdown-142325

Michler, J., & Kilic, T. (2020). *Socioeconomic impacts of COVID-19 in four African countries: Watch the event recording*. The World Bank. https://www.worldbank.org/en/programs/ lsms/brief/socioeconomic-impacts-of-COVID-19-in-four-african-countries-watch-the-event-recording

Moseley, W. G., & Battersby, J. (2020). The vulnerability and resilience of African food systems, food security, and nutrition in the context of the COVID-19 pandemic. *African Studies Review*, *63*(3), 449–461. doi:10.1017/asr.2020.72

Mviena, J. L., Fanne, M., Gondo, R., Mwamelo, A., Esso, L., Epée, E., Mballa, G. A. E., & Boum, Y. (2020). How mental health care is changing Cameroon because of the COVID-19 pandemic. *The Lancet. Psychiatry*, *7*(10), E62–E63. doi:10.1016/S2215-0366(20)30390-4 PMID:32949524

Nicola, M., Alsafi, Z., Sohrabi, C., Kerwan, A., Al-Jabir, A., Iosifidis, C., Agha, M., & Agha, R. (2020). The socio-economic implications of the coronavirus pandemic (COVID-19): A review. *International Journal of Surgery*, *78*, 185–193. doi:10.1016/j.ijsu.2020.04.018 PMID:32305533

Omigbodun, O., & Abdulmalik, J. (2020). The pandemic will affect the mental health of these groups. *African Arguments*. https://africanarguments.org/2020/04/the- pandemic-will-affect-the-mental-health-of-these-groups/

Owings, L. (2020). Africa 'not ready' for COVID-19 mental health issues. *Sci. Dev. Net*. https://www.scidev.nt/sub-saharan-africa/news/afric-not-ready-for-COVID-19-mental-health-issue

PHAC. (n.d.). *Healthy living*. Government of Canada. https://www.canada.ca/en/public-health/services/health-promotion/healthy-living-html#

Polizzi, C., & Lynn, S. J. (2020). Your coping and resilience strategies might need to shift as the COVID-19 crisis continues. *The Conservation*. https://theconservation.com/your-coping-and-resilience-strategies-might-need-to-shift-as-the-COVID-19-crisis-continues-140507

Reinsdorf, M., Tebrake, J., O'Hanlon, N., & Graf, B. (2020). CPI weights and COVID-19 household expenditure pattern. *Statistics: Special Series on COVID-19*. https://www.imf.org/~/media/files/publications/covid19-special-notes/en-special-series-0n-COVID-19-cpi-weights-and-COVID-19-expenditure-patterns.ashx

Riddell, S., Goldie, S., Hill, A., Eagles, D., & Drew, T. W. (2020). The effect of temperature on persistence of SARS-CoV-2 on common surfaces. *Virology Journal, 17*(1), 145. doi:10.118612985-020-01418-7 PMID:33028356

Roman, N. V., Mthembu, T. G., & Hoosen, M. (2020). Spiritual care – 'Adeeper immunity' – A response to COVID-19 pandemic. *African Journal of Primary Healthcare and Medicine, 12*(1), 2456. doi:10.4102/phcfm.v12i1.2456 PMID:32634003

Sasson. (2012). Food security for Africa: an urgent global challenge. *Agriculture and Food Security, 1*(2).

Serafini, G., Parmigiani, B., Amerio, A., Aguglia, A., Sher, L., & Amore, M. (2020). The psychological impact of COVID-19 on the mental health in the general population. *QJM: An International Journal of Medicine, 113*(8), 531–537. doi:10.1093/qjmed/hcaa201 PMID:32569360

Simpson, E., & Conner, A. (2020). *Fighting coronavirus misinformation and disinformation – Preventive product recommendations for social media platforms*. Technology Policy: Centre for American Progress. https://www.americanprogress.org/issues/technology-policy/reports/2020/08/18/488714/fighting-coronavirus-misinformation-disinformation/

Sohrabi, C., Alsafi, Z., O'Neill, N., Khan, M., Kerwan, A., Al-Jabir, A., Iosifidis, C., & Agha, R. (2020). World Health Organisation declares global emergency: A review of the 2019 novel coronavirus (COVID-19). *International Journal of Surgery, 76*, 71–76. doi:10.1016/j.ijsu.2020.02.034 PMID:32112977

The National Academies. (n.d.). Encountering microbes – Entering the human host. *Infectious Diseases*.https://needtoknow.nas.edu/id/infection/encountering-microbes/entering-the-human-host/#

Tull, M. T., Edmonds, K. A., Scamaldo, K. Y., Richmond, J. R., Rose, J. P., & Gratz, K. L. (2020). Psychological outcomes associated with stay-at-home orders and the perceived impact of COVID-19 on daily life. *Psychiatry Research, 287*, 113098. doi:10.1016/j.psychres.2020.113098

UNDP. (2020). *COVID-19: Socio-economic impact*. United Nations Development Program. https://www.undp.org/content/undp/en/coronavirus/socio-economic-impact-of-COVID-19.html

UNESCO (2020). *Socio-economic and cultural impacts of COVID-19 on Africa – UNESCO responses*. United Nations Scientific and Cultural Organisation.

UNICEF. (2020). *Key messages and actions for COVID-19 prevention and control in schools*. United Nations Children Education Fund/World Health Organisation. https://www.who.int/key-messages-and-actions-for-COVID-19-preventiopn-and-control-in-schools

Voinsky, I., Baristaite, G., & Gurwitz, D. (2020). Effects of age and sex on recovery from COVID-19: Analysis of 5769 Israeli patients. *The Journal of Infection*, *81*(2), e102–e103. doi:10.1016/j.jinf.2020.05.026 PMID:32425274

WEF. (2020). *Fighting COVID-19 could cost 500 times as much as pandemic prevention measures*. World Economic Forum. https://www.weforum.org/agenda/2020/08/pandemic-fight-costs-500x-morethen-preventing-one-futurity

WHO. (2020a). *Impact of COVID-19 on people's livelihoods, their health and our food system*. Joint statement by ILO, FAO, IFAD and WHO: World Health Organisation. https://www.who.int/news/item/13-10-2020-impact-of-COVID-19-on-people's-livelihoods-their-health-and-our-food-systems

WHO. (2020b). *COVID-19 cases top 10 000 in Africa*. World Health Organisation: Regional Office for Africa. https://www.afro.who.int/news/COVID-19-cases-top-10000-africa#

WHO. (2020c). *A second COVID-19 case is confirmed in Africa*. World Health Organisation: Regional Office for Africa. https://www.afro.who.int/news/secon-COVID-19-cases-confirmed-in-africa

WHO. (2020d). *Weekly bulletin on outbreaks and other emergencies*. World Health Organisation: Regional Office for Africa. https://apps.who.int/iris/bitstream/handle/10665/331892/OEW17-2026042020.pdf

WHO. (2020e). *COVID-19: vulnerable and high risk group*. World Health Organisation. https://www.who.int/westernpacific/emergencies/COVID-19information/high-risk-group#

WHO. (2020f). *COVID-19 in Africa: Marking six months of response*. World Health Organisation: Regional Office for Africa. https://www.afro.who.int/COVID-19-africa-marking-six-months-response

WHO. (2020g). *Managing the COVID-19 infodemic: Promoting healthy behaviours and mitigating the harm from information dissemination*. World Health Organisation: https://www.who.int/news/iten/23-09-2020-managing-the-COVID-19-infodemic-promoting-healthy-behaviours-and-mitigating-the-harm-from-misinformation-and-disinformation

World Bank. (2020). *World Bank predicts sharpest decline of remittance in recent history*. https://www.wordbank.org/en/news/press-relase/2020/04/22/world-bank-predicts-sharpest-decline-of-remittances-in-recent-history

Wu, Y., Jing, W., Liu, J., Ma, Q., Yuan, J., Wang, Y., Du, M., & Liu, M. (2020). Effects of temperature and humidity on the daily cases and new deaths of COVID-19 in 166 countries. *The Science of the Total Environment*, *729*, 139051. Advance online publication. doi:10.1016/j.scitotenv.2020.139051 PMID:32361460

Wyper, G. M. A., Assuncao, R., Cuschieri, S., Devleesschauwer, B., Fletcher, E., Haagsma, J. A., & Grant, I. (2020). Population vulnerability to COVID-19 in Europe: A burden of disease analysis. *Archives of Public Health*, *78*, 27. doi:10.118613690-020-0043-y

Ziet, M., Zucker, J., & Tatonetti, N. P. (2020). Associations between blood type and COVID-19 infection, incubation and death. *Nature Communications*, *11*(1), 5761. doi:10.103841467-020-19623-x PMID:33188185

KEY TERMS AND DEFINITIONS

COVID-19: It is caused by a coronavirus called SARS-CoV-2 which is a new virus. On contracts this virus through contact with another person who has the virus.

Food Insecurity: It is the state of having less reliable access to a sufficient quantity of affordable and nutritious food for healthy living and improved quality of life.

Gross Domestic Product (GDP): It is the total market value of all final goods and services produced within a country's borders during a specific time period. It is considered to be a broad measure of overall domestic production and determination of the state of the economy.

Meta-Analysis: It is a statistical analysis that examines data from a number of studies concerning the same subject as a means to determine the overall trends.

Remittances: It is a non-commercial transfer of money by a foreign worker or by a citizen with family ties overseas that is used for the purpose of household income in their home country.

SARS-CoV-2: It is a virus with origins from the severe acute respiratory syndrome–related coronavirus (SARSr-CoV). This virus is largely responsible for the COVID-19 pandemic.

Sub-Sahara Africa: It is the area of the African continent that lies south of the Sahara. Based on the classification by the United Nations, it consists of African countries that are fully or partially south of the Sahara.

APPENDIX

Table 1. Covıd-19 cases in Africa, as at December 13, 2020

No	Country	Cases	Recoveries	Deaths
1	South Africa	852,965	760,118	23,106
2	Morocco	397,597	353,098	6,589
3	Egypt	121,089	104,710	6,898
4	Ethiopia	116,297	92,449	1,803
5	Tunisia	110,393	84,218	3,836
6	Algeria	91,638	60,028	2,584
7	Kenya	91,526	72,596	1,586
8	Libya	89,880	59,839	1,278
9	Nigeria	72,757	65,850	1,194
10	Ghana	52,933	51,676	327
11	Uganda	27,071	9,744	220
12	Cameroon	25,143	23,851	443
13	Cote d'Ivoire	21,639	21,261	133
14	Sudan	21,147	12,227	1,344
15	Zambia	18,217	17,339	366
16	Madagascar	17,587	16,992	259
17	Senegal	17,061	16,059	349
18	Mozambique	16,812	14,795	140
19	Namibia	16,269	14,582	160
20	Angola	16,161	8,841	366
21	Congo-Kinshasa	14,342	12,465	352
22	Guinea	13,420	12,657	79
23	Botswana	12,501	9,940	37
24	Cape Verde	11,302	10,922	110
25	Zimbabwe	11,219	9,359	307
26	Mauritania	10,780	8,022	222
27	Gabon	9,330	9,182	63
28	Swaziland	6,714	6,331	127
29	Rwanda	6,528	5,892	56
30	Malawi	6,063	5,491	186
31	Congo-Brazzaville	6,049	4,988	99
32	Djibouti	5,725	5,612	61

continues on following page

Table 1. Continued

No	Country	Cases	Recoveries	Deaths
33	Mali	5,721	3,566	189
34	Equatorial Guinea	5,185	5,058	85
35	Central African Republic	4,936	1,924	63
36	Somalia	4,579	3,529	121
37	Burkina Faso	3,894	2,858	71
38	Gambia	3,779	3,645	123
39	Togo	3,221	2,745	66
40	South Sudan	3,206	3,043	62
41	Benin	3,090	2,972	44
42	Guinea Bissau	2,444	2,337	44
43	Sierra Leone	2,440	1,850	75
44	Lesotho	2,250	1,319	44
45	Niger	2,199	1,276	80
46	Chad	1,751	1,603	102
47	Liberia	1,676	1,358	83
48	São Tomé and Príncipe	1,009	947	17
49	Burundi	728	640	1
50	Eritrea	711	564	0
51	Comoros	628	606	7
52	Mauritius	515	478	10
53	Tanzania	509	183	21
54	Seychelles	187	182	0
55	Western Sahara	10	8	1

Source: Data from allAfrica/Africa CDC

Chapter 4
Adverse Economic Impacts on the Occupationally Insecure Workforce in Thailand Amid the Pandemic

Jason Hung
https://orcid.org/0000-0002-0267-3925
University of Cambridge, Thailand

ABSTRACT

The author suggests a range of public policies that the Thai government should employ so as to help Thai nationals and smaller-size businesses weather the storm of the pandemic. As the Thai economy is significantly tied to its tourism development, it is not pragmatic for Thai authorities and nationals to aim at full economic recovery in the short- and mid-term. In the short-term, Thai authorities should help local businesses and nationals to satisfy household subsistence. Then, the Thai government should create more job opportunities for the Thai workforce and financially support local businesses in the short- and mid-term. Concurrently, the Thai government should expand their delivery of social protection schemes to Thai nationals, helping local populations obtain basic social welfare services that are conducive to their survival. In the longer-term, the Thai government should welcome international tourisms in phases, and co-build transport infrastructures with neighbouring countries in order to prepare a full re-opening of national borders in due course.

DOI: 10.4018/978-1-7998-6900-9.ch004

INTRODUCTION

Thriving Tourism in Thailand

In 2019, Thailand and Bangkok—the capital of the country—were the ninth most visited country and the second most visited city, respectively, in the world, with a total of some 38 million and 26 million arrivals (Street, 2019; Wright, 2020). Thailand is a Southeast Asian country, hosting a population of 69.3 million, known for its tourism and hospitality. Not only does Thailand welcome inbound travels, but also the fairly large population size suggests that the country has plentiful demand for domestic tourism (Fitch Solutions, 2020). The revenues of the Thai tourism industry increased by 8.2 percent in 2018, reaching a total of US$ 116.1 billion (MarketLine, 2020) (see Tables 1 and 2). The lucrative revenues represented a compound annual growth rate (CAGR) of 6.8 percent from 2014 to 2018. Comparatively, the tourism industries of China and Indonesia, the largest East Asian and Southeast Asian countries, grew only by 5.6 percent and 4.5 percent, respectively, in terms of CAGR during the same course (MarketLine, 2020).

Table 1. Thailand travel and tourism industry value 2014-18 (CAGR: 2014-18)

Year	$ Billion	THB Billion	€ Billion	Percent Growth
2014	89.2	2,883.0	75.6	-
2015	93.0	3,006.6	78.8	4.3
2016	99.3	3,209.4	84.1	6.7
2017	107.3	3,467.2	90.0	8.0
2018	116.1	3,752.0	98.4	8.2

Source: MarketLine

Table 2. Thailand travel and tourism industry geography segmentation

Geography	US$ Billion in 2018
China	975.8
Japan	485.2
India	213.4
Thailand	116.1
Indonesia	63.1
Rest of Asian-Pacific countries	1570.9
Total	3,424.5

Source: MarketLine

In 2019, tourism uptick was decreasingly positive, at 4.3 percent year-on-year, since mainland Chinese tourists shunned Thailand as a travel destination after the 2018 Phuket ferry disaster, wherein two tourist boats capsized during a sudden storm resulting in 47 deaths, alongside the then rising Thai currency–BHAT (THB). Despite these challenges, Thai tourism has proved its resilience, where the industry enjoyed a double-digit annual growth rate during the years despite the Bangkok bombing in 2015 and the death of the country's monarch (i.e., King Bhumibol Adulyadej) in 2016 (Fitch Solutions, 2020).

To stimulate domestic and inbound travels, Thailand launched a series of policies. For example, the Tourism Authority of Thailand (TAT) has regularly organised the Thailand Tourism Festival in Lumphini Park, Bangkok, in order for tourists to explore Thai cultures. Moreover, the government has removed the visa extension fees and reduced the visa on arrival application fees from 21 countries, including China and India. Such policies have prompted international tourists to stay longer and consume more in the country (MarketLine, 2020). Their consumptions include spending on food and accommodations, where the food services and hotels/motels segments of the industry earned as much as US$ 28.7 and US$ 28.3 billion tourism-related revenues respectively (MarketLine, 2020) (see Table 3). Thai government's endeavors to boost its countries' tourism development suggest the importance of tourism economy for economic sustainability and growth. Such an understanding motivates the design of this reviewed chapter where existing literature and reports are studied to explore how heavily the outbreak of COVID-19 has impacted the Thai economy.

Table 3. Thailand travel and tourism industry category segmentation

Category	2018	
	US$ Billion	**%**
Foodservice	28.7	24.7
Hostels & Motels	28.3	24.3
Casino & Gaming	25.5	22.0
Travel Intermediaries	23.0	19.8
Airlines	10.4	8.9
Passenger Rail	0.2	0.2
Total	116.1	99.9

Source: MarketLine

On one hand, Thailand's travel and tourism industry had been growing between 2014 and 2018, demonstrating that the country could continue to capitalize on the industry to earn lucrative revenues (see Figure 1). On the other hand, the growth rates had been flattening during the course, possibly leading to uncertainty of the Thai economy, should any regional or global challenges discouraging international travels and tourism and domestic consumption occur in the proceeding years. The occurrence of one of the arguably most sizable public health challenges in modern history—the outbreak of the coronavirus (COVID-19)—from December 2019, has caused a cloud of uncertainty and financial difficulties towards the development of the Thai economy. In this chapter, the author summarizes and evaluates the existing literature and reports, outlining and analysing how the public health crisis has had an adverse influence on the Thai economy in the first few months of the outbreak of the pandemic due to Thailand's undue reliance on tourism. The author then suggests public policies that help local businesses and Thai nationals to weather the storm of economic hardships.

Figure 1. Thailand travel and tourism industry value: $ billion, 2014-18

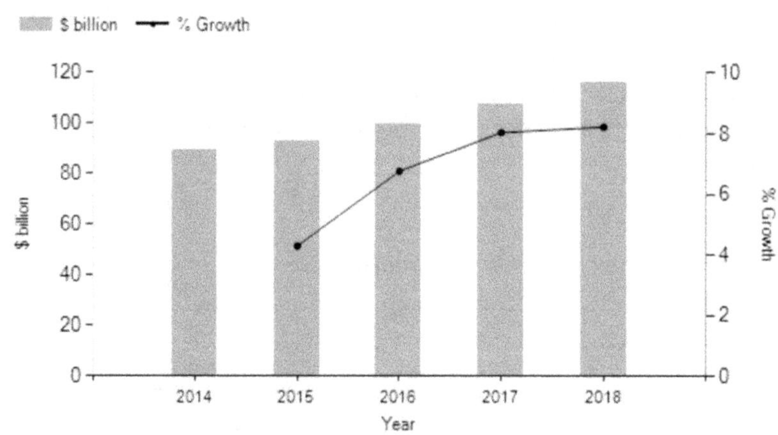

COVID-19

In Southeast Asia, Thailand is the first country to report a case of COVID-19 (Dechsupa et al., 2020). A Chinese national tested positive on January 13, 2020. On March 1, 2020, Thailand's Ministry of Public Health classified COVID-19 as a dangerous communicable disease under the Communicable Disease Act B. E. 2558 (2015). On March 26, 2020, the Thai Prime Minister announced a nationwide state of emergency (Open Development Thailand, 2020). Since then, COVID-19 testing, treatment, quarantine, and hospital facilities have been expanded, travel bans have been issued, and curfew was employed, from April 3, to June 15, 2020 (Bangkok Post Online Reporters, 2020; World Bank Group, 2020). The government established that all individuals countrywide must wear a facemask and practice social distancing (Dechsupa et al., 2020).

The confirmed COVID-19 cases within the country rocketed from 177 in total, as of March 17, 2020, to 2,700, as of April 17, 2020. As of October 29, 2020, the total number of cases reached as many as 3,763, with 59 deaths from the virus recorded. Bangkok, Phuket, Chiang Mai, and Pattaya are known as the major tourist spots in Thailand. It was noteworthy that the distribution of COVID-19 confirmed cases were primarily located in these tourist-popular regions (Tantrakarnapa et al., 2020). Bangkok (1,557 cases), Phuket (227 cases), Chonburi (i.e., the province where Pattaya is situated) (86 cases), and Chiang Mai (54 cases), in total, comprised half of the COVID-19 cases in Thailand, as of October 29, 2020 (Department of Disease Control, Thai Government, 2020) (see Figures 2 and 3). The skewed distribution of COVID-19 cases in tourist-popular regions implicated that the majority of COVID-19 cases were either imported or disseminated through the prevalence of tourism-related activities. Such activities included sex tourism, the operation of pubs and nightclubs, and the business of massage shops. Unfortunately, there was an absence of official sources indicating the proportion of COVID-19 cases that were linked to tourism-related entertainment industries. Otherwise, interventions, if necessary, could have been designed and applied in order to curb the outbreak of COVID-19 within such a sector and, therefore, within the country to some extent.

As Figures 2 and 3 show, the total COVID-19 cases in Thailand spiked between mid-March and mid-April 2020. Since then, the cases have been rising steadily and slowly. The figures revealed that the outbreak of COVID-19 within the country was nearly under control, but has yet to be fully contained. Opening up the borders for international travel and welcoming inbound travels travellers might be seen as a source of imported COVID-19 cases, adding uncertainty to the development of the public health crisis in Thailand and potentially threatening Thai travel and tourism industry in the longer-term. Thailand faced a tug of war between whether they should open the borders to international tourists to restore the local economy and whether they should restrict international travel to ensure a second wave of COVID-19 would not occur as an avoidance of further economic loss. Only by guaranteeing the COVID-19 spread was in check, could Thailand resume inbound travel in phases and gradually attain economic recovery. As mentioned, there was a skewed distribution of COVID-19 cases in tourist-popular regions. Campaigning for mass inoculations to realize herd immunity (vaccinating 70% of the population) nationwide would be unrealistic in the foreseeable future, especially when developed economies have had a more significant edge in purchasing sufficient COVID-19 vaccines and a more organised set of state policies for mass vaccination) in Thailand. The Thai government, yet, could focus on prioritising local citizens residing and working in tourist-popular regions. The goal is to enable these areas to open their doors to international tourism at a much faster pace than the rest of the country. International tourists arriving in these regions should be geographically confined, for example, they should be barred from inter-provincial travels. In so doing, Thailand could continue to earn a satisfactory amount of national revenues from tourism while minimizing the threats of imported COVID-19 cases and the need for a second nationwide lockdown.

Figure 2. Total COVID-19 cases in Thailand

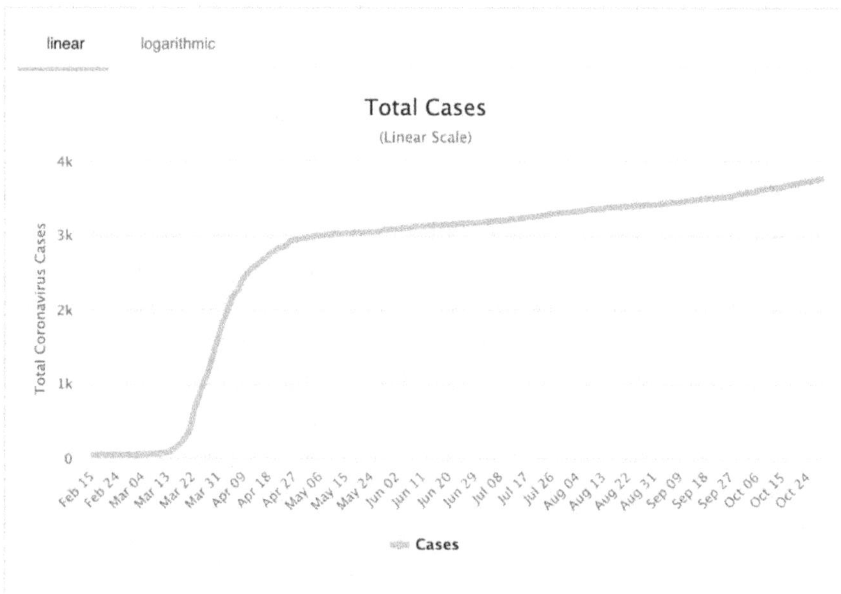

According to Chart 1 in Figure 4, the outbreak of the COVID-19 was under control after high-risks and business places, including massage shops, brothels, and nightclubs, were closed and a curfew was placed. However, there is a lack of public information addressing whether any entertainment businesses breached the laws and opened to customers during the curfew. If unauthorized business operation occurred, it was possible to result in mass contagion with COVID-19, and the application of the curfew would be void. Therefore, Thai authorities must strictly sanction unauthorized business operations and customers involved. Financial penalties, imprisonment, and immediate deportation (if the persons violating the laws are foreign nationals) are among the sanctions that should be applied. Convenient stores, supermarkets, and other outlets selling alcohol should be strictly restrained as to when alcohol can be sold. For example, alcohol can only be sold in by outlets between 16:00 and 19:00 each day. Such restrictions could help minimize the chances of customers purchasing alcohol and violating the social distance rules by collectively partying in private accommodations or hotels.

Figure 3. Daily new COVID-10 cases in Thailand

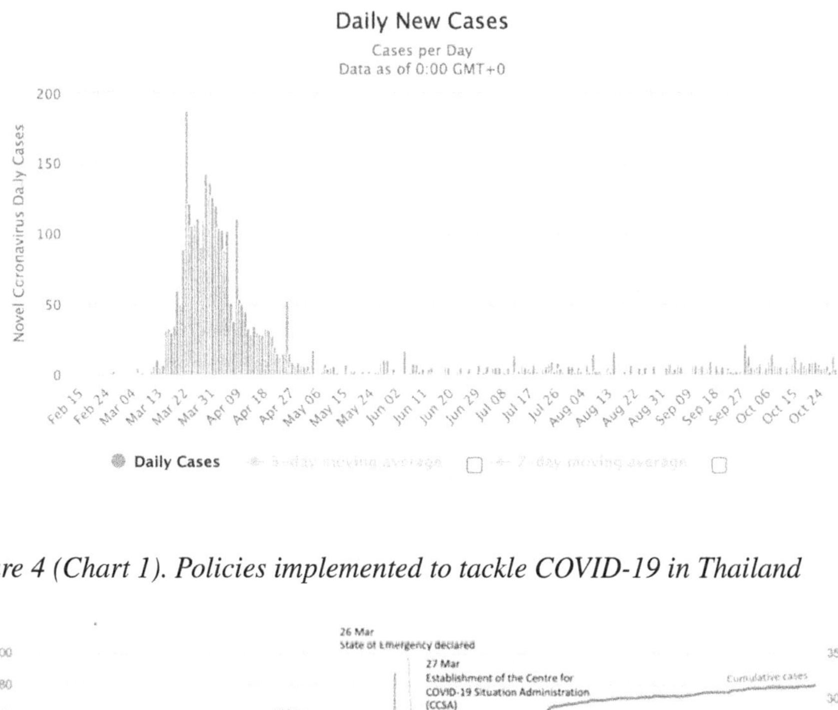

Figure 4 (Chart 1). Policies implemented to tackle COVID-19 in Thailand

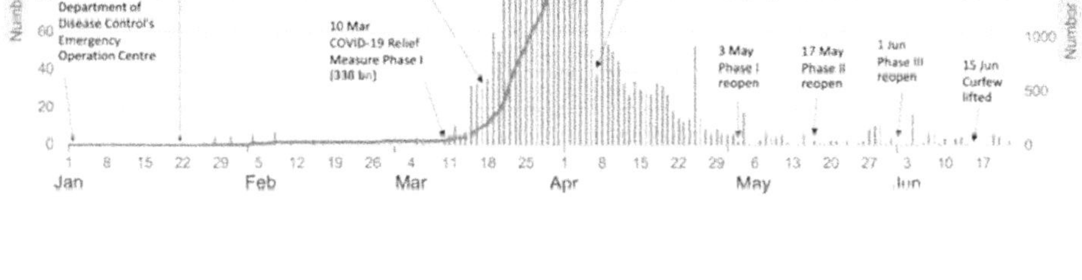

Additionally, if a second wave of COVID-19 outbreak takes place in the future, Thai authorities may have to re-apply such restrictive policies, including a curfew, as a response. However, travel and tourism always requires outdoor activities. Restriction on individuals' mobility would bar such activities, lessening the recreational advantages of Thailand to attract international travellers and inflicting economic challenges on tourism-related businesses countrywide. With a minimal amount of inbound tourism revenues amid the pandemic, let alone the above suggestion of prioritising the mass inoculation in, and opening up, tourist-popular regions, Thailand should seek alternative approaches to ensure that local citizens, especially those who are economically and occupationally vulnerable, can be financially at ease to some extent. Two of the approaches that the author discusses below, is for the Thai government to boost public investment and deliver financial relief packages.

Although Thai authorities have nearly contained the spread of COVID-19, they have decided to extend the implementation of the state of emergency for an additional month, from October 31 to November 30, 2020 (Meechukhun, 2020). Such a policy is conducive to the prevention of the local COVID-19 spread at the expense of restricting tourists' mobility and entertainment activities, and therefore, minimising the recovery of the Thai economy from the travel and tourism industry. If a state of emergency continues to apply, a larger scale of public investment and financial assistance will be required to help local citizens weather the storm of the public health and financial crisis.

Thailand's Tourism and Economy

The world economy has severely been contracting, as individual governments have employed containment measures, leading to disruptions of global economic activities. Overall, manufacturing, employment, private consumption, private investment, and merchandise exports have significantly been affected. Both Thailand and its trading partner economies would enter into some extent of recession in 2020. They have also been potentially subject to a more severe and prolonged outbreak of the pandemic than previously assessed, due to an emergence of the next wave of COVID-19, putting the global financial system in peril as a result of the growing level of risks of defaults or credit rating downgrades among governments and corporates (Bank of Thailand, 2020). It is noteworthy that inbound travellers will plausibly have lower financial capacity to consume in Thailand once the global pandemic is contained, if global financial downturn persists.

Under the climate of the COVID-19 pandemic, public health and economic challenges are intertwined. Not only is mortality of COVID-19 inequitably allocated to vulnerable populations, the outbreak and spread of the virus also adversely affects these cohorts the most, from an economic perspective (Shadmi et al., 2020). These vulnerable groups include individuals living in crowded areas, those with lower socioeconomic status, and migrants. One of the negative economic impacts hitting these populations in low-and-middle income countries has been the reduction or loss of income sources due to economic downtown, resulting in the encounters of food insecurity and difficulties in child caring, among others (Shadmi et al., 2020). In this reviewed essay, the author addresses how the Thai travel and tourism industry had been shrinking in 2019 and has substantially been contracting since the outbreak of COVID-19. The author indicates how the Thai economy has been particularly vulnerable amid the public health crisis, due to its extensive reliance on the then thriving travel and tourism industry.

Among all 10 countries in Southeast Asia, Thailand only had the fifth place for most COVID-19 cases region wide, which means the confirmed COVID-19 cases were much fewer than those in the Philippines (153,660), Indonesia (135,123), Singapore (55,580), and Malaysia (9,149) (Centre for Strategic and International Studies, 2020). However, Thailand is the Southeast Asian economy that is the most dependent upon tourism revenues. As a consequence of the pandemic, foreign arrivals decreased by 66 percent in the first six months of 2020 in Thailand, to 6.69 million. A sum of 1.6 trillion BHAT (US$ 51.50 billion) in revenue was wiped out in the industry of tourism in Thailand during this period, and the country has experienced its worst economic crisis in several decades (Tourism-reliant Thailand, 2020). As the pandemic has persisted in the second half of 2020, financial loss in the industry will continue. The author restrictively explores the economic impacts of COVID-19 on financially insecure businesses, which are on the verge of liquidation, and on the occupationally insecure workforce (those facing underemployment or who are on the brink of unemployment) in Thailand. To mitigate the economic challenges the most vulnerable cohorts have faced, the author explains how the Thai government has endeavoured to deliver financial relief packages as interventions that aim to minimize the adverse economic impacts caused by the outbreak of COVID-19 and the shrinking travel and tourism industry.

Thailand's Shrinking Tourism Industry

The Thai economy was subject to pre-existing vulnerabilities before the outbreak of COVID-19. These vulnerabilities included U.S.-China trade tensions, droughts of 2019, which affected agricultural production and slowed public investments. The country's economic growth reduced from 4.2 percent, in 2018, to 2.4 percent, in 2019, according to the World Bank Group (2020). The COVID-19 pandemic has further compounded economic development, resulting in a growth contraction of 1.8 year-on-year in the first quarter of 2020 (World Bank Group, 2020). The growth contraction was attributed primarily to the shrinking tourism and business travel sector. Since travel restrictions were applied, the number of flight arrivals in Thailand plummeted sharply in February, March, and especially April 2020. The amount of flight arrivals in April 2020 was over 10 times less than that in January of the same year (see Figure 5). Additionally, the number of tourist arrivals in Thailand in February and March of 2020 resulted in a twofold decline from the preceding month (see Figure 6). Overall speaking, international tourism receipts were forecast at -80.5 percent year-on-year in USD and -79.6 percent year-on-year in THB (see Table 4).

Figure 5. Number of aircraft arriving in Thailand declined sharply in March 2020, as travel restrictions began

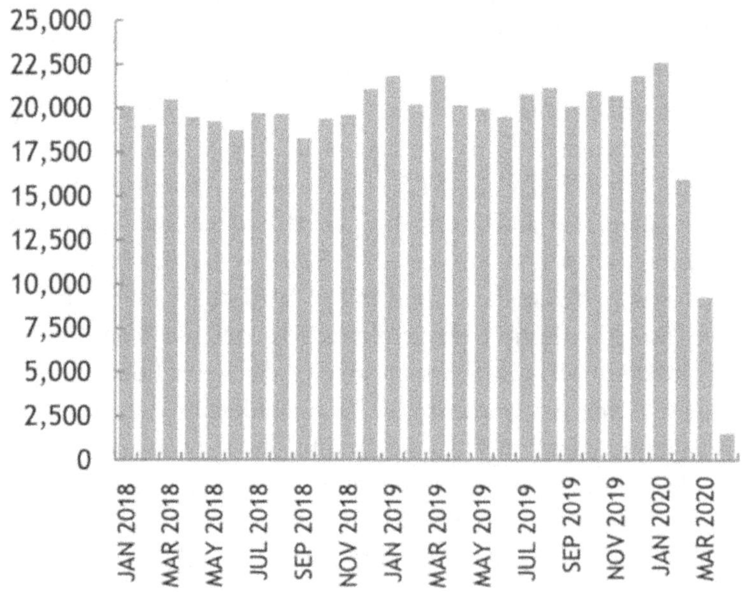

In Phuket, the second most popular destination for international travellers after Bangkok, for example, streets, restaurants, and beaches have become deserted, bars have been empty, and nearly 3,000 hotels have been closed (Hung, 2020a). Once regional mass inoculation is reached, areas, such as Phuket, could gradually re-open tourism-related businesses. However, a significant proportion of laborers working in these tourist-popular cities, islands, or provinces are internal or foreign migrant workers. It is necessary for the Thai government to prioritize fully vaccinating these workers, even if they hold foreign nationalities, in order to facilitate their return to these tourist-concentrated regions for work. As fully vaccinated workers still face a certain extent of risks for COVID-19 contraction, the Thai government should legally require all internal and foreign migrant workers to undertake government-funded COVID-19 tests regularly. Such a measure is essential to ensure no mass outbreak of COVID-19 can be seen in these tourist-popular regions, for the purpose of avoiding another wave of lockdown and travel restrictions regionwide.

Figure 6. Number of aircraft arriving in Thailand declined sharply in March 2020, leading to sharp decline in tourist arrivals

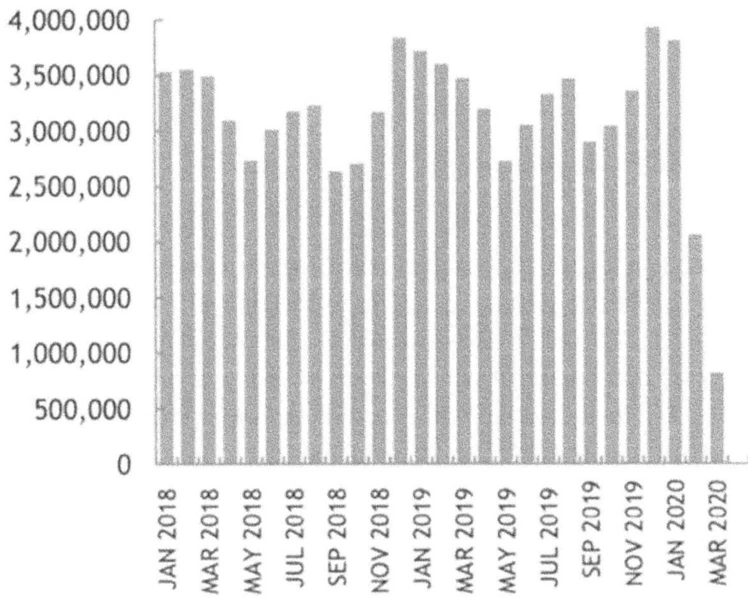

In Thailand, border closures have crippled the travel and tourism and food services industries. Flight suspensions and travel restrictions remained applicable in the third quarter of 2020, and are expected to extend into the fourth quarter (Fitch Solutions, 2020). Business owners in the food services industry may need to boost domestic consumption in order to increase their earnings by, for example, partnering with more food delivery services giants, including *Grab Food* and *Food Panda*, and advertising on social media to sell their food online. Major social media platforms, including Facebook and Instagram, are common virtual spaces where food storeowners can promote and sell their goods. Especially when digital transactions and parcel and food deliveries have already been mature in Thailand in the pre-pandemic epoch, storeowners should instrumentalise such online resources to establish e-commerce businesses, selling food and other items.

Table 4. Key forecasts (Thailand 2018-2024)

Indicator	2018	2019e	2020f	2021f	2022f	2023f	2024f
International tourism receipts, USD bn	65.24	66.91	13.4	22.12	33.87	48.15	66.14
International tourism receipts, USD bn, % y-o-y	5.0	2.6	-80.5	69.6	53.1	42.1	37.4
International tourism receipts, THB bn	2,107.98	2,077.29	423.82	703.39	1,034.82	1,468.57	2,000.81
International tourism receipts, THB bn, % y-o-y	-0.1	-1.5	-79.6	66.0	47.1	41.9	36.2
Total arrivals, '000	38,178.19	39,760.00	8,621.53	13,695.51	20,115.47	28,405.78	38,749.94
Total arrivals, '000, y-o-y	7.3	4.1	-78.3	58.9	46.9	41.2	36.4

e/f = Fitch Solutions estimate/forecast.
Source: National sources, Fitch Solutions

In the second quarter of 2020, an estimated figure of over six million individuals working in the travel and tourism and food services industries were left unemployed (Fitch Solutions, 2020). The Thai Hotel Association estimated that the country has a total of 66,000 hotels, of which merely 17,000 are properly registered. The remaining 49,000, including AirBnB accommodations and guesthouses, are semi-legal due to non-registration. The hotel sector encompasses 1.6 million workers of whom 55 percent are employed by registered hotels. Amid the pandemic, 50 percent of registered hotels are shuttered due to an insufficient amount of customers, implying that some 50 percent of employees in registered hotels have been laid off or furloughed (Jansenn, 2020). Despite the absence of relevant estimation among unregistered hotels, it is likely that a higher proportion of employees have been fired or asked to take unpaid leave as a result of the lack of labour contract protection, relative to their counterparts working in registered hotels.

To protect informal workers in the housing industry, it is necessary for the Thai government, through amending relevant laws and regulations, to ensure that employees working in unregistered accommodations sign a labor contract and receive occupational benefits, as many as their formal worker counterparts do. Employers in the informal sector who attempt to occupationally exploit their employees by, for example, failing to offer a labor contract, should receive criminal sanctions. By massifying the arrangement of labor contracts, the Thai government can therefore systematically subsidise laborers wages. In doing so, hotels and other tourism-related organisations could ease their financial burdens from delivering wages to all employees. Simultaneously, laborers are less likely to be fired or underemployed due to the shortage of financial resources faced by their affiliated workplaces, prompting a higher degree of occupational security.

Since the second quarter of 2020, a number of hotels in Bangkok, Phuket, and Koh Samui have been opening their doors to domestic tourists in phases; yet, the demand levels have been unsatisfactory. Hotels have been attempting to reduce operating costs and limiting cash expenditures (Fitch Solutions, 2020). These operating hotels have been expected to face cash flow difficulties, and they may continue to encounter financial barriers to operation unless the inflow of international tourists is retrieved. A majority of hotels, alternatively, remain closed and have suspended construction work on new establishments in order to limit cash loss. The Thai government should proactively publicly invest in construction projects by, for example, partnering with private property developers or giving out loans to those developers to complete the construction work as originally scheduled. Not only does supporting construction projects create temporary job opportunities, but, once the construction work concludes and the pandemic is contained, a substantial number of job vacancies will be produced in the long run. Moreover, by creating more job opportunities, Thailand can minimize the unemployment rates in future years and, thus, the amount of social and financial assistance distributed to unemployed cohorts. In the pre-pandemic epoch, foreign migrant workers shared a significant proportion of labour in the construction sector in Thailand. It is necessary for the Thai government, in the midst of the pandemic, to require property developers to prioritise the employment of local laborers. Such a suggested policy is conducive to minimize local labor unemployment or underemployment, alongside easing the amount of financial relief packages the Thai government has to deliver to local workers.

A significant number of smaller-size unregistered hotels and family-owned accommodations will encounter temporary or even permanent closures due to unbearable operating costs and a reduced level of cash flow (ibid). Based on the forecasts of Fitch Solutions (2020), domestic spending on hotels and restaurants is expected to drop by 40.7% year-on-year in 2020, to reach THB 1.1 trillion (US$ 33.2 billion). Such a forecast was down from THB 1.8 trillion (US$ 58.5 billion) in 2019. The number of registered hotels in Thailand is also expected to fall to 13,500 and 14,650 in 2020 and 2021, from an estimated figure of 15,000 in 2019. Total overnight stays by hotel customers will not expectedly resume to 2019s level (386 million) by 2024, and the occupancy rate of hotel rooms is expected to be lower in each year between 2020 and 2024 than in 2019 (see Table 5 and Figure 7). Since Thai economy is overwhelmingly dependent on tourism, especially international tourism, the TAT and Thai authorities should encourage, and potentially subsidise domestic travels and consumption, and open the borders to international travellers from low-risk countries as soon as possible. For the subsidization of domestic travel and consumption, the Thai government could consider designing a financial relief package where vouchers, in lieu of cash hand-outs, are distributed to Thai nationals. It is the utmost urgency for Thailand to stimulate domestic consumption on local, smaller-size businesses rather than on larger-size, international brands. Therefore, designing a digital voucher allocation system for Thai nationals where their domestic consumption on non-international chain stores is subsidized could be beneficial to the survival of smaller-size, local businesses.

Figure 7. Overnight stays and total domestic spending on hotels and restaurants, 2018-2024

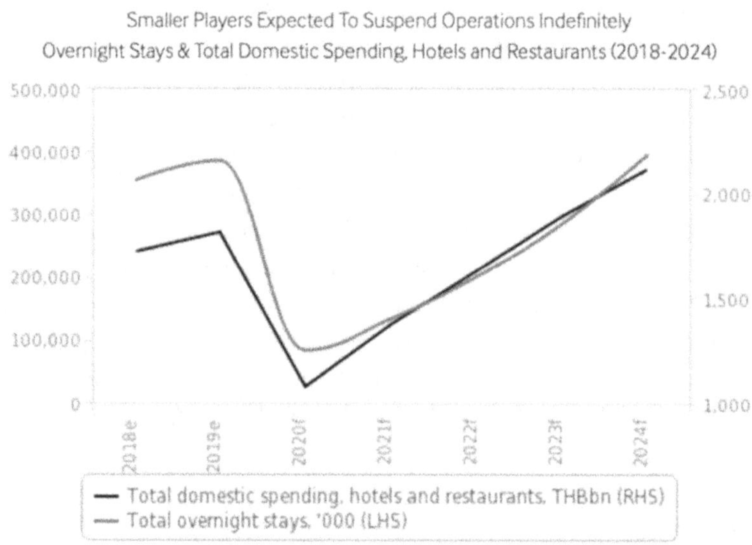

Talks of "travel bubble" formation with countries which were considered at low risk, including South Korea and New Zealand, halted as second waves of COVID-19, which led to renewed lockdowns, were seen in these overseas countries (Carminati, 2020). Even if international travellers can come to Thailand, the contemporarily extremely low rate of mass vaccination will deepen tourists' concerns, causing their delay to travel abroad (SCB Thailand, 2020). If the lack of international tourists continues by the end of 2020, the National Economic and Social Development Council expects that a total of 14 million in the Thai workforce will face unemployment. In the first two quarters of 2020, the unemployment rate in the country raised by 1.95 percent, which was the highest in 11 years. Those who were still employed were inclined to suffer from reduced work hours. The amount of furloughed workers could rise to 2.5 million, implicating the vulnerability of the labour market to some extent (SCB forecasts greater contraction, 2020). In the future, upon the formation of "travel bubbles," Thai authorities should ensure that a set of strict and sufficient quarantine resources and facilities are in place. If the formation of "travel bubbles" does not explicitly raise the number of COVID-19 cases, Thailand can give potential "travel bubble" partner countries and international travellers confidence that Thailand is well-equipped and prepared enough to contain the spread of COVID-19. As an outcome, the revenues from the travel and tourism industry will recover sooner than expected. It is necessary for Thai authorities to prepare for the worst. Despite the sufficiency of quarantine resources contemporarily, partially opening the door to international tourism will pose a large public health threat. In addition, COVID-19 could potentially mutate (Callaway, 2020), lessening the protection from vaccination and application of social distancing rules. Therefore, spare quarantine facilities should be built as soon as possible, even though such establishments might be deemed redundant currently.

Table 5. Hotel accommodation (Thailand 2018-24)

Indicator	2018e	2019e	2020f	2021f	2022f	2023f	2024f
Hotels and food sector annual wages, USD	4,927	5,481	6,128	6,195	6,450	6,996	7.728
Total domestic spending hotels and restaurants, THB bn	1,723.53	1,816.89	1,077.66	1,374.67	1,631.35	1,893.10	2,116.56
Total domestic spending, hotels and restaurants, THB bn, % y-o-y	6.8	5.4	-40.7	27.6	18.7	16.0	11.8
Number of hotels and establishments, '000	14.04	15,04	13.50	14.65	15.11	15.52	15.95
Total overnight stays, '000	354,675.4	385,937.1	84,107.8	133,997.9	201.129.9	285.368.2	394,977.8
Average length of stay, nights	9.3	9.7	9.8	9.8	9.9	9.9	10.0
Hotel rooms, '000	567.04	602.10	549.43	591.54	609.96	628.17	644.45
Occupancy rate, %	66.1	66.7	37.1	46.1	54.4	60.0	65.6

e/f = Fitch Solutions estimate/forecast.
Source: National sources, Fitch Solutions

Figure 8. Domestic demand drivers worsened with mobility restriction

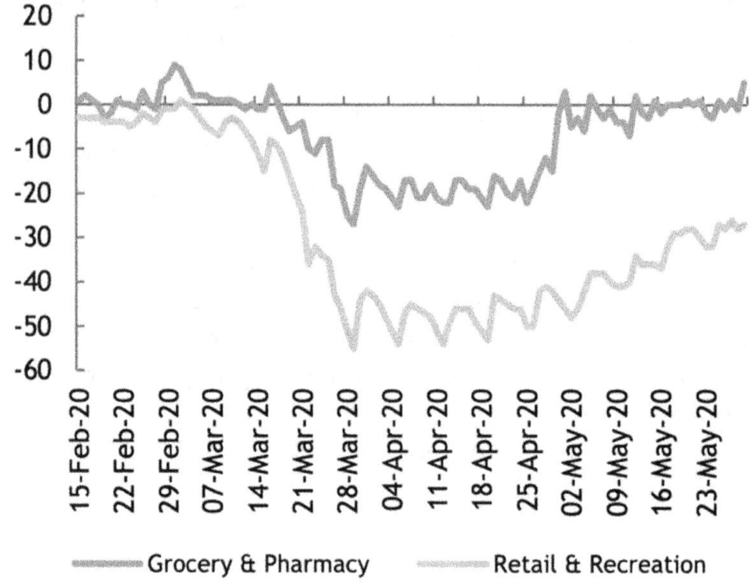

Figure 9. Growth of the private consumption index has begun to slow (% change, year-on-year), 2019-2020 (Q1)

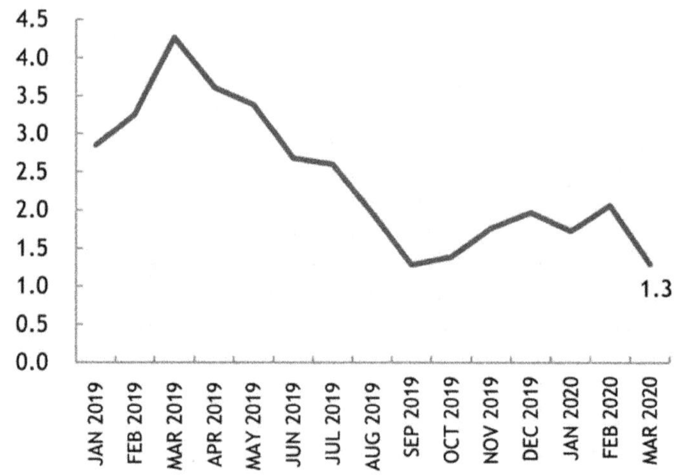

Currently, under the economic contraction, private consumption in Thailand, especially for retail and recreational services, will curtail due to weakening salary levels and employment status, alongside the sluggish investor sentiment amidst rising economic and public health uncertainty (Bank of Thailand, 2020). As per the data from the Google Community Report, because of the mobility restriction, domestic demands on grocery and pharmacy, and especially retail and recreation, fell sharply in April 2020 (see Figure 8) (World Bank Group, 2020). The Bank of Thailand indicated that the growth of the private consumption index in the country fell from nearly 4.5 in March 2019 to 1.3 in March 2020 (see Figure 9) (World Bank Group, 2020). Such figures hint the importance of allocating digital vouchers to Thai nationals, where such e-assets can be used to purchase goods from non-international chain stores.

The reducing private consumption is reflected in the sales of durables, where a nearly 12 percent decline in year-on-year terms occurred in the first quarter of 2020 (World Bank Group, 2020). In 2020, private consumption is projected to fall by 4 percent (World Bank Group, 2020). Thailand may need to wait until 2024 to recover to 2019 level of tourism spending. By far, the primary attributor to the decline in private consumption was the lack of spending by tourists. The non-residents expenditure index in the first quarter of 2020 was -44.2, significantly lower than 3.2 and -7.0 in the third and fourth quarters of 2019, respectively (see Table 6).

Table 6. Private consumption declined, dragged down by lower spending by tourists

% y-o-y	Q1 2019	Q2 2019	Q3 2019	Q4 2019	Q1 2020
Private consumption index	4.3	2.7	1.3	2.0	1.3
Non-durables index	2.7	3.6	1.9	1.2	0.6
Semi-durables index	1.8	1.1	0.4	-0.7	-2.2
Durables index	5.9	0.5	-3.4	-8.9	-12.0
Services index	3.9	3.3	2.1	2.1	-9.2
Non-residents expenditure index	-1.4	5.6	3.2	-7.0	-44.2

Source: Bank of Thailand, 2020; World Bank staff calculations

By 2024, it is expected that Thailand will lose a total of THB 4.8 trillion (US$ 160 billion) from the plunge of visitor spending due to the COVID-19 outbreak ("Thailand's tourism recovery," 2020). Encouraging public expenditure would therefore be necessary to weather the storm of economic contraction. As the Siam Commercial Bank Economic Intelligence Centre forecasts, the increase in growth domestic product (GDP) in terms of private consumption and investments, exports, and imports will all turn from positive to negative. Yet, public consumption and investments will rise by 1.1 percent (to 2.5 percent) and 4.4 percent (to 4.6 percent), respectively (see Figure 10) (Fitch Solutions, 2020). A growth of public consumption and investments serve as the foundation of economic sustainability of Thailand in the long-term; while stimulating private consumption, for example, by issuing digital vouchers, which can help provide financial relief for local business owners and Thai nationals or help them make ends meet in the short- and mid-term. Both public and private investments should be arranged concurrently in order for Thai nationals to weather the storm of the pandemic and for Thailand to strengthen its economic and occupational potentials in the post-pandemic epoch.

Figure 10. Projected increase rate of GDP in 2020

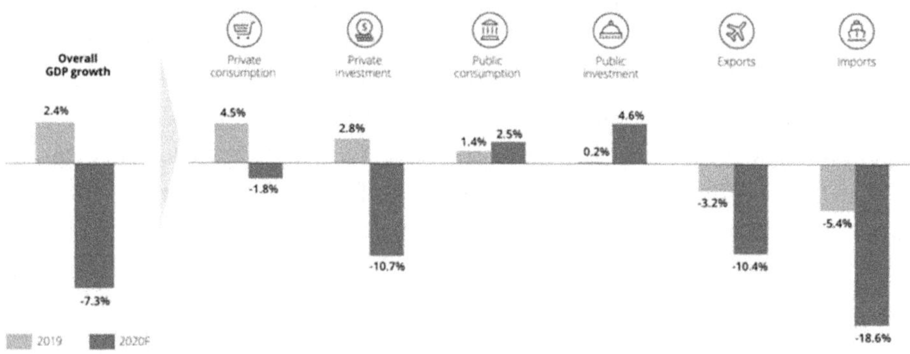

It is noteworthy that the reduced spending on hospitability and tourism will likely weigh on the infrastructure pipeline in 2020. Transportation and accommodations under construction may therefore experience postponements or delays (Fitch Solutions, 2020). However, Thai authorities should endeavor to make sure that the construction of transport infrastructure could be completed on time, in order to boost the demand for domestic travels. Once such projects conclude and COVID-19 outbreaks in neighboring countries are nearly contained, inbound travels by neigboring countries' visitors, such as those from Malaysia, Vietnam, Cambodia, and Indonesia, can be facilitated. Therefore, building transport infrastructures will pave the way to boost travel and tourism revenues once the public health crisis is in check. Thailand should discuss with neighbouring countries to collectively demand the allocation of funding by the Association of Southeast Asian Nations (ASEAN) and/or the Asian Development Bank (ADB), to collaboratively construct cross-national transport infrastructure and boost regional economic growth in due course.

Within Thailand, Airports of Thailand (AT) decided to consume THB 140 billion (US$ 4.3 billion) to expand the Survarnabhumi Airport in Bangkok, in anticipation of the rising passenger arrivals in the future. The estimated construction completion date will be in 2021 (Fitch Solutions, 2020). As one of the most visited cities for tourism, expanding the capacity of the major airport will give Thailand an edge to raise the number of aircraft arriving in the country, in addition to the amount of tourist arrivals on a daily basis, when international travel and tourism resume. In the long-term, as a country relying heavily on tourism for economic growth, increasing public investment is deemed an ultimate strategy for Thailand to restore and strengthen its economy. In the shorter-term, such public investment will create job vacancies, which are exactly needed, as millions of Thai nationals have lost their jobs amid the pandemic.

To restore inbound tourism and private consumption, Thai authorities have particularly focused on attracting visitors of Chinese nationality, as the largest source of international tourists in Thailand. The number of outbound tourists from China grew eightfold, from less than 11 million in 2003 to almost 87 million in 2018. Chinese visitors accounted for more than 25 percent of all tourists in Thailand, Myanmar, and Vietnam, among other Asian countries (Asian Development Bank, 2020). After the outbreak of the pandemic, the number of Chinese visitors and tourists of alternative nationalities have largely reduced, leading to the shrinking tourism industry in Thailand and wider developing Asia. According to the World Tourism Organisation, Thailand ranked ninth in international tourism recipients by percentage of the GDP in 2017, in which international tourism comprised some 13% of the national GDP (Asian Development Bank, 2020). The Asian Development Bank's staff estimated that the decline in tourism revenues from Chinese nationals alone, by percentage of the national GDP, was already between 0.8 percent and 2.4 percent from January to February 2020, during which the development of COVID-19 within the country was still pre-mature (Asian Development Bank, 2020). It is plausible to expect that the tourism revenue from Chinese nationals by percentage of the national GDP has been falling exponentially since March 2020, as the COVID-19 cases in the country spiked between March and April 2020, and travel restrictions have been applied since March 2020.

In 2020, the total number of Chinese visitors is forecast at 1.7 million, down from 11.0 million in 2019. Despite the sharp reduction of Chinese tourists in 2020, the forecast of the number of Chinese visitors in Thailand at least doubles that of each of the remaining top 10 of Thailand's inbound source market (see Figure 11). Thailand reduces entry barriers for Chinese passport holders by, for example, removing their visa fees and partnering with China to establish the Special Tourist Visa Programme (STVP). Since the second quarter of 2020, the TAT has been working to invite more Chinese visitors to Thailand, and the introduction of the

STVP is one of its relevant endeavours (Fitch Solutions, 2020). Thailand has only recorded a handful of domestic confirmed COVID-19 cases since June 2020. In addition, China's local outbreaks have swiftly dissipated after Chinese authorities proactively tested entire cities where outbreaks occurred and quarantined those who had been in contact with COVID-19 patients. As a result, Thailand and China co-introduced the STVP, allowing a small number of Chinese nationals to visit Thailand. Thirty-nine Chinese visitors flew from Shanghai to Bangkok on October 20, 2020; the first of such arrivals since international tourism was banned earlier in 2020. They were required to comply with a 14-day quarantine rule. If everything goes as planned and no local outbreaks occur in Thailand as a result of the trickle of Chinese tourists, it is expected that a greater flow will be welcomed—helping to restore the Thai economy (Hung, 2020a). It is a wise decision for Thailand to attract Chinese nationals as a first batch of international tourists to the country amid the pandemic. First, China is by far the biggest inbound source market. If the first batch of Chinese tourists can travel safely into Thailand, it is likely that a fairly large number of Chinese tourists would prefer traveling to Thailand, rather than to other low-risk countries in the next months, if not years. Second, China swiftly recovered from COVID-19, and economic activities have resumed in the second quarter of 2020, while many countries in the rest of the world continue to battle with the COVID-19 outbreak. Therefore, Chinese tourists should have a higher purchasing ability and willingness, relative to their counterparts from higher COVID-19 risk countries.

Figure 11. Top 10 inbound source markets of Thailand

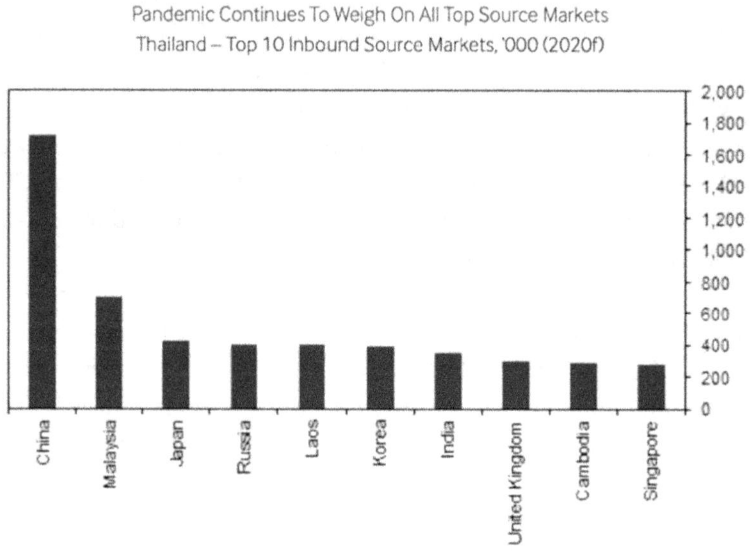

Thai authorities have declared that their borders will remain closed to international tourism, with the exception of welcoming a small amount of targeted tourists, including high net worth individuals and Chinese nationals, to their country until next year. This suggests that travel agencies, hotels, airlines, and related tour services will miss out the traditional revenue-generating October-January peak season (Fitch Solutions, 2020; Jansenn, 2020). For example, Pattaya's restaurants financially struggled during the Chinese "Golden Week" (October 1 to October 7) in 2020. Restaurants in Pattaya used to earn THB 300,000 (US$ 9,500) per day during 2019s "Golden Week," but no Chinese visitors were found in the same course of 2020 (Duangdee, 2020). Attracting ultra-high net worth individuals to visit Thailand will stimulate the spending on expensive hotels, luxurious accommodations, and high-end hospitability services, in order to drive the revenue recovery of Thailand. Such a policy can also ensure that social distancing rules are in place by keeping crowd numbers in check. Additionally, even if Thailand failed to welcome as many Chinese visitors in the upcoming years' during "Golden Week" than they did in 2019, restoring even a portion of inbound travellers from China will enable local Thai businesses to maintain a satisfactory amount of revenue. Upon fully opening borders to international tourism, Thai businesses and nationals should not aim at earning a lucrative amount of tourism-related revenues, as they were benefitted in the pre-pandemic epoch. They should, alternatively, focus on earning a sufficient amount of financial revenue for household survival and subsistence, especially when uncertainty on international travels remains.

Disadvantaged Populations in Thailand

The pandemic, where social distancing and staying at home rules have been strictly applied, has worsened the occupational security faced by vulnerable populations. These include migrant workers, informal laborers, older individuals, and those who are disabled, among others (Thailand's parliament approves, 2020). In the first quarter of 2020, more than 170,000 formal workers filed for unemployment benefits and the average number of work hours dropped year-on-year. The National Economic and Social Development Council estimated that 8.4 million jobs in Thailand were at risk in the second and third quarters of 2020, and six million farmers had already been at risk from droughts before the outbreak of COVID-19 (World Bank Group, 2020). The ten occupations with the largest shares of daily or hourly workers in the informal sector resulted in a reduction of 435,000 employees between the first quarter of 2019 and the first quarter of 2020 (United Nations Thailand, 2020). More than half of all employed laborers in the country were working informally (in 2018, 21.2 million and 17.1 million were working in the informal and formal sectors, respectively), meaning that they were not covered by any social security scheme or unemployment benefits. The pandemic and weakening economy exposes them to further occupational insecurity, if they become underemployed or unemployed. The median wage and salary levels for informal workers are lower than for their formal worker counterparts. Such earning gaps are particularly explicit in the transport and finance sectors, among other industries (World Bank Group, 2020). The loss of income among informal laborers is likely to push many over the poverty threshold, where the share of working poor in the country is expected to grow from 4.7 percent to over 11 percent of total employment in 2020 (United Nations Thailand, 2020). Therefore, it is necessary for the Thai government to provide social security programs and unemployment benefits to informal workers, especially amid the pandemic. Otherwise, informal workers and their households may not even be able to make ends meet. The Thai government should also endeavor to formalize informal workers' employment status (including keeping their employment records in the government's database). In so doing, financial relief packages distributed to such workers will be more organized and convenient.

Low-paid and low-skilled workers in labor-intensive sectors, particularly working for accommodation, food services, and retail trade industries, are also among the most vulnerable cohorts (United Nations Thailand, 2020). Due to the nearly banned international tourism and low level of domestic consumption, low-paid and low-skilled workers are unlikely to secure their income sources. It is therefore crucial for the government to raise their levels of public investment for the purpose of creating labor-intensive jobs for those who lose their work or income sources due to the pandemic.

Internal migrant workers and their households are occupationally and financially disadvantaged, as well. Households without working adults are largely dependent on remittance income sources transferred by their working household members in cities. In Thailand, about 13% of households have an absence of working members. In these households, remittance income comprises nearly two-thirds of their total household income. As lockdowns and social distancing rules apply, and travel and tourism industry rapidly contracts, many working members return to rural areas to live with their families (World Bank Group, 2020). Losing the remittance income sources, these families can hardly sustain their usual standard of living and, worse still; an increasing proportion of them may fall into poverty. Despite their loss of income sources, the Thai government should strengthen their social protection schemes, distributing a range of social welfare services, including healthcare insurance, housing subsidies, and unemployment insurance to Thai households to support their subsistence.

Since March 2020, 70 percent of the workforce countrywide has seen their average monthly income fall by 47 percent; 11 percent of small businesses are on the brink of permanent closure and 75 percent of small tourism-related businesses have been subject to a drop in revenue by no less than three-quarters (Jansenn, 2020). Currently, Thailand's household debts total some 80 percent of GDP, while household debts in emerging market countries, on average, only represent some 40 percent of GDP. The average household debt per person for Thai households is approximately US$ 2,021, whereas the average household financial assets per person are approximately US$ 1,941 (United Nations Thailand, 2020). In the worst-case scenario, if Thailand applies another lockdown, the economic consequences will be catastrophic, especially to the occupationally insecure populations (Thailand's real crisis, 2020).

Even if Thailand and most of their major inbound source markets have been effectively containing the spread of COVID-19 within their borders, international tourism revenues shall take a long time to be fully recovered (OECD, 2020). This is because weakening income levels and employment status has widely been seen in Asia Pacific (APAC) (Thailand's tourism recovery, 2020). Therefore, not only shall mass tourism take time to be restored in Thailand, but also tourists may plausibly consume less in the country.

Interventions to Mitigate Covid-19 Relevant Economic Downturn

Since the economic downturn has persisted, the Ministry of Finance and the Bank of Thailand have launched a large relief package totalling THB 1.9 trillion (US$ 62 billion), which comprises 12 percent of the GDP (World Bank Group, 2020). Such a package offers subsidies, loans, and funds to support socio-economic rehabilitation from COVID-19 impacts (see Table 7). These include the following measures:

- The provision of soft loans, special tax measures, and debt relief for small and medium enterprises (SMEs) and business operators
- A monthly hand-out of THB 5,000 (US$ 163) to each of 15 million self-employed and laid-off workers for up to three months (totalling some THB 225 billion, that is US$ 7 billion)
- A partial wage compensation up to a maximum of THB 15,000 (US$ 490) to each eligible worker in the formal sector
- A fund of THB 5,000 (US$ 163) per individual to farmers
- A THB 1,000 (US$ 33) per month cash transfer to each child, the disabled, and elderly (World Bank Group, 2020; Open Development Thailand, 2020)

The relief package benefitting vulnerable businesses and workers is detailed in the following subsections.

Table 7. Thailand's fiscal stimulus

Phase	Total Value By Phase (THB bn)	Measures	Value (THB bn)
Phase 1		Soft loans for entrepreneurs	150
Phase 1		Soft loans for companies to hire workers	30
Phase 1	338	Electrical and water guarantee deposit refunds	36
Phase 1		Tax breaks and delays	79
Phase 1		Other expense reductions	43
Phase 2		Cash hand-outs *	45
Phase 2		Soft loans for individuals	62
Phase 2	126	Loans for SMEs	10
Phase 2		Tax break and delays	5
Phase 2		Other expense reductions	4
Phase 3		Increase in cash hand-outs **	225
Phase 3		Other health-related plans and financial aids to affected individuals	375
Phase 3	1,900	Economic and social rehabilitation projects	400
Phase 3		Soft loans for SMEs provided by the Bank of Thailand	500
Phase 3		Buying of corporate bonds by the Bank of Thailand	400

Note:
* Cash hand-out of THB 5,000 per person for 3 months, covering 3 mn people
** Phase cash hand-outs extended to 6 months from 3 months, covering the total of 9 million people from previously 3 million people
Source: Fiscal Policy Office

Funds to Ease Access to Finance for Firms

About 25 percent of the financial resources of the relief package have been distributed to the provision of soft loans and restructuring or deferral of debt obligations. These include giving out THB 150 billion (US$ 5 billion) in low-interest loans by the Government Saving Bank, THB 30 billion (US$ 980 million) by the Social Security Office, and THB 500 billion (US$ 16 billion) through commercial banks' SME lending programs (who are also issuing a six-month moratorium on principal interest payments to eligible SMEs) (World Bank Group. 2020).

The Bank of Thailand has established a corporate bond market stabilization fund to help companies rollover maturing bonds (comprising 2.4 percent of GDP) and fund soft loans to SMEs (comprising 2.9 percent of the GDP) (World Bank Group. 2020).

For the tax relief measures, policies include deferring payment of corporate taxes, reducing the withholding rate temporarily, cutting social security contributions, and expanding payroll tax deductions for eligible SMEs (World Bank Group. 2020).

Cash Hand-Out Scheme

After the three-month cash hand-out to self-employed and laid-off workers, the scheme, however, halted abruptly on July 31, 2020, as the COVID-19 impact on local economy has persisted. Such a termination of the scheme renders an absence of alternative income source to about 14 million recipients. The Thai government is considering issuing a new scheme, allocating THB 3,000 (US$ 98) per month to each recipient. However, recipients will be required to submit an online application form. Those without Internet or computer access may face substantial barriers to the application of cash hand-out (Thailand's real crisis, 2020).

To further socially protect the most vulnerable populations, the Ministry of Finance has prioritised the cash hand-out given to disabled and alternative underprivileged populations. In order to further extend the social protection in the mid- and long-term, the Ministry guarantees that a minimum financial package will continue to be distributed to the most vulnerable cohorts, and an effective delivery mechanism for social protection programmes will be constructed and organised (Thailand's parliament approves, 2020). According to the social impact assessment conducted in rural areas by Oxford Policy Management, the poverty rate dropped by 2 percent from 11 percent to 9 percent due to the delivery of the relief package. The package negates the loss in income in the short-term, and results in a rise in rural consumption and decline in rural poverty (United Nations Thailand, 2020).

Other social benefits provided by the government include offering personal loans, reducing and postponing employees' contribution to the Social Security System, delaying and reducing utility bills, cutting rent for public housing, exempting tax on risk payments for medical workers, and deducing health insurance premium (United Nations Thailand, 2020).

Public Investment Programs

Such programs aim at helping rehabilitate the economy through projects that build community infrastructure, strengthen local economic competitiveness, and create jobs (World Bank Group, 2020).

CONCLUSION

In this chapter, the author suggests a range of public policies that the Thai government should employ to help Thai nationals and smaller-size businesses weather the storm of the pandemic. As the Thai economy is significantly tied to its tourism development, it is not pragmatic for Thai authorities and nationals to aim at full economic recovery in the short- and mid-term. In the short-term, Thai authorities should help local businesses and nationals to satisfy household subsistence. Then, the Thai government should create more job opportunities for the Thai workforce and financially support local businesses in the short- and mid-term. Concurrently, the Thai government should expand their delivery of social protection schemes to Thai nationals, helping local populations obtain basic social welfare services that are conducive to their survival. In the longer-term, the Thai government should welcome international tourisms in phases, and co-build transport infrastructures with neighboring countries to prepare a full reopening of national borders in due course.

REFERENCES

Asadullah, M. N., & Bhula-or, R. (2020, April 28). *Why COVID-19 will worsen inequality in Thailand*. The Diplomat. https://thediplomat.com/2020/04/why-COVID-19-will-worsen-inequality-in-thailand/

Asian Development Bank. (2020, March). *The Economic Impact of the COVID-19 Outbreak on Developing Asia*. ADB briefs No. 128. doi:10.22617/BRF200096

Bangkok Post Online Reporters. (2020, June 12). *Curfew ending, country remains closed to outsiders*. Bangkok Post. https://www.bangkokpost.com/thailand/general/1933820/curfew-ending-country-remains-closed-to-outsiders

Bank of Thailand. (2020). *BOT press release – Monetary policy report, June 2020*. Monetary Policy Strategy Division, Bank of Thailand.

Callaway, E. (2020, September). *The Coronavirus is Mutating - Does it Matter?* Nature. https://www.nature.com/articles/d41586-020-02544-6

Carminati, D. (2020, September 23). *Thailand's Economy and the Pandemic: Facing Delays and Difficult Choices*. Global Risk Insights. https://globalriskinsights.com/2020/09/thailands-economy-and-the-pandemic-facing-delays-and-difficult-choices/

Centre for Strategic and International Studies. (2020). *Southeast Asia COVID-19 tracker.* CSIS. https://www.csis.org/programs/southeast-asia-program/southeast-asia-COVID-19-tracker-0

Channel News Asia. (2020, August 6). *Tourism-reliant Thailand shelves "Travel Bubble" Plan as Asia COVID-19 cases rise.* https://www.channelnewsasia.com/news/asia/thailand-COVID-19-tourism-travel-bubble-asia-cases-12995474

Chiang Rai Times. (2020, September 11). *Thailand's real crisis is its contracting economy not COVID-19.* https://www.chiangraitimes.com/economy-business/thailands-real-crisis-is-its-contracting-economy-not-COVID-19/

Dechsupa, S., Assawakosri, S., Phakham, S., & Honsawek, S. (2020). Positive impact of lockdown on COVID-19 outbreak in Thailand. *Travel Medicine and Infectious Disease*, *36*(4), 101802. doi:10.1016/j.tmaid.2020.101802 PMID:32569811

Department of Disease Control, Thai Government. (2020, October 29). *COVID-19 situation reports.* https://covid19.ddc.moph.go.th/en

Duangdee, V. (2020, October 6). *"Golden week" ghost town: Thailand's Pattaya party zone struggles with no Chinese tourists.* South China Morning Post. https://www.scmp.com/week-asia/economics/article/3104289/golden-week-ghost-town-thailands-pattaya-party-zone-struggles

English, K. (2020, April). *Chaos at Ministry as protesters demand 5,000 Bhat cash relief.* Khaosod English. https://www.khaosodenglish.com/politics/2020/04/14/chaos-at-ministry-as-protesters-demand-5000-baht-cash-relief/#search/project-syndicate.org/_blank

Fitch Solutions. (2020). *Thailand tourism report: Includes 5-year forecasts to 2024.* Fitch Solutions Group Limited.

Hung, J. (2020a, October 23). *A trickle of Chinese tourists return to Thailand, with hopes of more to come.* The Diplomat. https://thediplomat.com/2020/10/a-trickle-of-chinese-tourists-return-to-thailand-with-hopes-of-more-to-come/

Hung, J. (2020b, April 1). *Delivery people are risking their lives to keep Asia running. Here's what people are doing to say thank you.* The Diplomat. https://thediplomat.com/2020/04/delivery-people-are-risking-their-lives-to-keep-asia-running-heres-what-people-are-doing-to-say-thank-you/

International Labour Organisation (ILO). (2021). *Triangle in ASEAN Quarterly Briefing Note.* https://www.ilo.org/wcmsp5/groups/public/---asia/---ro-bangkok/documents/genericdocument/wcms_735108.pdf

Jansenn, P. (2020, August 14). *Thailand's COVID success turns economic failure.* Asia Times. https://asiatimes.com/2020/08/thailands-covid-success-turns-economic-failure/

MarketLine. (2020). *Travel & tourism in Thailand.* MarketLine Industry Profile.

Meechukhun, N. (2020, October 26). *Thailand's centre for COVID-19 situation administration agrees to extend emergency decree nationwide for another month.* The Pattaya News. https://thepattayanews.com/2020/10/26/thailands-center-for-COVID-19-situation-administration-agrees-to-extend-emergency-decree-nationwide-for-another-month/

Open Development Thailand. (2020, May 16). *COVID-19 in Thailand.* https://thailand.opendevelopmentmekong.net/topics/pandemics-COVID-19/

Organisation for Economic Co-operation and Development (OECD). (2020). *OECD Economic Surveys Economic Assessment Thailand.* https://www.oecd.org/countries/thailand/oecd economic-surveys-thailand-2020-ad2e50fa-en.htm

Reuters. (2020, May 31). *Thailand's parliament approves $58 billion economic package to east virus impact.* In *Reuters*. https://www.reuters.com/article/us-health-coronavirus-thailand-idUSKBN237047

Shadmi, E., Chen, Y., Dourado, I., Faran-Perach, I., Fuler, J., Hangoma, P., Hanvoravongchai, P., Obando, C., Petrosyan, V., Rao, K., Ruano, A., Shi, L., Souza, L., Spitzer-Shohat, S., Sturgiss, E., Suphanchaimat, R., Uribe, M., & Willems, S. (2020). Health equity and COVID-19: Global perspectives. *International Journal for Equity in Health, 19*(104), 104. Advance online publication. doi:10.118612939-020-01218-z PMID:32586388

Street, F. (2019, December 3). *The most visited cities in the world 2019.* CNN Travel. https://edition.cnn.com/travel/article/most-visited-cities-euromonitor-2019/index.html

Tantrakarnapa, K., Bhopdhornangkul, B., & Nakhaapakorn, K. (2020). Influencing factors of COVID-19 spreading: A case study of Thailand. *Journal of Public Health: From Theory to Practice.* doi:10.1007/s10389-020-01329-5

Thailand, S. C. B. (2020). *Thailand after COVID-19 prepare to get through the Economist's perspective. Part 1: The impact of the economy and the Thai labour market.* https://www.scb.co.th/en/personal-banking/stories/business-maker/thailand-after-covid-ep1.html

The Nation Thailand. (2020, September 14). *SCB forecasts greater contraction of Thai economy in aftermath of COVID-19.* https://www.nationthailand.com/business/30394513?utm_source=homepage&utm_medium=internal_referral

United Nations Thailand. (2020). *Socio-economic response to COVID-19.* https://reliefweb.int/report/thailand/socio-economic-response-COVID-19

Weekly, T. T. R. (2020, September 28). *Thailand's tourism recovery four years away.* https://www.ttrweekly.com/site/2020/09/thailands-tourism-recovery-four-years-away/

World Bank Group. (2020). *Thailand economic monitor: Thailand in the time of COVID-19.* The World Bank.

Wright, S. (2020, June 5). *The world's most visited countries.* https://www.worldatlas.com/articles/10-most-visited-countries-in-the-world.html

KEY TERMS AND DEFINITIONS

Economic Inequality: It is the unequal distribution of income and opportunity between people in a country. To ameliorate economic inequality, governments can provide educational opportunities, enhancing skills, and other forms of training programs to lift people out of poverty.

Inbound Tourism: These are visits to a country by people who are not residents of the country.

Occupational Insecurity: It is also known as job insecurity which is probability that a person will keep their job or their chances of losing it.

Outbound Tourism: These are visits by residents of a country outside of a country.

Remittances: It is a sum of money sent that is sent via mail or electronic means in payment for goods or services. This could also be sent as a gift.

Small and Medium Enterprises (SMEs): They are businesses that maintain revenues, assets, or a number of employees below a certain threshold. SMEs vary from country to country.

Chapter 5
The Effect of the COVID-19 Pandemic on International Stock Exchanges

Hakan Altin
https://orcid.org/0000-0002-0012-0016
University of Aksaray, Turkey, Turkey

ABSTRACT

It is possible to define the concept of risk in various ways. Risk is the deviation possibility of the realized value from the expected value. It has two components, nonsystematic risk and systematic risk. Despite this, pandemics are risk factors that cannot be anticipated. They have deeply affected economies and financial markets under every condition. The importance of the detection of the COVID-19 pandemic comes from the selection of monetary and fiscal policies to be applied by governments during the rehabilitation process of economies. Equity share markets provide important information regarding the future of a company or economy. The reason for this is that the current value of an equity share is dependent on the deducted calculation of the cash flows of the equity share to be provided in the future. The actual price of the equity share is determined according to supply and demand under market conditions.

DOI: 10.4018/978-1-7998-6900-9.ch005

INTRODUCTION

It is possible to define the concept of risk in various ways. Risk is the deviation possibility of the realized value from the expected value. It has two components, nonsystematic risk and systematic risk. While this risk can be decreased, it cannot be completely eliminated. All markets are affected by the systematic risk factors. Despite this, pandemics are defined as unpredictable risk factors that do not take place in existent risk groups, that occur over wide areas, that involve multiple countries and continents, and that affect individuals and the majority of the society.

If a pandemic occurs only in a specific region, its economic impact will not be so great. However, it deeply affects the economies and financial markets in every situation. This impact occurs as the costs and profits of companies, the consumption and saving habits of individuals, the monetary and fiscal policies of governments, the labor force markets, and the money and capital markets are affected. Recession is experienced in general economic balance. If a pandemic occurs in a slumped economy due to recession, it increases the impact of the recession. It increases the worries of decision makers regarding the rehabilitation of the economy.

Humankind has struggled with many pandemics with a global dimension in history, and humans have overcome them by using their collective knowledge and intelligence against these pandemics. Today, collective knowledge and intelligence are needed in the struggle against the pandemic. Three important pandemics have been experienced all over the world in the recent past, severe acute respiratory syndrome (SARS), avian influenza (bird flu), and coronavirus (COVID- 19).

SARS, the first of the above-mentioned pandemics, emerged in the state of Guangdong in southern China in November 2002. The World Health Organization (WHO) published a global warning about SARS on March 12th and suggested a delay of all travel to the regions where SARS was observed. The first impact of the pandemic was experienced in the trade and tourism sectors. It then had a negative impact on Asia and the global equity share markets. Sharp decreases were seen in the equity share prices. However, while SARS negatively affected the economy for short term, it did not have any significant impact on domestic and foreign investment.

Bird flu, the second above-mentioned pandemic, emerged in Vietnam in December 2003. The first impact of the pandemic was experienced in international trade, and its second impact was experienced in the labor force market in the issue of labor force efficiency and quality. However, although the bird flu was a highly infectious disease, it did not have a high fatality rate and thus had a limited impact on the economy. As in SARS, the bird flu pandemic negatively affected the economy for only a short term.

COVID-19, the third pandemic mentioned above, emerged for the first time in the city of Wuhan in China on December 31st, 2019. It expanded rapidly all over the world and deeply and negatively affected the economic system on a global scale. WHO classified the COVID-19 epidemic as a global emergency on January 30th, 2020. Governments have taken strict precautions to decrease the fatal impact of the pandemic including border closures, travel restrictions, social distance, and quarantine which have caused a decrease in the need for goods and service in all economic sectors. A decrease has been seen in both labor force demand and labor force supply in the labor force markets. Countries have faced an intensive unemployment problem. Conversely, increasing demands have been observed in medical materials and food sectors. The global economic crisis triggered by COVID-19 today is very different from the pandemics of the past because COVID-19 is an epidemic that caused the sudden stoppage of global economic activities because it is spread from person to person via droplets. It is clear that this pandemic will not go away in a short period of time. COVID-19 pandemic has affected the international equity share markets. The detection of this impact is important governments play an important role in selecting the monetary and fiscal policies to be applied during the rehabilitation process of the economies. The impact of COVID-19 on 39 international stock exchange indexes was examined in this study, and findings are shared below.

Literature Review

The impact of severe acute respiratory syndrome (SARS), avian influenza (Bird Flu) and the coronavirus pandemic (COVID-19) on economies and financial markets are summarized in Table 1.

THE PURPOSE AND SCOPE OF THE STUDY

The aim of this study was the determination of the impact of COVID-19 pandemic on international stock exchanges. Within this framework, 39 international stock exchange indexes conducting transactions in global markets were examined. The examined period was between December 1, 2019 – May 31, 2020. This period was divided into three equal sub-periods and classified as before the pandemic, during the pandemic, and after the pandemic.

The implementation part of the study consists of four stages. Abstract statistics were in the first stage. Abnormal return was calculated for each stock exchange in the second stage. The statistical significance of the results was examined in the third stage. Theoretical and conceptual explanations were made regarding the possible equity share prices in the pandemic periods.

Table 1. Impacts of pandemics on economies and financial markets

No	Authors	Type of Pandemic	Purpose of the Study	Results
1.	Lee & McKibbin (2004a)	Severe Acute Respiratory Syndrome (SARS)	The evaluation of the global cost of the epidemic	If the repetition threat of SARS and similar diseases is real, the risk estimated regarding the economic activity both in the region and the world may be much higher.
2.	Lee & McKibbin (2004b)	SARS	The determination of the impact of the epidemic on the economies of China and Hong Kong	The estimated costs are based on the fixed exchange rate regime applied in China and Hong Kong.
3.	Siu & Wong (2004)	SARS	The impact of the epidemic on the Hong Kong economy	Local consumption, tourism, and air travel export have been seriously affected for the short term. A supply-based shock has not been experienced.
4.	Day, Mckay, Ishman & Chung (2004)	SARS	The examination of the natural risks and hardships in the developing market	It is necessary to prepare an emergency plan to cope with these kinds of epidemics.
5.	Au, Ramasamy, & Yeung (2005)	SARS	The examination of its impact on the travel of tourists to Hong Kong	All kinds of external shocks such as SARS have a permanent impact on the number of tourist entrances.
6.	Khoon (2006)	SARS	The examination of the social ecology of the epidemic in Malaysia	Its most important impact is expected to be on the tourism sector and subsidiary sectors.
7.	Chen (2007)	SARS	The impact of the epidemic on Chinese hotel equity share returns	SARS epidemic negatively affects hotel equity shares.
8.	Chen, Jang, & Kim (2007)	SARS	The impact of the epidemic on Taiwanese hotel equity shares	Seven hotel companies open for public experienced sharp decreases in their returns and equity share prices during SARS epidemic period.
9.	Wong (2008)	SARS	The estimation of the impact of the epidemic on the real estate prices and sales in Hong Kong	The expected price decrease remains weak. This situation stems from the properties of the real estate market peculiar to itself.
10.	Chen, Chen, Tang, & Huang (2009)	SARS	The examination of whether the epidemic has had positive impacts on Taiwanese stock exchange	It shows that SARS crisis has caused negative impacts on the tourism and wholesale and retail sectors. However, biotechnology sector was positively affected by the impacts of SARS crisis.
11.	Chen, Lee, Lin, & Chen, (2018)	SARS	The examination of the impact of the epidemic on the long-term relation between China and four Asian stock exchanges	The existence of the cointegration relation changing over time in the equity share indexes weakens the relationship among the stock exchanges.

continues on following page

Table 1. Continued

No	Authors	Type of Pandemic	Purpose of the Study	Results
12.	Jonung & Roeger (2006)	Bird Flu (Avian Influenza)	The estimation of the possible macroeconomic impacts of the pandemic in European Union	It will not pose any serious threat for the European macroeconomy.
13.	Chang, Lee, Lin, & Hsu (2007)	Bird Flu	Analysis of the potential results of the bird flu epidemic on the macroeconomy and individual industries of Taiwan	Domestic consumption, exports, and labor force demand will decrease.
14.	Suder & Inthavong, (2008)	Bird Flu	The examination of at what degree the bird flu disease has affected the poultry farming business	Consumer behavior has not significantly changed. It has not caused to job losses.
15.	Göktaş, Koker, & Alemdar (2008)	Bird Flu	How the most important crisis in Turkish white meat sector until now has been managed	The success of the management of bird flu crisis in Turkey is directly related to the fulfillment of the principles of crisis management.
16.	Ishida, Ishikawa, & Fukushige, (2010)	Bird Flu	Examination of the impacts of bovine spongiform encephalopathy (BSE) and bird flu on the meat demand of the consumers in Japan	The fear of BSE and bird flu causes a decrease in demand for cattle meat and chicken and causes an increase in the demand for pork meat and fish.
17.	Thurlow (2010)	Bird Flu	The impact of the bird flu epidemic on Kenya economy	It has not sharply decreased economic growth. In addition, it significantly worsens poverty.
18.	Karki (2017)	Bird Flu	The assessment of the economic and social impacts of the bird flu epidemic in Nepal	Mostly the small-scale merchant farmers and butchers were affected from this epidemic.
19.	Menard, Thompson, English, Hughes, Griffith, Smith, % Jensen (2020)	Bird Flu	The impact of bird flu on the poultry farming industry in Tennessee	If it is thought that animal diseases generally affect only the production and prices, its more impact may be experienced in the relationship between economies and sectors.
20.	Al-Awadhi, Saifi, Awadhi, & Alhamadi (2020)	Coronavirus Pandemic (COVID-19)	The impact of Coronavirus on Chinese stock exchange	The daily growth in total cases and death cases has a significantly negative impact on the equity share returns.
21.	Ramelli and Wagner (2020)	COVID-19	The assessment of the risk perception of the investors	Investors have been worried about the survival chances of the companies with high debt and little cash.
22.	Corbet, Hou, Hu, Lucey, & Oxley (2020)	COVID-19	The examination of the status of the companies using the expression of coronavirus in their institutional identities	This relationship has been found negative in terms of the companies.

continues on following page

Table 1. Continued

No	Authors	Type of Pandemic	Purpose of the Study	Results
23.	Nicola, Alsafi, Sohrabi, Kerwan, Al-Jabir, Iosifidis, & Agha (2020)	COVID-19	The examination of the socioeconomic impact of COVID-19	There is a need for a wide socioeconomic development plan containing the sector plans and encouraging entrepreneurship.
24.	Ding, Levine, Lin, & Xie (2020)	COVID-19	The determination of the share price reactions given to COVID-19 cases	The companies with stronger economic conditions (more cash, less debt, and higher profit) are stronger against COVID-19.
25.	Sansa (2020)	COVID-19	The impact of COVID-19 on the financial markets in China and the USA.	There is a positive and significant relationship between COVID-19 cases and the Shanghai stock exchange and New York Dow Jones.
26.	Salisu & Vo (2020a)	COVID-19	The impact of health news on the equity share returns during COVID-19 period	Health news has a positive impact on the equity share returns.
27.	Salisu, Ebuh, & Usman (2020b)	COVID-19	The examination of the causality relationship among interest, petroleum price, exchange rate, and equity share returns after the declaration of COVID- 19 pandemic	Petroleum is an important input in the production conducted by most companies. With this assumption, it affects the expected cash flows, costs, returns, dividends, and equity share prices of the companies.
28.	Salisu, Akanni, & Raheem (2020c)	COVID-19	The determination of the relationship between the global fear index-GFI and commodity price returns during COVID-19 epidemic	There is a positive relationship between the global fear index-GFI and commodity price returns. As the fear of COVID-19 increases, commodity returns (profits) increase.
29.	Topcu & Gulal (2020)	COVID-19	The determination of the impact of COVID-19 on the developing stock exchanges	It is seen that the negative impact of the epidemic on the developing stock exchanges gradually decreased during the examined period.
30.	Liu, Manzoor, Wang, Zhang, & Manzoor, (2020)	COVID-19	The assessment of the short-term impact of the coronavirus epidemic on the leading stock exchange indexes	It is seen that stock exchanges have rapidly decreased after the virus epidemic.
31.	Kartal, Depren, & Depren (2020)	COVID-19	The examination of the reasons for main stock exchange index changes during COVID-19 period	The changes in the XU100 index before and after the pandemic could be explained with the number of foreign investors in the equity share market, CDS spreads, interest rates of the state bonds, and MSCI developing markets index.
32.	Czech, Wielechowski, Kotyza, Benešová, & Laputková (2020)	COVID-19	The assessment of the short-term impact of COVID-19 on financial markets in Visegrad states	There is a significant negative relationship between Visegrad stock exchange indexes and COVID-19 spreads.

continues on following page

Table 1. Continued

No	Authors	Type of Pandemic	Purpose of the Study	Results
33.	Altig, Baker, Barrero, Bloom, Bunn, Chen, & Mizen (2020)	COVID-19	The determination of various economic uncertainty scales for the USA and England before and during COVID-19 epidemic	All precautions show great uncertainty bounces as a reaction to the pandemic and its economic impacts.
34.	Iqbal, Fareed, Shahzad, He, Shahzad, & Lina (2020)	COVID-19	The relationship between the air temperature, COVID-19, and the Chinese economy	The exchange rate and the COVID-19 epidemic have a negative, but limited impact on Chinese export economy. Also, the increase in temperature does not have a significant impact on slowing down the new COVID-19 infections.
35.	Griffith, Levell, & Stroud (2020)	COVID-19	The revelation of how this impact changes among the sectors using the data regarding the equity share prices in London Stock Exchange	Tourism and entertainment (including air travel), fossil fuel production and distribution, banking, insurance, retailers (except for food and drug retailers) and some big production industries are among the most affected sectors.
36.	Yang, Sha, Liu, Li, Lan, Guan, & Wang (2020)	COVID-19	Formation of collective view, data collection, analysis and sharing regarding the global health emergency	Changing consumer needs, interruption of supply chain, employment losses, and economic recession are widely affected from the epidemic.
37.	Mazur, Dang, & Vega (2020)	COVID-19	The impact of COVID-19 on the American stock exchange performance	It is seen that the equity shares of natural gas, food, health, and software have provided a high positive return, but they have significantly decreased in the sectors of petroleum, real estate, entertainment, and accommodation.
38.	Alam, Alam, & Chavali (2020)	COVID-19	The examination of the impact of the quarantine period caused by COVID-19 on Indian stock exchange	The market has given a significantly positive reaction during the current market limitation period. But the investors have shown panic behavior before the limitation.
39.	Chang, McAleer, & Wang (2020)	COVID-19	The impact of COVID-19 on both fossil fuel and renewable energy sectors	These markets have the risk of herd behavior.
40.	Ozili (2020)	COVID-19	The impact of coronavirus on African economy	Precautions peculiar to the state have been taken by many African states. These precautions have affected the African economy. It is possible for all the African states to undergo an inevitable recession when the pandemic ends.

continues on following page

Table 1. Continued

No	Authors	Type of Pandemic	Purpose of the Study	Results
41.	Bashir, Benjiang, & Shahzad (2020)	COVID-19	Socioeconomic and environmental impacts of COVID-19	This epidemic has caused serious demographic changes and unemployment. Economic activities have been stopped to save human life. Transportation and travel industries have been most seriously affected because the global tourism has been almost zero in recent months. But, limited economic activities have contributed to a cleaner environment.
42.	McKibbin & Fernando (2020)	COVID-19	The impact of COVID 19 on macroeconomic and financial markets	Economic costs increase when the epidemic has turned into pandemic. It is an efficient reaction to put the affected people in quarantine and decrease large scale social interaction.
43.	Narayan, Phan, & Liu (2020)	COVID-19	The impact of the governmental reactions of G7 states to the coronavirus pandemic on the stock exchange returns	Limitations, travel prohibitions, and economic incentive packages form a positive impact on G7 stock exchanges.
44.	Cox, Greenwald, & Ludvigson (2020)	COVID-19	The examination of the role of the different causal factors in the sharp V action of the US stock exchange during the first stages of COVID-19	There is the phenomenon of avoidance of risk on the first basis of this action. This action cannot be explained with traditional monetary policy.
45.	Bieszk-Stolorz & Dmytrów, (2020)	COVID-19	The assessment of the power of the reaction of the world stock exchanges to coronavirus epidemic	The decreased intensity and risk of the equity share indexes show changes from continent to continent.
46.	David, Inácio Jr, & Machado (2020)	COVID-19	The dynamic relationship between the pandemics (i.e., COVID-19, EBOLA, MERS, and SARS) and the important stock exchange indexes (i.e., Dow-Jones, S&P 500)	The shocks caused by the diseases have significantly affected the market. Recovery will take a longer time when COVID-19 and other pandemics are compared.

MSCI World Index was used as a representation of all the market in the calculation of the abnormal return. The MSCI World Index was determined as approximately 23 and was calculated upon the market values of American, European and Middle Eastern, and Pacific countries. It covers 85% of the public companies.

METHOD

The method used in the study consists of four stages:

Stage 1: Analysis of the abstract statistics.
Stage 2: Calculation of the abnormal return (AR) for stock exchange indexes.

$$R_{it} = \left(\frac{last\ price - initial\ price}{initial\ price} \right) \times 100 \quad (1)$$

$$R_{mt} = \left(\frac{last\ price - initial\ price}{initial\ price} \right) \times 100 \quad (2)$$

$$AR = R_{it} - R_{mt} \quad (3)$$

Stage 3: Testing of the statistical significance of the obtained results.

Two-Sample Kolmogorov-Smirnov Test

H_0: Two samples have been taken from the universes with the same distribution.
H_1: Two samples have been taken from the universes with different distribution.

Levene Test

H_0: The universe variances of the two samples are equal.
H_1: The universe variances of the two samples are not equal.

Wald-Wolfowitz Test

H_0: The two samples have the same distribution.
H_1: The two samples do not have the same distribution.

Stage 4: Explanation of the changes in equity share prices.

$$\hat{P}_0 = \frac{D_1}{r_s - g} \tag{4}$$

$$\hat{r}_s = \frac{D_1}{\hat{P}_0} + g \tag{5}$$

$$\hat{P}_0 = \frac{D_1}{(1+r_s)^1} + \frac{D_2}{(1+r_s)^2} + \frac{D_3}{(1+r_s)^3} + \ldots + \frac{D_n}{(1+r_s)^n} \tag{6}$$

ANALYSIS OF THE MODEL

Before the pandemic, while 29 out of the examined 39 international stock exchange indexes provided a positive return (profit), 10 provided a negative return. All stock exchange indexes provided negative returns during the pandemic period. After the pandemic, while 36 stock exchange indexes provided positive return, three of them provided negative return. The highest variability was experienced in the pandemic periods in all stock exchange indexes. Stock exchange indexes gave mixed results in the issue of the abnormal returns.

When the case numbers regarding COVID- 19 pandemic were examined, it was seen that the first five states are respectively America, India, Brazil, France, and Russia. The reaction given by the stock exchanges of these states to the pandemic is as follows.

Table 2. S&P500 abnormal return results

Variables	Before Pandemic	Pandemic Period	After Pandemic
Minimum	-0.0177	-0.1198	-0.0307
Maximum	0.0101	0.0938	0.0703
Median	0.0013	-0.0033	0.0045
Mean	0.0011	-0.0050	0.0054
Std. Dev.	0.0061	0.0448	0.0198
Abnormal Return	Yes	Yes	Yes
Statistical Significant	Yes	Yes	Yes

According to Table 2; the minimum and maximum return statistics occurring before the pandemic in S&P500 were 0.13% and 0.45% before and after the pandemic, showing a negative return with -0.33% during the pandemic period. While the mean value showed a positive return with a0.11% and 0.54% before and after the pandemic, it showed a negative return with -0.50% during the pandemic period. When the standard deviation statistics were examined, it was detected that the highest variability was experienced during the pandemic period with 4.48%. On the other hand, returns or losses were experienced in every examined period. However, these returns and losses did not prevent the experience of an abnormal return. The returns or losses experienced in the S&P500 index were in a better condition when compared to the returns and losses experienced in the market. The obtained results were statistically significant.

The explanation of the decreases seen in the equity share prices during COVID-19 crisis is as follows. Firstly, the COVID-19 crisis prevented companies from making a sufficient profit. This situation has negatively affected the companies both in the obtainment of profit and in the distribution of profit share. Secondly, the companies that cannot make sufficient amounts of money gave up on their new investment (growth) decisions. Companies have reached reduction decisions. Thirdly, recession has been experienced in both supply and demand aspects in the labor force market. Fourthly, great losses have been experienced in household incomes as in the companies. This situation has caused demand shocks. Fifthly, recessions have been seen in economies on a global scale. On the other hand, this chain of relationships has not been experienced to the same degree in all sectors. For instance, health and food sectors have got the best of the pandemic period. Similar results are valid for all stock exchange indexes.

Table 3. CNX abnormal return results

Variables	Before Pandemic	Pandemic Period	After Pandemic
Minimum	-0.0191	-0.1298	-0.0574
Maximum	0.0158	0.0662	0.0876
Median	0.0009	-0.0041	0.0050
Mean	0.0001	-0.0088	0.0044
Std. Dev.	0.0071	0.0383	0.0249
Abnormal Return	No	No	No
Statistically Significant	Yes	Yes	Yes

According to Table 3; the minimum and maximum return statistics occurring before the pandemic in CNX were -1.91 percent and 1.58 percent. These statistics were -12.98 percent and 6.62 percent during the pandemic period. They were -5.74 percent and 8.76 percent after the pandemic. While the median value showed a positive return with 0.09 percent and 0.50 percent before and after the pandemic, it showed a negative return with -0.41 percent during the pandemic period. While the mean value showed a positive return with 0.01 percent and 0.44 percent before and after the pandemic, it showed a negative return with -0.88 percent during the pandemic period. When the standard deviation statistics was examined, it was detected that the highest variability was experienced during the pandemic period with 3.83 percent. On the other hand, returns or losses were experienced in every examined period. However, abnormal return were not experienced. The obtained results were statistically significant.

Table 4. BOVESPA abnormal return results

Variables	Before Pandemic	Pandemic Period	After Pandemic
Minimum	-0.0160	-0.1444	-0.0563
Maximum	0.0253	0.1395	0.1036
Median	0.0000	-0.0092	-0.0015
Mean	0.0013	-0.0128	0.0069
Std. Dev.	0.0099	0.0536	0.0324
Abnormal Return	Yes	No	Yes
Statistically Significant	Yes	Yes	Yes

According to Table 4; the minimum and maximum return statistics occurring before the pandemic in BOVESPA were -1.60% and 2.53%. These statistics were -14.44% and 13.95% during the pandemic period. They were -5.63 percent and 10.36 percent after the pandemic. The median value was 0.00 percent and -0.15 percent before and after the pandemic. It was -0.92 percent during the pandemic period. The mean value was 0.13 percent and 0.69 percent before and after the pandemic. It showed the negative return with -1.28 percent during the pandemic period. When the standard deviation statistics was examined, it was detected that the highest variability was experienced during the pandemic period with 5.36 percent. On the other hand, returns or losses were experienced in every examined period. There are complex results in the issue of the abnormal return. The obtained results are statistically significant.

Table 5. CAC40 abnormal return results

Variables	Before Pandemic	Pandemic Period	After Pandemic
Minimum	-0.0268	-0.1228	-0.0424
Maximum	0.0127	0.0839	0.0516
Median	0.0004	0.0009	0.0038
Mean	0.0001	-0.0065	0.0030
Std. Dev.	0.0078	0.0391	0.0215
Abnormal Return	No	No	No
Statistically Significant	Yes	Yes	Yes

According to Table 5; the minimum and maximum return statistics occurring before the pandemic in CAC40 were -2.68 percent and 1.27 percent. These statistics are -12.28 percent and 8.39 percent during the pandemic period. They were -4.24 percent and 5.16 percent after the pandemic. The median value was 0.04 percent, 0.09 percent, and 0/38 percent before, during and after the pandemic. While the mean value was 0, 1 percent and 0.30 percent before and after the pandemic, it showed a negative return with -0.65 percent during the pandemic period. When the standard deviation statistics was examined, it was detected that the highest variability was experienced during the pandemic period with 3.91 percent. On the other hand, returns or losses were experienced in every examined period. However, an abnormal return was not experienced. The obtained results were statistically significant.

Table 6. RTSI abnormal return results

Variables	Before Pandemic	Pandemic Period	After Pandemic
Minimum	-0.0362	-0.1302	-0.0762
Maximum	0.0113	0.0171	0.0469
Median	0.0027	-0.0072	0.0084
Mean	0.0015	-0.0092	0.0057
Std. Dev.	0.0110	0.0468	0.0272
Abnormal Return	Yes	No	Yes
Statistically Significant	Yes	Yes	Yes

According to Table 6; the minimum and maximum return statistics occurring before the pandemic in RTSI were -3.62 percent and 1.13 percent. These statistics were -13.02 percent and 1.71 percent during the pandemic period. They were -7.62 percent and 4.69 percent after the pandemic. While the median value showed a positive return with 0.27 percent and 0.84 percent before and after the pandemic, it showed a negative return with -0.92 percent during the pandemic period. While the mean value showed a positive return with 0.15 percent and 0.54 percent before and after the pandemic, it showed a negative return with -0.92 percent during the pandemic period. When the standard deviation statistics as examined, it was detected that the highest variability was experienced during the pandemic period with 4.68 percent. On the other hand, returns or losses were experienced in every examined period. There were complex results regarding the issue of the abnormal return. The obtained results were statistically significant.

CONCLUSION

Equity share markets provide important information regarding the future of a company or economy because the current value of an equity share is dependent on the deducted calculation of the cash flows of the equity share to be provided in the future. The actual price of the equity share is determined according to the supply and demand under market conditions. The investment decision was reached by comparing the current value (estimated value, calculated value, and real value) of the equity share found by calculation to the market price of the equity share. Therefore, the fluctuations experienced in the equity share markets show the behavior of the individuals and the degree to which the sectors are affected.

The impact of COVID-19 pandemic on the economic and financial markets is as follows. Most of the companies have either stopped working or have had to work at a reduced rate during the period of the applied restrictions. This situation has forced companies to decrease labor costs. The most affected sectors are transportation and tourism. Individuals have been obliged to stay away from social life. The general wealth level of society has decreased. Companies have been unsuccessful in the issue of cash and profit making. They have given up on new investments and growth. Also, great decreases have been seen in the prices of bond returns and petroleum and equity share.

Recovery in the economic and financial markets will occur after the COVID-19 pandemic during which restrictions will be loosened and rehabilitation will start. A new balancing is expected to be seen in economics in the spring period of 2021 for three important reasons. First, vaccination studies will reach a certain level in this period. Second, there is an expectation of a natural decrease regarding the epidemic in summer period. Third, more information will be known regarding the treatment of COVID-19 in the winter period of 2021. In this way, the case numbers will come under control.

Consequently, humankind has been exposed to many pandemics in history. These pandemics are unpredictable risk factors, and coping with these kinds of unpredictable risk factors depends on the knowledge and experiences obtained in the past. Rehabilitation will occur with the knowledge and intelligence of humankind that will be used collectively during the difficult days of the pandemic process. Although it is not possible to return to the old normal, a new rehabilitation will be experienced both in household and economies as life goes on. Generally, it appears that the impact seems less in the markets of the states where necessary precautions regarding the impact of COVID-19 were taken on time.

REFERENCES

Al-Awadhi, A. M., Al-Saifi, K., Al-Awadhi, A., & Alhamadi, S. (2020). Death and contagious infectious diseases: Impact of the COVID-19 virus on stock market returns. *Journal of Behavioral and Experimental Finance*, *27*, 100326. doi:10.1016/j.jbef.2020.100326 PMID:32292707

Alam, M. N., Alam, M. S., & Chavali, K. (2020). Stock Market Response during COVID-19 Lockdown Period in India: An Event Study. *The Journal of Asian Finance, Economics, and Business*, *7*(7), 131–137. doi:10.13106/jafeb.2020.vol7.no7.131

Altig, D., Baker, S., Barrero, J. M., Bloom, N., Bunn, P., Chen, S., ... Mizen, P. (2020). Economic uncertainty before and during the COVID-19 pandemic. *Journal of Public Economics*, *191*, 104274. doi:10.1016/j.jpubeco.2020.104274 PMID:32921841

Au, A. K., Ramasamy, B., & Yeung, M. C. (2005). The effects of SARS on the Hong Kong tourism industry: An empirical evaluation. *Asia Pacific Journal of Tourism Research*, *10*(1), 85–95. doi:10.1080/1094166042000330236

Bashir, M. F., Benjiang, M. A., & Shahzad, L. (2020). A brief review of socio-economic and environmental impact of COVID-19. *Air Quality, Atmosphere & Health*, *13*(12), 1–7. doi:10.100711869-020-00894-8 PMID:32837620

Bieszk-Stolorz, B., & Dmytrów, K. (2020). Survival analysis in assessment of influence of the SARS-CoV-2 pandemic on probability and intensity of decline in the value of stock indices. Research Square, 1-9. doi:10.21203/rs.3.rs-41942/v1

Chang, C. C., Lee, D. H., Lin, H. C., & Hsu, S. S. (2007). *The potential economic impact of avian flu pandemic on Taiwan* (No. 381-2016-22318). Academic Press.

Chang, C. L., McAleer, M., & Wang, Y. A. (2020). Herding behavior in energy stock markets during the Global Financial Crisis, SARS, and ongoing COVID-19. *Renewable & Sustainable Energy Reviews*, *134*, 110349. doi:10.1016/j.rser.2020.110349 PMID:34234619

Chen, C. D., Chen, C. C., Tang, W. W., & Huang, B. Y. (2009). The positive and negative impacts of the SARS outbreak: A case of the Taiwan industries. *Journal of Developing Areas*, *43*(1), 281–293. doi:10.1353/jda.0.0041

Chen, M. H. (2007). Macro and non-macro explanatory factors of Chinese hotel stock returns. *International Journal of Hospitality Management*, *26*(4), 991–1004. doi:10.1016/j.ijhm.2006.04.002 PMID:32287850

Chen, M. H., Jang, S. S., & Kim, W. G. (2007). The impact of the SARS outbreak on Taiwanese hotel stock performance: An event-study approach. *International Journal of Hospitality Management*, *26*(1), 200–212. doi:10.1016/j.ijhm.2005.11.004 PMID:32287849

Chen, M. P., Lee, C. C., Lin, Y. H., & Chen, W. Y. (2018). Did the SARS epidemic weaken the integration of Asian stock markets? Evidence from smooth time-varying cointegration analysis. Economic research-. *Ekonomska Istrazivanja*, *31*(1), 908–926. doi:10.1080/1331677X.2018.1456354

Corbet, S., Hou, Y., Hu, Y., Lucey, B., & Oxley, L. (2020). Aye Corona! The contagion effects of being named Corona during the COVID-19 pandemic. *Finance Research Letters*, 101591. PMID:32837362

Cox, J., Greenwald, D. L., & Ludvigson, S. C. (2020). What Explains the COVID-19 Stock Market? (No. w27784). National Bureau of Economic Research.

Czech, K., Wielechowski, M., Kotyza, P., Benešová, I., & Laputková, A. (2020). Shaking Stability: COVID-19 Impact on the Visegrad Group Countries' Financial Markets. *Sustainability*, *12*(15), 6282. doi:10.3390u12156282

David, S. A., Inácio, C. M. C. Jr, & Machado, J. A. T. (2020). The recovery of global stock markets indices after impacts due to pandemics. *Research in International Business and Finance*, 101335. PMID:34173412

Day, B., Mckay, R. B., Ishman, M., & Chung, E. (2004). The new normal: Lessons learned from SARS for corporations operating in emerging markets. *Management Decision*, *42*(6), 794–806. doi:10.1108/00251740410542357

Ding, W., Levine, R., Lin, C., & Xie, W. (2020). *Corporate immunity to the COVID-19 pandemic (No. w27055)*. National Bureau of Economic Research. doi:10.3386/w27055

Göktaş, A., Koker, N. E., & Alemdar, Y. M. (2008). How to manage reputation during crisis: An analysis of Turkish white meat sector during the avian influenza (bird flu) crisis. *Journal of Yaşar University*, *3*(12), 1760–1786.

Griffith, R., Levell, P., & Stroud, R. (2020). The Impact of COVID-19 on Share Prices in the UK. *Fiscal Studies*, *41*(2), 363–369. doi:10.1111/1475-5890.12226

Iqbal, N., Fareed, Z., Shahzad, F., He, X., Shahzad, U., & Lina, M. (2020). Nexus between COVID-19, temperature and exchange rate in Wuhan City: New findings from Partial and Multiple Wavelet Coherence. *The Science of the Total Environment*, *729*, 138916. doi:10.1016/j.scitotenv.2020.138916 PMID:32388129

Ishida, T., Ishikawa, N., & Fukushige, M. (2010). Impact of BSE and bird flu on consumers' meat demand in Japan. *Applied Economics*, *42*(1), 49–56. doi:10.1080/00036840701564392

JonungL.RoegerW. (2006). The macroeconomic effects of a pandemic in Europe-A model-based assessment. Available at SSRN 920851. doi:10.2139/ssrn.920851

Karki, S. (2017). Effects of highly pathogenic avian influenza H5N1 outbreak in Nepal from financial and social perspectives: A case study. *Nepalese Veterinary Journal*, *34*, 26–35. doi:10.3126/nvj.v34i0.22861

Kartal, M. T., Depren, Ö., & Depren, S. K. (2020). The determinants of main stock exchange index changes in emerging countries: Evidence from Turkey in COVID-19 pandemic age. *Quantitative Finance and Economics*, *4*(4), 526–541. doi:10.3934/QFE.2020025

Khoon, C. C. (2006). *Risk Perception and coping responses in a SARS outbreak in Malaysia* (Vol. 2006). World Scientific. doi:10.1142/9789812773395_0018

Lee, J. W., & McKibbin, W. J. (2004). Globalization and disease: The case of SARS. *Asian Economic Papers*, *3*(1), 113–131. doi:10.1162/1535351041747932

Lee, J. W., & McKibbin, W. J. (2004, April). Estimating the global economic costs of SARS. In *Learning from SARS: preparing for the next disease outbreak: workshop summary* (pp. 92–109). National Academies Press.

Liu, H., Manzoor, A., Wang, C., Zhang, L., & Manzoor, Z. (2020). The COVID-19 outbreak and affected countries stock markets response. *International Journal of Environmental Research and Public Health, 17*(8), 2800. doi:10.3390/ijerph17082800 PMID:32325710

Mazur, M., Dang, M., & Vega, M. (2020). COVID-19 and the march 2020 stock market crash. Evidence from S&P1500. *Finance Research Letters*, 101690. PMID:32837377

McKibbin, W. J., & Fernando, R. (2020). *The global macroeconomic impacts of COVID-19: Seven scenarios.* Centre for Applied Macroeconomic Analysis, CAMA Working Paper, 1-45.

Menard, J., Thompson, J., English, B. C., Hughes, D., Griffith, A. P., Smith, A., & Jensen, K. (2020). Economic Impacts from an On-Farm Highly Pathogenic Avian Influenza Event in Tennessee. *The Review of Regional Studies, 50*(2), 282–300. doi:10.52324/001c.14168

Narayan, P. K., Phan, D. H. B., & Liu, G. (2020). COVID-19 lockdowns, stimulus packages, travel bans, and stock returns. *Finance Research Letters*, 101732. PMID:32843886

Nicola, M., Alsafi, Z., Sohrabi, C., Kerwan, A., Al-Jabir, A., Iosifidis, C., Agha, M., & Agha, R. (2020). The socio-economic implications of the coronavirus pandemic (COVID-19): A review. *International Journal of Surgery (London, England), 78*, 185–193. doi:10.1016/j.ijsu.2020.04.018 PMID:32305533

Ozili, P. K. (2020). COVID-19 in Africa: socioeconomic impact, policy response and opportunities. *Policy Response and Opportunities.*

Ramelli, S., & Wagner, A. F. (2020). *Feverish stock price reactions to COVID-19.* Discussion Paper DP14511, 7, 1-61.

Salisu, A. A., Akanni, L., & Raheem, I. (2020c). The COVID-19 global fear index and the predictability of commodity price returns. *Journal of Behavioral and Experimental Finance, 27*, 100383. doi:10.1016/j.jbef.2020.100383 PMID:32835013

Salisu, A. A., Ebuh, G. U., & Usman, N. (2020b). Revisiting oil-stock nexus during COVID-19 pandemic: Some preliminary results. *International Review of Economics & Finance, 69*, 280–294. doi:10.1016/j.iref.2020.06.023

Salisu, A. A., & Vo, X. V. (2020a). Predicting stock returns in the presence of COVID-19 pandemic: The role of health news. *International Review of Financial Analysis, 71*, 101546. doi:10.1016/j.irfa.2020.101546

Sansa, N. A. (2020). The Impact of the COVID-19 on the Financial Markets: Evidence from China and USA. *Electronic Research Journal of Social Sciences and Humanities, 2.*

Siu, A., & Wong, Y. R. (2004). Economic impact of SARS: The case of Hong Kong. *Asian Economic Papers, 3*(1), 62–83. doi:10.1162/1535351041747996

Suder, G., & Inthavong, S. (2008). New health risks and sociocultural contexts: Bird flu impacts on consumers and poultry businesses in Lao PDR. *Risk Analysis: An International Journal, 28*(1), 1–12. doi:10.1111/j.1539-6924.2008.00997.x PMID:18304102

Thurlow, J. (2010). *Implications of avian flu for economic development in Kenya (No. 951). International Food Policy Research Institute.* IFPRI.

Topcu, M., & Gulal, O. S. (2020). The impact of COVID-19 on emerging stock markets. *Finance Research Letters, 36*, 101691. doi:10.1016/j.frl.2020.101691 PMID:32837378

Wong, G. (2008). Has SARS infected the property market? Evidence from Hong Kong. *Journal of Urban Economics, 63*(1), 74–95. doi:10.1016/j.jue.2006.12.007 PMID:32287489

Yang, C., Sha, D., Liu, Q., Li, Y., Lan, H., Guan, W. W., ... Wang, Z. (2020). Taking the pulse of COVID-19: A spatiotemporal perspective. *International Journal of Digital Earth, 13*(10), 1–26. doi:10.1080/17538947.2020.1809723

KEY TERMS AND DEFINITIONS

AEX: It is an index representing the 25 most traded equity shares traded in the Holland stock exchange.

BIST100: It is an index used to measure the performance of the highest 100 equity shares in terms of the market and transaction volume traded in the Istanbul Stock Exchange.

BOVESPA: It is an index representing the 68 highest companies in terms of the market and transaction volume in the Brazil Stock Exchange.

CAC40: It is an index representing the 40 most important equity shares among the greatest 100 market values of the French stock exchange.

CNX: It is an index covering the greatest and most liquid 50 equity shares consisting of Indian companies.

DAX: It is an index representing 30 of the greatest and most liquid German companies traded in the Frankfurt Stock Exchange.

FTSEMIB: It is an index representing the 40 most equity shares in the Italian Stock Exchange.

RTSI: It is an index consisting of the 50 most liquid equity shares listed on the Russian Stock Exchange.

S&P 500: It is an index consisting of the 500 greatest American companies and covering approximately 75 percent of the equity share market.

SSEC: It is an index containing all equity shares in the Shanghai Stock Exchange.

APPENDIX 1

International Stock Exchanges

Table 7. International stock exchanges

No	Symbol	Description
1	AEX	Amsterdam Index
2	AMMANINDX	Amman General Index
3	AORD	All Ordinaries Australia
4	ATX	ATX Index Vienna
5	BEL20	Brussels BEL 20 Index
6	BIST	BIST100 Istanbul
7	BOVESPA	Bovespa, Sao Paulo Index
8	BUX	Budapest BUX
9	CAC40	Paris CAC 40 Index
10	CNX	Indian S&P CNX NIFTY 50
11	DAX	Germany
12	EGX30	Egypt EGX30 Index
13	FTSEMIB	FTSE MIB Index Italy
14	HEX25	OMX Helsinki 25
15	HSI	Hong Kong Hang Seng Index
16	IBE35	IBEX 35 Index Madrid
17	ITSEC	T300 Comp. Toronto
18	JKSE	Jakarta Composite
19	KLSE	Kuala Lumpur Composite
20	KOSPI	Seoul Composite
21	MERV	Buones Aires Stock Exchange MERVAL
22	MSCIWO	MSCI World PR USD
23	NIKKEI225	Nikkei 225 Index
24	OW20	WIG20 Warsaw
25	PSI20	Lisbon PSI 20 Index
26	PX50	PX50 Prag
27	QATARINDX	Qatar Index
28	RTSI	Russia RSI Index
29	SASEINDX	Saudi Arabia Tadawul index

continues on following page

Table 7. Continued

No	Symbol	Description
30	SASX10	SASE Index Sarajevo
31	SENS	Bombay SENSEX
32	SINGT	Straits Times Singapore Exchange
33	SMI	Swiss Market Indicator
34	S&P500	America 500 Index
35	SSEC	Shanghai Composite
36	SZCOMP	Shenzhen Composite China
37	TA100	Tel-Aviv TASE100
38	TOTX	Total Index, Oslo
39	TWII	Taiwan Weighted

APPENDIX 2

Abnormal Returns

Table 8. MSCIWO benchmark index

Variables	Before Pandemic	Pandemic Period	After Pandemic
Minimum	-0.0164	-0.0991	-0.0310
Maximum	0.0098	0.0877	0.0589
Median	0.0004	-0.0042	0.0043
Mean	0.0007	-0.0054	0.0046
Std. Dev.	0.0051	0.0344	0.0173

Table 9. AEX abnormal return results

Variables	Before Pandemic	Pandemic Period	After Pandemic
Minimum	*-0.0253*	-0.1120	-0.0332
Maximum	0.0184	0.0897	0.0391
Median	-0.0001	0.0002	0.0030
Mean	0.0001	-0.0046	0.0033
Std. Dev.	0.0082	0.0356	0.0189
Abnormal Return	No	Yes	No
Statistically Significant	Yes	Yes	Yes

Table 10. AMMANDX abnormal return results

Variables	Before Pandemic	Pandemic Period	After Pandemic
Minimum	-0.0039	-0.0490	-0.0145
Maximum	0.0128	0.0038	0.0103
Median	-0.0001	-0.0052	0.0000
Mean	0.0021	-0.0094	-0.0007
Std. Dev.	-0.0039	-0.0490	-0.0145
Abnormal Return	Yes	No	No
Statistically Significant	Yes	Yes	Yes

Table 11. AORD abnormal return results

Variables	Before Pandemic	Pandemic Period	After Pandemic
Minimum	-0.0172	-0.0952	-0.0487
Maximum	0.0157	0.0656	0.0424
Median	0.0014	-0.0013	0.0034
Mean	0.0008	-0.0066	0.0035
Std. Dev.	0.0075	0.0363	0.0174
Abnormal Return	Yes	No	No
Statistically Significant	Yes	Yes	Yes

Table 12. ATX abnormal return results

Variables	Before Pandemic	Pandemic Period	After Pandemic
Minimum	-0.0149	-0.1365	-0.0697
Maximum	0.0138	0.1074	0.0419
Median	-0.0001	-0.0044	0.0081
Mean	-0.0003	-0.0104	0.0038
Std. Dev.	0.0067	0.0426	0.0256
Abnormal Return	No	No	No
Statistically Significant	Yes	Yes	Yes

Table 13. BEL20 abnormal return results

Variables	Before Pandemic	Pandemic Period	After Pandemic
Minimum	-0.0248	-0.1421	-0.0474
Maximum	0.0152	0.0764	0.0538
Median	0.0010	0.0005	0.0075
Mean	0.0001	-0.0070	0.0034
Std. Dev.	0.0071	0.0392	0.0243
Abnormal Return	No	No	No
Statistically Significant	Yes	Yes	Yes

Table 14. BIST100 abnormal return results

Variables	Before Pandemic	Pandemic Period	After Pandemic
Minimum	-0.0200	-0.0807	-0.0273
Maximum	0.0453	0.0598	0.0281
Median	0.0016	-0.0032	0.0041
Mean	0.0023	-0.0066	0.0047
Std. Dev.	0.0107	0.0269	0.0125
Abnormal Return	Yes	No	Yes
Statistically Significant	Yes	Yes	Yes

Table 15. BOVESP abnormal return results

Variables	Before Pandemic	Pandemic Period	After Pandemic
Minimum	-0.0160	-0.1444	0.0563
Maximum	0.0253	0.1395	0.1036
Median	0.0000	-0.0092	-0.0015
Mean	0.0013	-0.0128	0.0069
Std. Dev.	0.0099	0.0536	0.0324
Abnormal Return	Yes	No	Yes
Statistically Significant	Yes	Yes	Yes

Table 16. BUX abnormal return results

Variables	Before Pandemic	Pandemic Period	After Pandemic
Minimum	-0.0132	-0.1155	-0.0482
Maximum	0.0105	0.0597	0.0487
Median	-0.0057	-0.0216	0.0051
Mean	-0.0038	-0.0190	0.0057
Std. Dev.	0.0068	0.0521	0.0230
Abnormal Return	Yes	No	Yes
Statistically Significant	Yes	Yes	Yes

Table 17. CAC40 abnormal return results

Variables	Before Pandemic	Pandemic Period	After Pandemic
Minimum	-0.0268	-0.1228	-0.0424
Maximum	0.0127	0.0839	0.0516
Median	0.0004	0.0009	0.0038
Mean	0.0001	-0.0065	0.0030
Std. Dev.	0.0078	0.0391	0.0215
Abnormal Return	No	No	No
Statistically Significant	Yes	Yes	Yes

Table 18. CNX abnormal return results

Variables	Before Pandemic	Pandemic Period	After Pandemic
Minimum	-0.0191	-0.1298	-0.0574
Maximum	0.0158	0.0662	0.0876
Median	0.0009	-0.0041	0.0050
Mean	0.0001	-0.0088	0.0044
Std. Dev.	0.0071	0.0383	0.0249
Abnormal Return	No	No	No
Statistically Significant	Yes	Yes	Yes

Table 19. DAX abnormal return results

Variables	Before Pandemic	Pandemic Period	After Pandemic
Minimum	-0.0399	-0.1224	-0.0274
Maximum	0.0577	0.1098	0.0141
Median	0.0097	-0.0013	0.0004
Mean	0.0058	-0.0063	0.0004
Std. Dev.	0.0228	0.0361	0.0085
Abnormal Return	Yes	No	No
Statistically Significant	Yes	Yes	Yes

Table 20. EGX30 abnormal return results

Variables	Before Pandemic	Pandemic Period	After Pandemic
Minimum	-0.0494	-0.1577	-0.0447
Maximum	0.0250	0.0915	0.0417
Median	0.0024	-0.0064	0.0032
Mean	0.0011	-0.0123	0.0027
Std. Dev.	0.0128	0.0449	0.0193
Abnormal Return	Yes	No	No
Statistically Significant	Yes	Yes	Yes

Table 21. FTSEMIB abnormal return results

Variables	Before Pandemic	Pandemic Period	After Pandemic
Minimum	-0.0231	-0.1692	-0.0478
Maximum	0.0261	0.0893	0.0326
Median	0.0003	0.0012	0.0050
Mean	0.0006	-0.0081	0.0026
Std. Dev.	0.0099	0.0421	0.0203
Abnormal Return	No	No	No
Statistically Significant	Yes	Yes	Yes

Table 22. HEX25 abnormal return results

Variables	Before Pandemic	Pandemic Period	After Pandemic
Minimum	-0.0225	-0.1013	-0.0423
Maximum	0.0182	0.0689	0.0518
Median	0.0024	-0.0036	0.0084
Mean	0.0019	-0.0069	0.0053
Std. Dev.	0.0075	0.0320	0.0210
Abnormal Return	Yes	No	Yes
Statistically Significant	Yes	Yes	Yes

Table 23. HSI Abnormal Return Results

Variables	Before Pandemic	Pandemic Period	After Pandemic
Minimum	-0.0282	-0.0486	-0.0556
Maximum	0.0257	0.0505	0.0221
Median	0.0014	-0.0028	0.0007
Mean	0.0000	-0.0038	0.0000
Std. Dev.	0.0118	0.0225	0.0161
Abnormal Return	No	Yes	No
Statistically Significant	Yes	Yes	Yes

Table 24. IBE35 abnormal return results

Variables	Before Pandemic	Pandemic Period	After Pandemic
Minimum	-0.0205	-0.1406	-0.0379
Maximum	0.0151	0.0782	0.0470
Median	-0.0016	0.0000	0.0040
Mean	0.0003	-0.0084	0.0021
Std. Dev.	0.0076	0.0381	0.0201
Abnormal Return	No	No	No
Statistically Significant	Yes	Yes	Yes

Table 25. ITSEC abnormal return results

Variables	Before Pandemic	Pandemic Period	After Pandemic
Minimum	-0.0097	-0.1234	-0.0312
Maximum	0.0083	0.1196	0.0506
Median	0.0010	0.0010	0.0048
Mean	0.0009	-0.0063	0.0045
Std. Dev.	0.0029	0.0463	0.0166
Abnormal Return	Yes	No	No
Statistically Significant	Yes	Yes	Yes

Table 26. JKSE abnormal return results

Variables	Before Pandemic	Pandemic Period	After Pandemic
Minimum	-0.0194	-0.0658	-0.0318
Maximum	0.0094	0.1019	0.0407
Median	0.0002	-0.0074	0.0034
Mean	-0.0016	-0.0088	0.0010
Std. Dev.	0.0071	0.0325	0.0176
Abnormal Return	No	No	No
Statistically Significant	Yes	Yes	Yes

Table 27. KLSE abnormal return results

Variables	Before Pandemic	Pandemic Period	After Pandemic
Minimum	-0.0167	-0.0526	-0.0222
Maximum	0.0141	0.0685	0.0210
Median	-0.0008	-0.0024	0.0041
Mean	-0.0006	-0.0036	0.0030
Std. Dev.	0.0065	0.0214	0.0098
Abnormal Return	No	Yes	No
Statistically Significant	Yes	Yes	Yes

Table 28. KOSPI abnormal return results

Variables	Before Pandemic	Pandemic Period	After Pandemic
Minimum	-0.0309	-0.0839	-0.0268
Maximum	0.0163	0.0860	0.0385
Median	0.0020	-0.0058	0.0048
Mean	0.0005	-0.0057	0.0050
Std. Dev.	0.0100	0.0330	0.0138
Abnormal Return	No	No	Yes
Statistically Significant	Yes	Yes	Yes

Table 29. MERVE abnormal return results

Variables	Before Pandemic	Pandemic Period	After Pandemic
Minimum	-0.0481	-0.1447	-0.0621
Maximum	0.0592	0.1025	0.1027
Median	-0.0001	-0.0068	0.0106
Mean	0.0035	-0.0134	0.0111
Std. Dev.	0.0222	0.0511	0.0329
Abnormal Return	Yes	Yes	Yes
Statistically Significant	Yes	Yes	Yes

Table 30. NIKKEI225 Abnormal return results

Variables	Before Pandemic	Pandemic Period	After Pandemic
Minimum	-0.0203	-0.0608	-0.0288
Maximum	-0.0064	0.0102	0.0001
Median	0.0003	-0.0059	0.0038
Mean	-0.0003	-0.0047	0.0052
Std. Dev.	0.0100	0.0285	0.0169
Abnormal Return	No	Yes	Yes
Statistically Significant	Yes	Yes	Yes

Table 31. OW20 abnormal return results

Variables	Before Pandemic	Pandemic Period	After Pandemic
Minimum	-0.0327	-0.1328	-0.0406
Maximum	0.0268	0.0654	0.0495
Median	-0.0001	-0.0054	0.0024
Mean	-0.0007	-0.0080	0.0041
Std. Dev.	0.0109	0.0369	0.0201
Abnormal Return	No	No	No
Statistically Significant	Yes	Yes	Yes

Table 32. PSI20 abnormal return results

Variables	Before Pandemic	Pandemic Period	After Pandemic
Minimum	-0.0204	-0.1218	-0.0291
Maximum	0.0124	0.0782	0.0462
Median	0.0002	-0.0007	0.0042
Mean	0.0006	-0.0058	0.0022
Std. Dev.	0.0058	0.0340	0.0154
Abnormal Return	No	No	No
Statistically Significant	Yes	Yes	Yes

Table 33. PX50 abnormal return results

Variables	Before Pandemic	Pandemic Period	After Pandemic
Minimum	-0.0213	-0.0784	-0.0286
Maximum	0.0109	0.0765	0.0434
Median	0.0003	-0.0046	0.0074
Mean	-0.0001	-0.0086	0.0041
Std. Dev.	0.0070	0.0298	0.0147
Abnormal Return	No	No	No
Statistically Significant	Yes	Yes	Yes

Table 34. QATARINDX abnormal return results

Variables	Before Pandemic	Pandemic Period	After Pandemic
Minimum	-0.0129	-0.0235	-0.0286
Maximum	0.0145	0.0214	0.0343
Median	0.0007	-0.0013	0.0023
Mean	0.0004	-0.0018	-0.0004
Std. Dev.	0.0063	0.0101	0.0103
Abnormal Return	No	Yes	No
Statistically Significant	Yes	Yes	Yes

Table 35. RTSI abnormal return results

Variables	Before Pandemic	Pandemic Period	After Pandemic
Minimum	-0.0362	-0.1302	-0.0762
Maximum	0.0113	0.0171	0.0469
Median	0.0027	-0.0072	0.0084
Mean	0.0015	-0.0092	0.0057
Std. Dev.	0.0110	0.0468	0.0272
Abnormal Return	Yes	No	Yes
Statistically Significant	Yes	Yes	Yes

Table 36. SASEINDX abnormal return results

Variables	Before Pandemic	Pandemic Period	After Pandemic
Minimum	-0.0248	-0.1543	-0.0727
Maximum	0.0273	0.0707	0.0337
Median	0.0012	-0.0002	0.0055
Mean	0.0005	-0.0062	0.0027
Std. Dev.	0.0108	0.0388	0.0208
Abnormal Return	No	No	No
Statistically Significant	Yes	Yes	Yes

Table 37. SASX10 abnormal return results

Variables	Before Pandemic	Pandemic Period	After Pandemic
Minimum	-0.0240	-0.0375	-0.0283
Maximum	0.0179	0.0211	0.0356
Median	-0.0017	0.0000	0.0000
Mean	-0.0027	-0.0012	-0.0006
Std. Dev.	0.0080	0.0116	0.0115
Abnormal Return	No	Yes	No
Statistically Significant	Yes	Yes	Yes

Table 38. SENS abnormal return results

Variables	Before Pandemic	Pandemic Period	After Pandemic
Minimum	-0.0190	-0.1315	-0.0594
Maximum	0.0155	0.0698	0.0897
Median	0.0002	-0.0040	0.0046
Mean	0.0002	-0.0086	0.0041
Std. Dev.	0.0070	0.0392	0.0257
Abnormal Return	No	No	No
Statistically Significant	Yes	Yes	Yes

Table 39. SINGT abnormal return results

Variables	Before Pandemic	Pandemic Period	After Pandemic
Minimum	-0.0181	-0.0735	-0.0260
Maximum	0.0091	0.0607	0.0410
Median	0.0004	-0.0055	0.0009
Mean	-0.0005	-0.0078	0.0020
Std. Dev.	0.0053	0.0312	0.0154
Abnormal Return	No	No	No
Statistically Significant	Yes	Yes	Yes

Table 40. SMI abnormal return results

Variables	Before Pandemic	Pandemic Period	After Pandemic
Minimum	-0.0160	-0.0964	-0.0248
Maximum	0.0139	0.0702	0.0272
Median	0.0014	-0.0010	0.0037
Mean	0.0010	-0.0045	0.0022
Std. Dev.	0.0066	0.0304	0.0137
Abnormal Return	Yes	Yes	No
Statistically Significant	Yes	Yes	Yes

Table 41. S&P500 abnormal return results

Variables	Before Pandemic	Pandemic Period	After Pandemic
Minimum	-0.0177	-0.1198	-0.0307
Maximum	0.0101	0.0938	0.0703
Median	0.0013	-0.0033	0.0045
Mean	0.0011	-0.0050	0.0054
Std. Dev.	0.0061	0.0448	0.0198
Abnormal Return	Yes	Yes	Yes
Statistically Significant	Yes	Yes	Yes

Table 42. SSEC abnormal return results

Variables	Before Pandemic	Pandemic Period	After Pandemic
Minimum	-0.0275	-0.0371	-0.0189
Maximum	0.0178	0.0315	0.0205
Median	0.0008	0.0008	0.0018
Mean	0.0010	-0.0010	0.0011
Std. Dev.	0.0085	0.0163	0.0082
Abnormal Return	Yes	Yes	No
Statistically Significant	Yes	Yes	Yes

Table 43. SZCOMP abnormal return results

Variables	Before Pandemic	Pandemic Period	After Pandemic
Minimum	-0.0345	-0.0493	-0.0203
Maximum	0.0193	0.0377	0.0318
Median	0.0038	0.0032	-0.0010
Mean	0.0055	-0.0007	0.0089
Std. Dev.	0.0109	0.0213	0.0120
Abnormal Return	Yes	Yes	Yes
Statistically Significant	Yes	Yes	Yes

Table 44. TA100 abnormal return results

Variables	Before Pandemic	Pandemic Period	After Pandemic
Minimum	-0.0263	-0.1089	-0.0458
Maximum	0.0111	0.0750	0.0541
Median	0.0012	-0.0031	0.0044
Mean	0.0005	-0.0094	0.0054
Std. Dev.	0.0072	0.0380	0.0228
Abnormal Return	No	No	Yes
Statistically Significant	Yes	Yes	Yes

Table 45. TOTX abnormal return results

Variables	Before Pandemic	Pandemic Period	After Pandemic
Minimum	-0.0204	-0.0936	0.0328
Maximum	0.0107	0.0602	0.0282
Median	0.0010	-0.0009	0.0049
Mean	0.0005	-0.0065	0.0028
Std. Dev.	0.0066	0.0343	0.0173
Abnormal Return	No	No	No
Statistically Significant	Yes	Yes	Yes

Table 46. TWII abnormal return results

Variables	Before Pandemic	Pandemic Period	After Pandemic
Minimum	-0.0575	-0.0583	-0.0282
Maximum	0.0133	0.0637	0.0231
Median	0.0020	-0.0033	0.0046
Mean	0.0000	-0.0042	0.0033
Std. Dev.	0.0117	0.0232	0.0121
Abnormal Return	No	Yes	No
Statistically Significant	Yes	Yes	Yes

APPENDIX 3

Statistical Significance Tests

Results are statistically significant at the significance levels of 1 percent, 5 percent, and 10 percent. Similar results are valid for all stock exchange indexes.

BEFORE PANDEMIC AND PANDEMIC PERIOD

Table 47. Two-sample Kolmogorov-Smirnov Test

Frequencies		
	X12	N
S&P500	1	38
	2	38
	Total	76

Table 48.

Test Statistics[a]		
		SP500
Most Extreme Differences	Absolute	.368
	Positive	.263
	Negative	-.368
Kolmogorov-Smirnov Z		1.606
Asymp. Sig. (2-tailed)		.012
a. Grouping Variable: X12		

Table 49. Independent sample T-Test

Group Statistics					
	X12	**N**	**Mean**	**Std. Deviation**	**Std. Error Mean**
S&P500	1	38	.001353	.0055848	.0009060
	2	38	-.005017	.0447571	.0072606

Table 50.

		Levene's Test for Equality of Variances	
		F	**Sig.**
S&P500	Equal variances assumed	29.789	.000
	Equal variances not assumed		

Wald-Wolfowitz Test

Table 51.

Frequencies		
	X12	N
S&P500	1	38
	2	38
	Total	76

Table 52.

Test Statistics[b,c]				
		Number of Runs	Z	Asymp. Sig. (1-tailed)
S&P500	Exact Number of Runs	23[a]	-3.695	.000
a. No inter-group ties encountered. b. Wald-Wolfowitz Test c. Grouping Variable: X12				

PANDEMIC PERIOD - AFTER PANDEMIC

Two-Sample Kolmogorov-Smirnov Test

Table 53.

Frequencies		
	X12	N
S&P500	1	38
	2	38
	Total	76

Table 54.

Test Statistics[a]		
		SP500
Most Extreme Differences	Absolute	.289
	Positive	.289
	Negative	-.132
Kolmogorov-Smirnov Z		1.262
Asymp. Sig. (2-tailed)		.083
a. Grouping Variable: X12		

Independent Sample T-Test

Table 55.

Group Statistics					
	X12	N	Mean	Std. Deviation	Std. Error Mean
S&P500	1	38	-.005017	.0447571	.0072606
	2	38	.005637	.0202644	.0032873

Table 56.

		Levene's Test for Equality of Variances	
		F	Sig.
S&P500	Equal variances assumed	8.853	.004
	Equal variances not assumed		

Wald-Wolfowitz Test

Table 57.

Frequencies		
	X12	N
S&P500	1	38
	2	38
	Total	76

Table 58.

Test Statistics[b,c]				
		Number of Runs	Z	Asymp. Sig. (1-tailed)
S&P500	Exact Number of Runs	31[a]	-1.848	.032

a. No inter-group ties encountered.
b. Wald-Wolfowitz Test
c. Grouping Variable: X12

Chapter 6
What Are the Potential Impacts of a Global Health Crisis on Economic Inequalities in Some Countries?

Ahmet Eren Yıldırım
Uşak University, Turkey

ABSTRACT

This study investigates the relationship between the COVID-19 crisis and economic inequalities in some developed and developing countries. Many institutions, like OECD, ILO, and UNDP, have released several reports deal with the relationship between COVID-19 and different kinds of inequalities. These reports generally emphasize the same problem. This study includes some indicators about the situation of education and gender inequalities in OECD countries. These indicators purely reveal that COVID-19 has negative effects on both education and gender inequalities in most of developed and developing countries. The main contribution of the study is to point out the importance of recovery policies the cover the inequality problems.

INTRODUCTION

The Global World has faced a global health problem, namely COVID-19, that has had deadly effects on humanity since the end of 2019. World Health Organization (WHO) declared this global health issue as a pandemic in March 2020. The COVID-19 pandemic has deeply affected humanity by covering all dimensions of life during this period. The first and most immediate action that governments took

DOI: 10.4018/978-1-7998-6900-9.ch006

was lockdowns for many sectors all around the world. These lockdowns directly affected the whole dimensions of daily life; all activities that can be together in a group have been banned. This process led to severe depression in both the production and consumption sectors. As expected, this kind of slowdown process mostly influenced low-income households almost all over the world. On the other hand, there have been vast income and wealth inequalities among the bottom and top of the distribution of household earnings for a very long-time. The high income and wealth inequalities have a negative effect on the socioeconomic structure of any society. Then, one can easily expect that the recent global health crisis would accelerate this effect.

Apart from income and wealth inequalities, the inequalities can be defined with social, cultural, racial, gender topics in the economics literature. Gender inequalities can usually be related to the employment opportunities in the labor market conditions. If anybody wants to decrease the gender inequalities in the labor market balance, there is the only way to solve this issue: increasing female employment. Territorial inequalities are another type of inequality in the related literature. Territorial inequality is also a critical indicator that deals with the development level of a country. All these types of inequalities are generally considered economic inequalities, and so, there may appear a strong relationship between the economic inequalities and COVID-19. Several studies have been conducted to investigate the socioeconomic impacts of the global health problem since the end of 2019 (Blundell et al., 2020; Furceri et al., 2020; Palomino et al., 2020; Papageorge et al., 2020; Stabile et al., 2020; Caitlin and Ravallion, 2020, Deaton, 2021). The common findings show that one of the main reasons for deepening the global health problem is the increasing inequality in the global economy. Then, some questions emerge: Has the COVID-19 negative impacted the socioeconomic structure of any country due to the increasing inequalities? If income and wealth inequalities were low, would COVID-19 still negatively affect the socioeconomic structure? By inspiring from these questions, this chapter focuses on the potential impacts of the current global health crisis on economic inequalities, such as education and gender inequalities, in the selected developed and developing countries.

Many international organizations like United Nations Development Programme (UNDP), International Labor Organization (ILO), and International Food Policy Research Institute (IFPRI) have published some reports on the relationship between the COVID-19 and inequalities recently. The UNDP reports revealed that the global human development index has started to decline in the last years, although it has had a development trend since 1990. Furthermore, this reduction draws attention to many cautions for all segments of society in the world. According to the details of the UNDP reports, the global per capita income is expected to fall by 4 percent. The UNDP argues that pandemics effects or expose the weaknesses of societies.

COVID-19 causes significant damage by affecting everyone regardless of the rich or poor societies because of the increasingly widening economic inequalities. The ILO reports emphasized the effects of COVID-19 on economic inequalities with the changing working conditions worldwide. According to the last report of the ILO on work, there are mainly three impacts of COVID-19 on working conditions. These are the closure of workplaces, loss of working-hour and decreasing income of labor. ILO also reports that the governments take some actions to fight this process; however, the interventions are not enough to prevent the increase in economic inequalities in rich countries and emerging countries. IFPRI reports presented the critical dimensions of the potential effects of COVID-19 on economic inequality. IFPRI has emphasized that the current pandemic is different from SARS, MERS, and avian influenza, which has occurred in previous ones regarding economic inequality. IFPRI points that COVID-19 has serious economic effects. First, the global stock markets have been damaged by the pandemic. Then, the economic activities have drastically slowed worldwide as movements were restricted to prevent the further spread of the virus. IFPRI provides three possible scenarios to examine the potential effects of COVID-19 on economic inequality. These are labor productivity shock, total factor productivity shock, and trade shock.

This study investigates the potential impacts of COVID-19 on economic inequalities by using the indicators of education and gender in the labor market conditions in developed and developing countries. In this context, the importance of this study is that it provides a perspective to the related literature in terms of reducing the socioeconomic effects of the pandemic in the last period when inequalities increased by analyzing the possible economic dimensions of COVID-19. The remainder of the study is structured as follows: the next section introduces the conceptual and descriptive analysis of selected indicators used in this study. Section 3 presents the relationship between COVID-19 and economic inequalities. Finally, section 4 discusses the policy implications and concludes.

THE EDUCATIONAL AND GENDER INEQUALITIES

This section presents a brief description of the concepts of education and gender inequalities and displays some descriptive trends reflecting these inequalities. These concepts are quite important in the context of socioeconomic development of societies, albeit discussed rarely in the studies that relate the economic inequalities. Moreover, explaining these inequalities will help to understand the effects of the global health crisis.

Educational Inequality

Educational inequality mainly emphasizes the opportunity equalities among the different income classes of any society. Inequality in education can be described in many ways. However, this study prefers a narrow definition to make a significant relationship with the COVID-19. The common definition is the unequal distribution of academic resources. Moreover, this situation also includes the school funding, qualified and experienced teachers, books, and technologies to access. According to Doyle (2020), when a school closure process due to any policy implication, the first and most important result is that inequality in education and skills increases. This result relates to the socioeconomic level of households. If a child is from the lower socioeconomic status of a society, his/her education is generally poor. The figures below provide some fundamental indicators that deal with the access to education in some developed and developing countries in the last decades. Figure 1 shows the participation rate of young people in formal education for many developed and developing countries between 2018 and 2020. Figure 2 displays the age range in which at least 90 percent of the population are enrolled for the last available years. Figure 3 gives the enrolment rates of young people in some countries.

Figure 1. The participation rate of young people in formal education (from 15 to 24 years)
Source: Eurostat

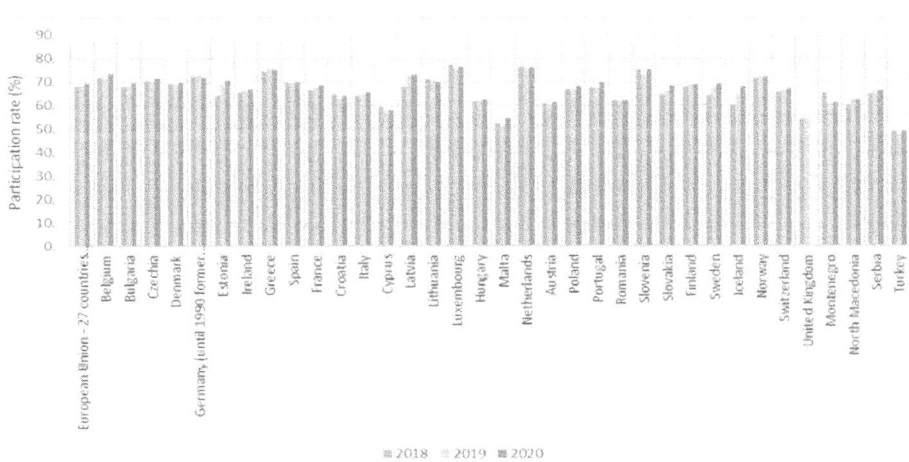

Figure 2. Age range in which at least 90 percent of the population are enrolled (2005, 2013, and 2019)
Source: OECD/UIS/Eurostat (2021)

	Number of years for which at least 90% of the population of school age are enrolled	Age range at which at least 90% of the population of school age are enrolled	Students as a percentage of the population of a specific age group											
			5 to 14	15 to 19	20 to 24	25 to 29	30 to 39	40 to 64	15 to 19	20 to 24	25 to 29	15 to 19	20 to 24	25 to 29
			2019						2013			2005		
	(1)	(2)	(3)	(4)	(5)	(6)	(7)	(8)	(9)	(10)	(11)	(12)	(13)	(14)
OECD — Countries														
Australia	13	5-17	100	88	55	26	15	7	86	48	21	82	44	21
Austria	13	4-16	99	80	36	18	6	1	79	35	18	m	m	m
Belgium	16	3-18	99	94	50	14	7	3	92	51	18	94	42	15
Canada [1]	11	5-15	100	72	36	11	5	1	73	33	11	m	m	m
Chile	13	5-17	98	82	44	15	6	1	78	41	16	m	m	m
Colombia	10	5-14	97	61	25	11	6	1	m	m	m	m	m	m
Costa Rica	12	4-15	97	64	23	11	2	3	m	m	4	m	m	a
Czech Republic	13	5-17	98	90	41	10	3	1	90	43	11	91	34	10
Denmark	15	3-17	100	86	53	28	9	2	88	57	32	84	48	27
Estonia	14	4-17	97	88	37	14	7	2	89	44	17	91	40	12
Finland	13	6-18	98	87	47	29	16	5	86	51	31	87	55	30
France	15	3-17	100	87	38	8	2	0	85	35	7	84	32	7
Germany	15	3-17	99	87	51	22	5	1	90	48	21	88	41	18
Greece	13	5-17	97	88	54	25	10	3	86	41	34	m	m	m
Hungary	13	4-16	95	83	34	10	4	1	87	42	12	87	38	13
Iceland	16	2-17	99	85	42	21	10	4	88	52	28	85	49	25
Ireland	15	3-17	100	94	43	12	6	3	94	37	9	89	32	10
Israel	15	3-17	96	66	21	19	6	2	65	22	22	m	m	m
Italy	15	3-17	99	86	38	13	3	1	78	37	14	82	33	10
Japarf	14	4-17	100	m	m	m	m	m	m	m	m	m	m	m
Korea	15	2-17	99	84	50	8	2	1	87	63	10	87	46	9
Latvia	15	4-18	99	92	46	16	6	1	94	46	12	m	m	m
Lithuania	14	5-18	100	93	44	11	5	1	94	52	16	98	49	15
Luxembourg	13	4-16	98	77	20	6	2	0	78	20	6	m	m	m
Mexico	9	5-13	100	63	26	10	4	2	54	21	6	48	17	5
Netherlands	14	4-17	100	92	m	m	m	m	91	49	13	m	m	m
New Zealand	12	5-16	99	82	43	19	12	5	84	38	16	74	41	21
Norway	17	2-18	99	87	47	19	8	3	87	43	18	89	46	20
Poland	14	5-18	97	92	48	11	3	1	90	56	13	92	50	10
Portugal	14	4-17	100	90	38	10	4	2	88	37	10	74	35	12
Slovak Republic	11	6-16	95	84	32	6	2	1	85	35	8	m	m	m
Slovenia	15	4-18	99	94	56	12	2	1	93	57	15	93	50	17
Spain	15	3-17	98	87	47	16	6	2	87	46	15	78	34	11
Sweden	17	2-18	99	88	44	26	16	5	86	42	28	m	m	m
Switzerland	13	5-17	100	85	41	18	5	1	86	38	16	83	31	13
Turkey	10	6-15	100	69	51	32	16	3	69	42	20	m	m	m
United Kingdom	15	3-17	97	83	33	10	6	2	81	31	11	m	m	m
United States	13	5-17	100	83	36	13	6	2	81	36	16	77	32	13
OECD average	14	4-17	99	84	41	16	6	2	84	42	16	84	40	14
Average for countries with available data for all reference years				87	44	15			86	44	16	84	40	15
EU22 average	14	4-17	98	88	43	15	6	2	88	44	16	88	41	15
Partners														
Argentina [1]	12	4-15	100	75	41	21	m	m	72	37	20	65	30	16
Brazil	13	4-16	99	69	29	14	8	3	69	27	14	m	m	m
China	18	2-19	m	m	m	m	m	m	m	m	m	m	m	a
India	18	2-19	m	m	m	a	m	m	m	m	m	m	m	a
Indonesia [1]	10	5-14	93	78	26	5	2	1	70	24	2	m	m	0
Russian Federation	11	7-17	98	88	38	7	2	0	84	32	10	m	m	m
Saudi Arabia	10	8-17	96	88	39	13	1	1	93	37	8	m	m	a
South Africa [1]	5	2-6	87	76	29	7	2	2	m	m	m	m	m	m
G20 average	13	m	m	m	m	m	m	m	m	m	m	m	m	m

According to Figure 1, Luxembourg, the Netherlands, and Slovenia are the top countries with the highest participation ratio among others informal education. On the contrary, Turkey and Malta have the lowest participation rates in formal education between 2018 and 2020. On the other hand, the participation rate of young people in formal education has dramatically decreased in some countries, Croatia, Cyprus, Lithuania, and Montenegro, in particular. Figure 2 shows that The Nordic Countries, like Finland, Norway, Sweden, Slovenia, and Poland, seem to have the highest age of enrolment in which at least 90 percent of their population while Iceland, Korea, Norway, and Sweden had the lowest age in 2019. On the other hand, Turkey, Costa Rica, Indonesia, Mexico, and Saudi Arabia are the lowest number of years for the school-age population to enroll at least 90 percent of their population. Figure 3 relates to the enrolment rates of 15-20 years old and displays the enrolment rate by level of education for 2013 and 2019. According to figure 3, many countries are greater than the average of OECD and EU22 countries at secondary school for 15 and 16ages. Ireland seems to be the best country by the full enrolment rate in secondary school enrollment at different ages, while Mexico and Colombia are the worst countries. Saudi Arabia is also another interesting sample by the full enrolment rate.

Figure 3. Enrolment rates of 15–20-years-old, by level of education, 2013 and 2019
Source: OECD (2021)

	2019														2013			
	Secondary	Secondary	Secondary	Post-secondary non-tertiary	Tertiary	Secondary	Post-secondary non-tertiary	Tertiary	Secondary	Post-secondary non-tertiary	Tertiary	Secondary	Post-secondary non-tertiary	Tertiary	All levels of education			
	Age 15	Age 16	Age 17			Age 18			Age 19			Age 20			Age 17	Age 18	Age 19	Age 20
	(1)	(2)	(3)	(4)	(5)	(6)	(7)	(8)	(9)	(10)	(11)	(12)	(13)	(14)	(15)	(16)	(17)	(18)
OECD Countries																		
Australia	100	99	88	1	5	36	3	36	20	4	49	17	3	50	90	74	70	66
Austria	95	90	74	0	13	44	1	29	21	1	32	10	1	32	89	74	51	41
Belgium	99	98	97	0	1	50	2	39	27	4	53	13	4	56	99	84	80	77
Canada	90	89	74	m	3	20	m	37	8	m	45	5	m	45	81	57	49	46
Chile	95	95	92	a	0	35	a	32	11	a	49	4	a	53	88	62	56	51
Colombia	86	75	42	0	13	21	0	23	10	0	28	5	0	27	m	m	m	m
Costa Rica	94	84	62	a	0	35	a	8	22	a	14	15	a	14	m	m	m	m
Czech Republic	99	97	94	m	0	87	m	1	47	m	24	13	m	43	96	90	72	57
Denmark	99	96	92	a	0	86	a	1	55	a	6	25	a	18	91	87	66	55
Estonia	98	96	93	0	0	88	0	2	32	1	27	12	2	35	95	88	69	57
Finland	98	96	97	0	0	96	0	1	33	0	13	16	0	25	95	94	51	48
France	97	95	90	0	3	30	1	48	11	0	56	5	0	51	91	77	64	53
Germany	98	94	88	4	1	65	7	9	38	11	21	22	13	30	94	86	74	64
Greece	99	97	94	0	1	13	13	50	7	12	52	7	10	56	97	74	68	66
Hungary	97	93	87	0	0	65	5	5	23	16	23	7	11	32	93	84	70	60
Iceland	99	95	90	0	0	81	0	1	50	0	10	26	0	21	90	83	74	54
Ireland	100	100	100	2	3	55	5	25	8	7	53	4	5	57	98	100	66	60
Israel	97	96	91	0	1	16	0	9	2	1	14	1	1	15	90	26	15	15
Italy	99	97	92[d]	x(3)	0	79[d]	x(6)	4	20[d]	x(9)	37	7d	x(12)	41	93	78	24	39
Japan	100	98	96	0	0	2	1	m	1	0	m	m	m	m	96	m	m	m
Korea	99	81	98	a	1	12	a	61	0	a	73	0	a	70	95	70	74	70
Latvia	98	97	95	0	1	88	0	4	35	3	39	11	3	48	98	93	83	59
Lithuania	100	100	98	0	1	89	1	6	21	6	45	5	6	52	98	95	79	68
Luxembourg	96	90	85	0	0	68	0	2	40	0	5	24	0	8	82	72	51	35
Mexico	81	75	62	a	4	25	a	24	11	a	31	6	a	31	57	41	34	30
Netherlands	100	99	89	a	8	62	a	26	40	a	40	25	a	47	96	86	78	68
New Zealand	99	96	83	4	2	26	9	30	10	11	41	7	10	44	92	67	59	54
Norway	100	95	94	0	0	91	0	0	39	0	18	20	0	35	93	90	57	53
Poland	95	95	94	0	1	92	0	3	44	3	34	10	6	46	96	93	72	66
Portugal	99	100	99	0	0	50	0	31	23	0	43	10	0	46	95	80	65	56
Slovak Republic	97	91	87	0	1	78	2	1	36	4	20	7	3	34	90	84	63	46
Slovenia	98	97	96	a	0	90	a	1	29	a	55	15	a	58	96	92	80	68
Spain	96	96	90	0	0	39	0	41	22	0	50	13	0	51	92	80	72	64
Sweden	99	99	98	0	0	96	0	1	32	1	14	17	1	23	98	96	43	40
Switzerland	97	99	91	0	0	78	1	4	48	1	12	21	1	22	91	86	63	46
Turkey	93	88	81	a	0	26	a	13	11	a	35	8	a	48	74	55	47	51
United Kingdom	99	97	90	a	3	33	a	36	16	a	47	10	a	47	90	67	59	53
United States	100	97	90	0	1	31	1	37	4	2	53	0	2	48	88	69	60	49
OECD average	97	94	88	0	2	55	2	18	24	3	34	12	2	39	91	78	62	54
EU22 average	98	96	92	0	2	69	2	15	29	3	34	13	3	40	94	86	65	57
Partners																		
Argentina[1]	94	87	82	a	0	37	a	19	18	a	34	8	a	38	78	54	47	41
Brazil	90	89	72	1	0	32	2	15	17	2	21	10	2	23	70	50	40	34
China	m	m	m	m	5	m	m	28	m	m	39	m	m	40	m	m	m	m
India	m	m	m	m	m	m	m	m	m	m	m	m	m	m	m	m	m	m
Indonesia[1]	100	94	81	a	0	54	a	3	41	a	17	11	a	25	82	55	45	30
Russian Federation	93	66	53	0	41	13	1	66	4	0	65	2	0	54	92	77	66	53
Saudi Arabia	100	100	100	0	1	28	0	34	12	0	51	12	0	45	92	98	81	42
South Africa[1]	70	75	76	0	2	67	1	8	45	3	10	30	4	12	m	m	m	m
G20 average	m	m	m	m	m	m	m	m	m	m	m	m	m	m	m	m	m	m

Gender Inequality

Gender inequality is another issue about economic inequalities. According to UNDP reports, gender inequality is a common problem faced by most societies by positioning males better than females on average in social, economic, and political hierarchies (UNDP, 2013). This study treats gender inequality in terms of labor market conditions. Therefore, UNDP reports are the main sources to exhibit the situation of gender inequality in this part of the study. Some international organizations and national strategy statements have aimed to reduce gender inequalities for about the last two decades. Especially, the UNDP has included the issue of gender inequality in the Millennium Development Goals. Goal 3 draws attention to this issue as globally. Gender inequality is an important issue that relates to women's participation in employment in the labor market. Figure 4 shows the spending time at the workplace between men and women.

Figure 4. Men vs. women in the workplace (2018, 2019, and 2020)
Source: OECD

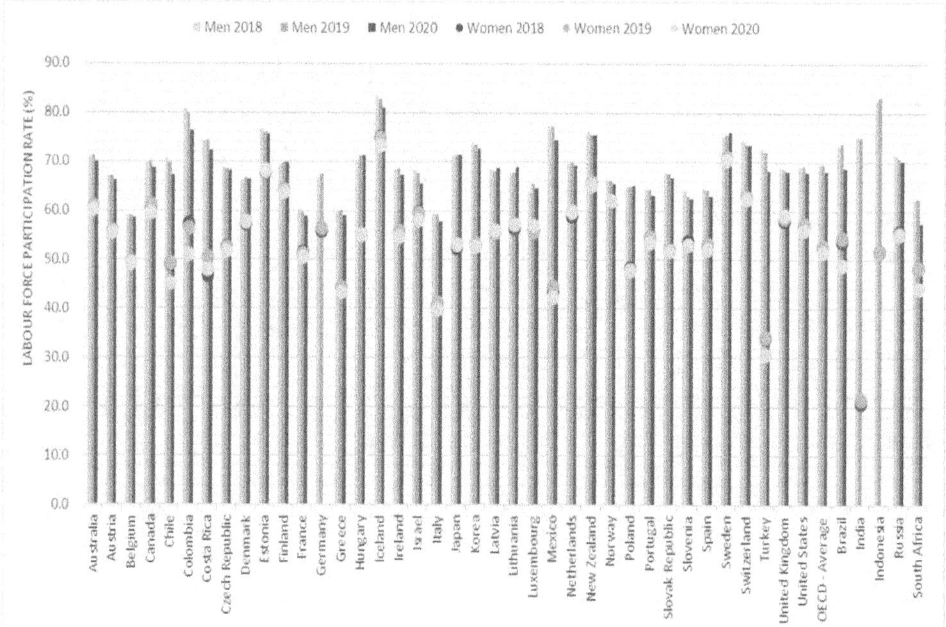

According to Figure 4, as in education inequality, developed countries like Norway, Sweden, Finland, and Estonia seem to be more equity than the average of OECD countries in gender equality in the workplace. However, Turkey and India are the highest unequal countries in providing opportunities to women in the workplace. Interestingly, one can easily be aware that there is a big gap between men and women in terms of spending time in the workplace in Japan.

Figure 5. The gender pay gap over time
Source: PayScale compensation data

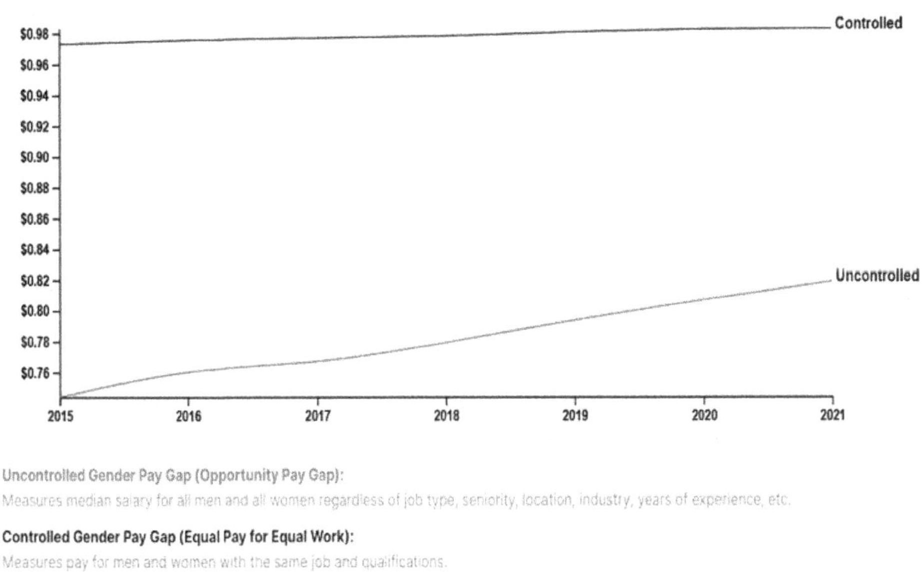

Figure 5 shows the pay gap between males and females under controlled and uncontrolled conditions, which means opportunity pay gap and equal pay for equal work, respectively. The controlled gender pay gap measures the payment for men and women with the same working conditions. The uncontrolled gender pay gap measures the payment in the median for men and women regardless of other factors like job type, seniority, location, experience (PayScale, 2021). Figure 5 indicates the increasing inequalities in working conditions between men and women.

THE RELATIONSHIP BETWEEN THE COVID-19 AND ECONOMIC INEQUALITIES

This section discusses the potential impacts of the COVID-19 pandemic on the inequalities in education and gender in some developed and developing countries. The COVID-19 has dominated all dimensions of life since the end of 2019; evidence points to this period. In a few months, the COVID-19 pandemic directly affected the education system and the labor market, albeit this issue is purely a health problem. When the pandemic started to spread worldwide, the governments decided to shut-down schools for all levels and locked down the workplaces where people worked together at the beginning of 2020. This process has emerged to a new implementation, which mainly prevents the crowds in education, working. As a result, distance education (or online education) gets popular globally, and education continues with this method. Meanwhile, the working conditions also changed, and most workplaces, particularly the food and supermarket sectors, continued to work in the distance.

Figure 6 shows the total net enrolment rate by primary education in most developing countries, and almost all countries have full enrolment in primary education, excluding Armenia, Azerbaijan, Burkina Faso, and Sub-Saharan Africa. Especially, one can easily be aware of the decrease in total enrolment from 2018 to 2020 in Armenia, Azerbaijan, Benin, Burkina Faso, and Kazakhstan. The lockdowns have deeply affected the daily routine of families recently. As a result of the COVID-19, education and learning have shifted from the classroom to the home. Distance education imposes many responsibilities and economic burdens on parents depending on the necessities of education. To efficient and productive distance education, many necessary tools will enable this process to be followed. Although the government partially meets such needs, these are met mainly by the families' economic means. The economic supports aimed at increasing children's success in education have helped to reduce inequalities, albeit temporarily, in both developed and developing countries. However, some children living in families in poor economic conditions in both developed and developing countries cannot fully enjoy their right to education during this period. Computers are one of the main necessary tools of students in this process. Figure 7 pictures the access to computers in OECD countries.

Figure 6. Total net enrolment rate by level of education (primary, both sexes) (2018, 2019, and 2020)
Source: UIS

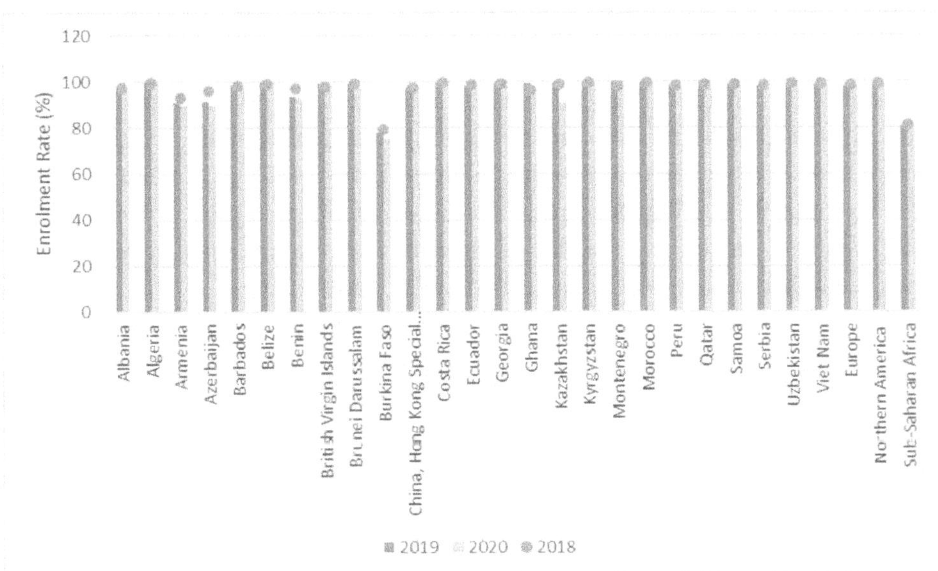

Figure 7. Access to a computer
Source: OECD (2020a)

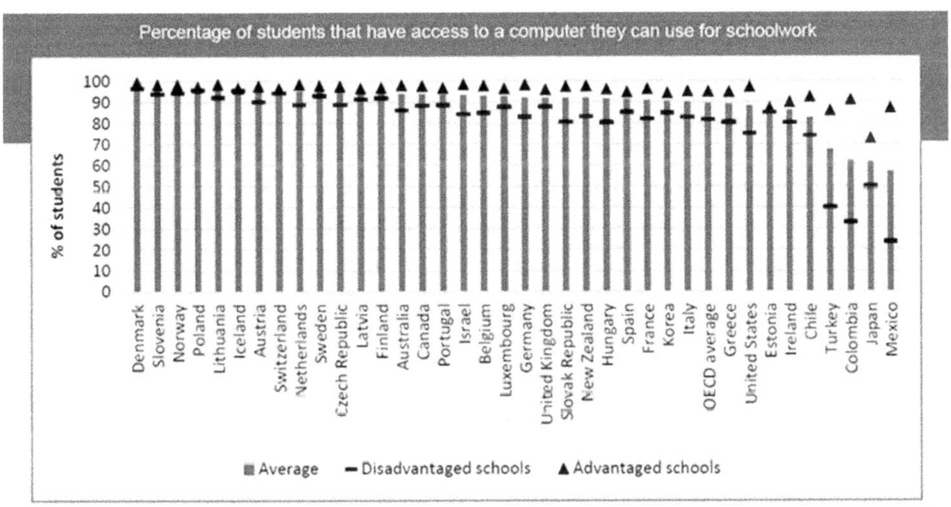

Note: socio-economically disadvantaged (advantaged) school is a school whose socio-economic profile (i.e. the average socio-economic status of the students in the school) is in the bottom (top) quarter of the PISA index of economic, social and cultural status amongst all schools in the relevant country/economy.

According to Figure 7, there is a growing reality about the unequal access to a computer among countries and the decreasing support for digital learning risks widening the learning gap. On OECD average, 9 out of 10 students have access to a computer and an internet at home. However, there is still great inequality between developed and developing countries. In addition, the students in advantaged schools are about 15 percent more likely to access a computer for schoolwork than their peers in disadvantaged schools. It should be noted that in many homes, computers may need to be shared between parents and children. This situation can make it difficult for many students to follow lessons in the distance education process. On the other hand, Denmark has the highest rate of student access to a computer. Mexico and Japan seem that the most unsuccessful country in this regard.

Another issue of distance education relates to the population of households. This issue is emphasized as overcrowded housing in OECD reports. Housing overcrowding may negatively affect the quality of education in distance learning, especially in low-income households. Figure 8 indicates the levels of overcrowded housing in OECD countries.

Figure 8. Housing overcrowding, total, percentage, 2018 and later
Source: OECD (2020)

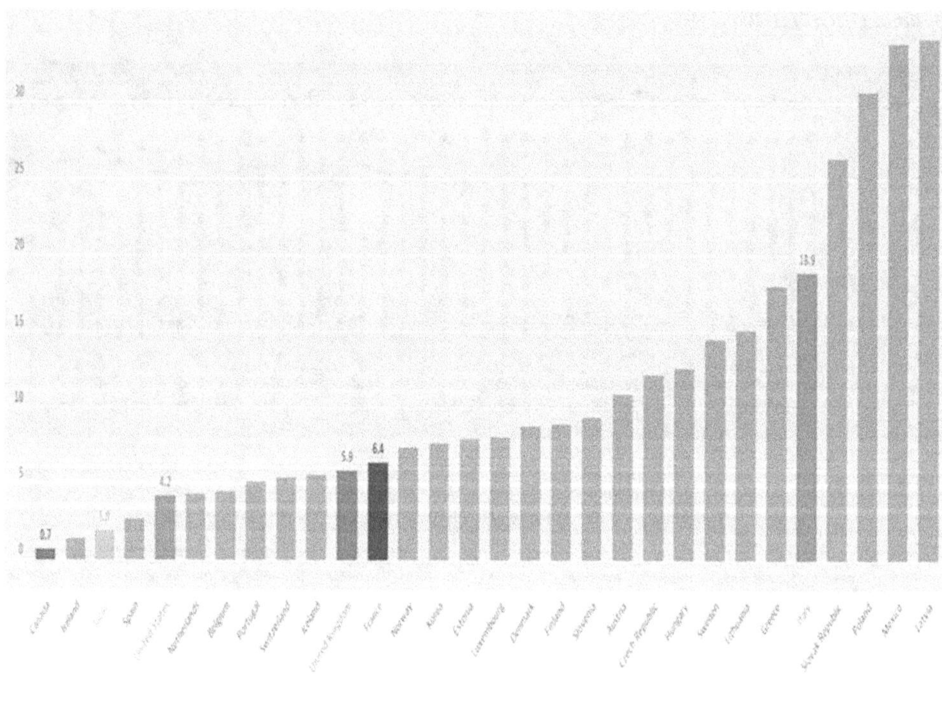

Housing overcrowding relates that people need sufficient space in their homes for privacy and health. Besides, the sufficient space in homes fulfills all the functions, such as studying, entertaining, and spending time with family. According to Figure 8, Canada seems to have the highest usage area per individual in family life by 0.7 percent. However, Latvia is the worst country among others, by about 35 percent.

This study stresses gender inequality in terms of worsening labor market conditions due to the COVID-19 pandemic. The COVID-19 caused many people to lose their jobs. However, this process mostly affected the female workers. This result can be seen in figure 4. Due to the COVID-19, the number of women in the workplace dramatically decrease in most countries from 2018 to 2020. Gender inequality in working life has been an ongoing problem for many years. The decrease in male employment is more than female employment in only Israel, France, Italy, and Mexico. The South American countries, like Chile, Brazil, and Costa Rica, are the worst in this issue. Additionally, Ecuador and Colombia are also the other countries where the decline in female employment is much higher than that of male employment. Figure 9 explains this dramatic change in the context of changing employment levels for some countries.

Figure 10 indicates the general employment, education, or training situation for the youth generation in the COVID-19 pandemic period. This figure shows many potential impacts of the COVID-19 on economic inequalities in developed and developing countries and presents the difference between males and females in youth not in employment, education, or training. Almost in all countries in the OECD, the youth women not in employment, education, or training between 20 and 24 are more than youth men in the same age group. Especially, Turkey, Mexico, and Colombia are the worst countries in terms of gender and education inequalities among the OECD countries. On the other hand, the Nordic countries, including Norway, Finland, and Denmark, are the best in gender and education inequality. However, according to this figure, Iceland is the most active country in OECD by about 93 percent level in youth in employment, education, or training. The second-best country in this regard is Sweden, with 90 percent.

The COVID-19 pandemic has seriously affected the inequalities in education and gender in both developed and developing countries. Accordingly, OECD, ILO, and UNDP have released some policy recommendations against this kind of economic inequalities in the period of COVID-19.

Figure 9. Decline in employment between 2019Q2 and 2020Q2, percent
Source: ILO (2020)

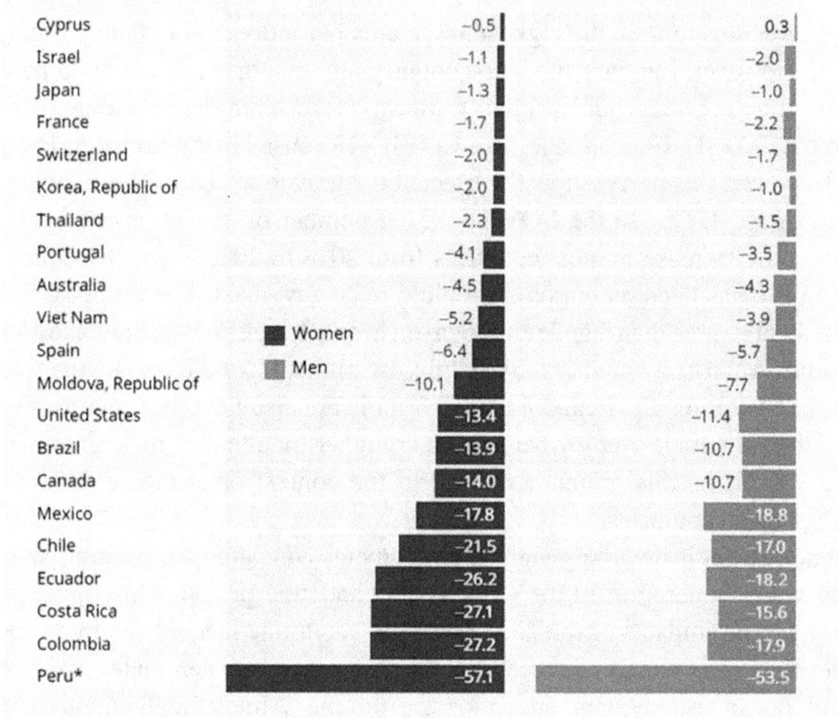

Figure 10. Youth not in employment, education, or training, % in the same age group
Source: OECD (2020)

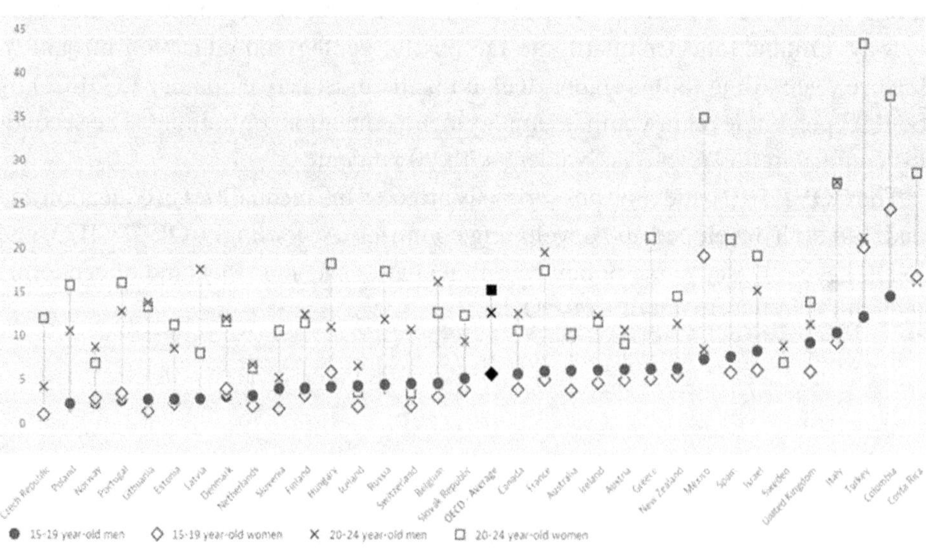

OECD released a report on the impacts of COVID-19 on student equity and inclusion about two months ago. This report mostly focuses on the vulnerable students and touches on the children from low-income and single-parent families. OECD highlights some policies to reduce inequality in education during school closures by scaling these policies according to their scope. Figure 11 presents the details of these policy suggestions. According to this figure, countries have developed specific and sometimes innovative policy initiatives such as providing equitable and inclusive access to digital learning tools and good learning conditions. Moreover, the countries ensure that socio-emotional needs are being met, offering equitable and inclusive access to extra services for vulnerable students, and ensuring support by and to teachers (OECD, 2020).

Going to school is a priority public right and the best public policy tool to improve skills. Although school time is fun and has an effect that can increase social skills and social awareness, when evaluated economically, increasing the child's skills is the main point of the time spent at school. A relatively short time at school can teach essential skills, while a short time away from school will result in some skills not being acquired.

Figure 11. Countries focus points in strategies of education continuity
Source: OECD (2020)

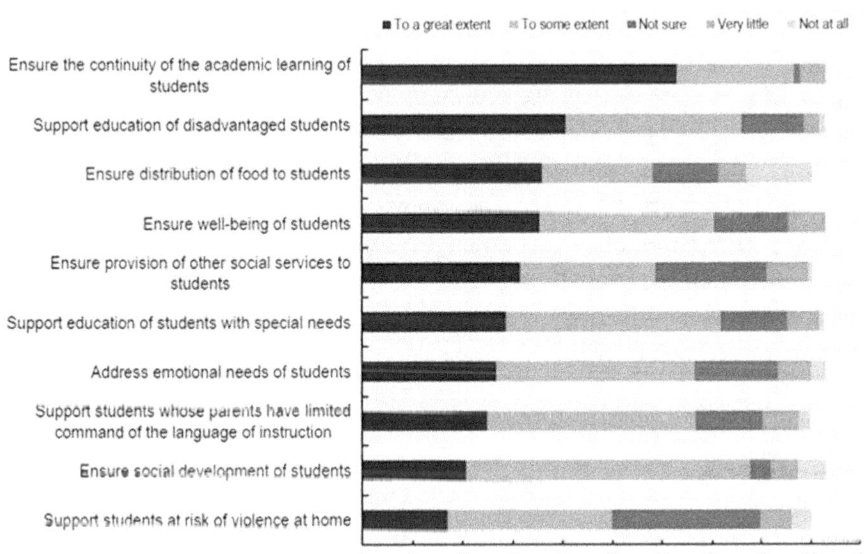

United Nations also released a report on the impact of COVID-19 on women. This report is quite important to investigate the potential impacts of COVID-19 on gender inequalities. There has been a focus on the five primary dimensions of gender discrimination in this report. The first and most important dimension is economic impacts. According to this report, emerging evidence on the impact of COVID-19 suggests that women's economic and productive lives will be affected disproportionately and differently from men. This situation causes less comfortable lives for women economically. As a result, women earn less, save less, work in less secure jobs, and are employed in the informal sector. When they become economically weak, they also become socially weak. Therefore, they have less access to social support, and the majority of those in this situation are single-parent households. Hence, their capacity to cope with economic shocks becomes less than that of men. United Nations (2020) proposes three crucial policy arguments to achieve successful economic equality recovery in communities facing the COVID-19 pandemic. These are[1]:

- Ensure women's equal representation in all COVID-19 response planning and decision-making
- Drive transformative change for equality by addressing the care economy, paid and unpaid
- Target women and girls in all efforts to address the socioeconomic impact of COVID-19

Figure 12 gives the comparing economic conditions between women and men during the COVID-19 period. According to this picture, there will be deep impacts of COVID-19 for women already living on the economic margins.

According to Figure 12, in the age range of 25 to 54, it can be seen that the labor force participation of men is about 1.5 times higher than women. Moreover, 740 million women are globally work in the informal economy under precarious conditions. The United Nations report reveals that women's economic conditions in working life are much worse than men's.

CONCLUSION

This study investigated the potential impacts of the global health crisis on some economic inequalities. Like OECD, ILO, and the UNDP, many institutions reported that the economic inequalities had reached a critical level recently. The first and most important conclusion of this study is a reciprocal negative relationship between the COVID-19 and economic inequalities. If there is substantial economic inequality in the global world, inequalities must be reduced to cope with its spread and effects on humanity when a global health crisis occurs. This study examined the recent developments in education and gender inequalities, which are among the economic inequalities most affected by the global health crisis during the COVID-19 outbreak. It revealed that the COVID-19 increases the inequality in education between the developed and developing countries. In this respect, it is an important contribution to the relevant literature by demonstrating that the rapid deepening of the pandemic is due to the increasing global economic inequality in recent years.

Figure 12. Some economic conditions between women and men
Source: UN Women Headquarters (2020)

The global health crises may have many post-pandemic effects that increase the negative effects of economic inequalities on social development in both developed and developing countries. Therefore, the governments should consider the possible negative effects of economic inequalities on societies and include precautions to reduce economic inequalities in social policies while deciding on social policies for the post-pandemic period.

REFERENCES

Blundell, R., Costa Diaz, M., Joyce, R., & Xu, X. (2020). COVID-19 and inequalities. *Fiscal Studies, 41*(2), 291–319. doi:10.1111/1475-5890.12232 PMID:32836542

Caitlin, S. B., & Ravallion, M. (2020). *Inequality and the coronavirus: Socioeconomic covariates of behavioral responses and viral outcomes across US counties*. NBER Working Paper 27549.

Deaton, A. (2021). *COVID-19 and global income inequality*. NBER Working Paper.

Doyle, O. (2020). *COVID-19: Exacerbating Educational Inequalities?* UCD Geary Institute for Public Policy.

Furceri, D., Loungani, P., Ostry, J. D., & Pizzuto, P. (2020). Will COVID-19 affect inequality? Evidence from past pandemics. *Covid Economics: Vetted and Real-Time Papers*, (12), 138–157.

ILO. (2020). *COVID-19 and the world of work* (6th ed.). ILO Monitor.

OECD. (2017). *The Pursuit of Gender Equality: An Uphill Battle*. OECD Publishing.

OECD. (2020a). Learning remotely when schools close: How well are students and schools prepared? Insights from PISA. In *Tackling Coronavirus (COVID-19): Contributing to a Global Effort*. OECD.

OECD. (2020b). The impact of COVID-19 on student equity and inclusion: supporting vulnerable students during school closures and school re-openings. In *Tackling Coronavirus (COVID-19): Contributing to a Global Effort*. OECD.

OECD. (2020c). *How's Life? 2020: Measuring Well-being*. OECD Publishing.

OECD. (2021). *Education at a Glance 2020: OECD Indicators*. OECD Publishing.

Palomino, J. C., Rodriguez, J. G., & Sebastian, R. (2020). Wage inequality and poverty effects of lockdown and social distancing in Europe. *European Economic Review*, 129. PMID:32836323

Papageorge, N. W., Zahn, M. V., Belot, M., van den Broek-Altenburg, E., Choi, S., Jamison, J. C., & Tripodi, E. (2021). *Socio-demographic factors associated with self-protecting behavior during the COVID-19 pandemic*. NBER Working Paper 27378.

PayScale. (2021). *The State of the Gender Pay Gap in 2021*. PayScale.

Stabile, M., Apouey, B. & Solal, I. (2020). *COVID-19, inequality, and gig economy workers*. VoxEU.org.

UN Women Headquarters. (2020). *Policy Brief: The Impact of COVID-19 on Women*. United Nations.

KEY TERMS AND DEFINITIONS

Educational Inequality: It is the unequal distribution of academic resources that would include school funding, qualified teachers, books (textbooks and library), and technology in disadvantaged communities.

Gender Inequality: It allows people to have different opportunities because of their perceived differences based on gender.

Gig Economy: It is a form of a labor market in which workers work on short-term contracts or doing freelance work as opposed to holding permanent jobs.

Inequality of Outcomes: It occurs when individuals do not possess the same level of material wealth or overall living economic conditions as others. That is, there are differences between individuals in their living conditions.

OECD Countries: The Organization for Economic Co-operation and Development (OECD) comprises of 37 countries that discuss and develop economic and social policy to improve economic welfare. The OECD are also economies that support free-market economies.

Well-Being: It is the state of being comfortable, healthy, or happy by an individual.

Chapter 7
Beyond Pandemic:
Accelerating Artificial Intelligence and Financial Analytics

Chabi Gupta
Christ University, India

ABSTRACT

As the COVID-19 pandemic continues to evolve even beyond a second wave, there is an urgent need for business organisations to rethink and reconfigure their strategies for long-term sustainability beyond the pandemic. Many organisations are already making changes in the way they run their businesses and the way they make decisions to emerge stronger. It can be observed that the pandemic has seriously affected the way business organisations are being operated. However, this research suggests during the discussion that what is required is a transformational change rather than a directed one for any business organisation. In the current scenario, AI is being seen as a key enabler for business organisations to be on the path to recovery. What the 'modus operandi' beyond the pandemic will be is a relevant issue for businesses indicating further need of research in this area. Using financial analytics and AI in combination will bring in a transformational change that might be viewed as the 'game changer' for businesses beyond the pandemic.

INTRODUCTION

The COVID-19 outbreak has imposed a heavy toll on financial and economic activity worldwide. The shock has been unpredictable and concurrent across many countries, and it has been characterized by significant uncertainty regarding its magnitude and

DOI: 10.4018/978-1-7998-6900-9.ch007

duration. First wave and then second wave. Even the possibility of a third wave. Uncertainties range from the infectiousness and long-term health effects of COVID-19 to the effectiveness of containment measures to the effectiveness of the vaccine. In addition to the uncertainty about COVID-19 itself, there is significant uncertainty about the pandemic's short- and long-run economic effects. The rapid transmission of the virus has caused people around the globe to simultaneously isolate following strict public health orders. Social distancing and other containment measures as a part of public policy are emergency protection measures saving precious lives, but they have contributed to a synchronized collapse in major economic activity. Major stock market indexes crashed at an unprecedented pace (Bragazzi, et al, 2020), erasing close to one-third of their value in just a matter of weeks and hitting industries across the board, reflecting expected losses in the corporate sector.

PREVIOUS EXPERIENCES – THE CASE FOR AI AND FINANCIAL ANALYTICS

Even prior to the COVID-19 pandemic's disastrous effect on the world economies, business leaders had started to increasingly embrace advanced analytics and artificial intelligence (AI), for good logic and reason. However, the pace at which it was being implemented was quite slow and even though financial analytics and AI adoption were progressing, it took a lot of time and a relaxed approach on the part of businesses.

The situation today has no time to relax. COVID-19 crisis has upended businesses as usual for communities and societies, which must now prioritize changes in their organizations to meet these new challenges. Specifically, governments and healthcare frontline workers, are leading massive efforts to support victims and their families and contain a virus that already has infected millions of people globally and claimed hundreds of thousands of lives. At the same time, business leaders must protect their employees and customers while managing the economic repercussions in the wake of mass economic lockdowns, increasing consumer fear, and continual uncertainty. The decisions they make today may alter their firm's trajectory for years to come and become a 'game changer' alternative to bankruptcy and closure. There is a need to seamlessly combine AI with human judgment and experience for long run sustainability (Ågerfalk, 2020). Min-Yuh Day and Tun-Keng Chang(2018) developed a portfolio optimization module which took the information from a variety of sources, such as stocks prices, investor profile and the other alternative data, and used them as input to calculate optimal weights of assets in the portfolio. Coombs, & Chopra (2019) discussed the benefits of AI for improving financial data analytics and decision-making, current and potential applications of AI within financial services, operational challenges and potential solutions for AI adoption, and concluded with the requirements for successful enterprise. („ 2020) studied the application of artificial intelligence and its powered technologies in the Indian banking and financial industry. Akter and Uddin (2020) researched transforming business using digital transformations with the application of AI, Blockchain, Cloud and Data analytics.

Some companies that are on the forefront of these trends and have already begun the AI journey will thrive in the post-crisis world. Again, history provides a guide: during the four previous global economic downturns, 14 percent of companies were actually able to increase both sales growth and profit margins, according to Boston Consulting Group research. (See Exhibit 1.) The majority of companies, however, are at the very early stages of the journey—or have yet to begin.

Figure 1.

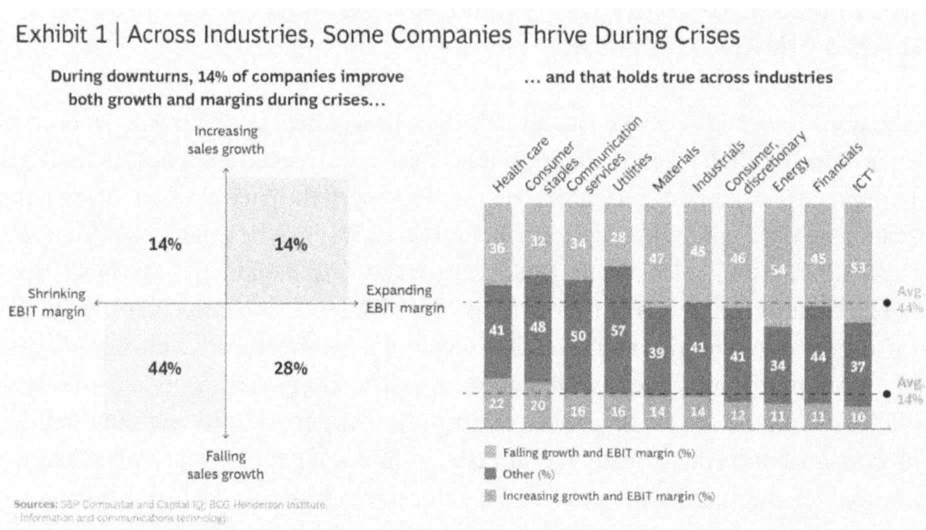

In these unpredictable times, where the change happens in days not weeks, it's not surprising that financial analytics, in particular, widely recognized for its number crunching, problem-solving and predictive abilities, has become an essential navigational tool. Financial Analytics supports numerous mandatory real time issues facing businesses today: forecasting demand, sales and service deliveries, identifying potential supply-chain disruptions, targeting support services to protect workers, analysing the numbers, predicting the effects of change and ultimately determining the effectiveness of crisis intervention strategies, to name a few. The foremost challenge in front of organisations who look to transform in the area of artificial intelligence and financial analytics is that the pandemic-induced behavioral and economic shifts have rendered some historical data useless. They need to work with this challenge. With a fully aligned systematic agenda and a clear view of the crucial mission, organizations will need to stand up financial analytics-driven solutions that enable strategic leaders to adjust their methologies amid the daily uncertainty of crisis's challenges and to prepare more effectively for the future.

DIGITAL IS HERE TO STAY

The turbulent times have demonstrated clearly that rapid, transformational change is both possible and pivotal for business survival (Sachdeva, 2020). Strategic leaders will need to shore up AI and financial analytics resources in most priority domains—for example, personalization, procurement, productivity, marketing or supply-chain optimization. Every sector and every business that wishes to sustain in the long run will now need to define its own priority domains based on what's most relevant to its value chains in the current environment and beyond. For some businesses, this will mean accelerating existing investments in the areas that traditionally drive value. However, in the next normal, we expect these virtual agents and chatbots to become even more critical as consumers increasingly migrate online. In other cases, organizations will need to invest capital in emerging value drivers. Going digital is no longer a strategy but a need. It is here to stay. For good. Obviously, some more complex challenges won't be solved quickly. But strategic leaders who learn from response to the crisis acknowledge seriously that the future will be quite different from the past, and there is an imperative need to build on the new—and practical, real-time ways of working will make potential businesses not only survive the unprecedented times but to also thrive (Bragazzi, et al, 2020; Agra, 2020).

ACCELERATING FINANCIAL ANALYTICS TO NAVIGATE COVID-19 AND THE NEXT NORMAL

Crisis are disruptive events that have profound consequences for society and the economy financially. It's important to move and think beyond a crisis and learn lessons as to how active intelligence can be leveraged to improve crisis management and decision making.

Business organizations are now gearing up analytics capabilities in a matter of weeks to effectively respond to COVID-19 crisis challenges and prepare for the future. It is but the need of the hour and something to add to inherent capabilities of the organisations to further add to their competitive advantage which will be the utmost differentiating factor in the long run. The pandemic and the ensuing supply chain disruption has exposed weak links in most business's supply chain, and its implications on the balance sheet of the business.

Still, spreadsheets are the predominant supply chain planning and execution tool in use by analysts around the world despite its obvious limitations. Most firms are still using data and obsolete technologies to analyse financial data. The relevant question which must be thought about is whether these firms can really afford to continue using static supply chain tools like spreadsheets and static weekly reports from their legacy ERP system to deal with another crisis or outbreak? Their intentions may be to migrate to latest technologies and using financial analytics tools but still this has not been able to materialize.

It is time to repair, reinvent and resurge ahead using the latest AI and leveraging financial analytics. (Bhushan, & Ghosh, 2020). There is a need for all small, medium and big corporates to decide to accelerate and thereby

1. Empower their business leaders with automated, accurate, reliable, spatial, predictive, descriptive and code-free visual analytics platforms and tools to enable them to accurately forecast and then position appropriate supply to respond to a rapidly changing landscape or crisis outbreak.
2. To empower data scientists with code-friendly, self-service AI+ Financial Analytics platforms which enable them to work with their machine learning and natural language processing (NLP) algorithms to enable a robust scenario, strategic planning and what-if analysis.
3. To empower and enable C-suite and business leaders with automated, accurate, reliable, and right time decision support, enabling practical actionable insights for them to make critical strategic, timely decisions that prevent supply chain disruption and minimize financial losses through leveraging financial analytics.

The next normal is when business organizations will effectively enhance their productivity and efficiency leveraging artificial intelligence and financial analytics amongst other technological advancements. Technology is the need of the hour and its here to stay. Thinking beyond the pandemic, artificial intelligence can further improve utilisation of critical resources by initiating automated, trigger-based alerts and actions based on dynamic data insights and analysis. The corporates will be able to tune in better and have highly sensitive data driven systems to respond to even the slightest hint of a crisis in the future. It will also make the businesses more competitive and be the differentiating factor in their capabilities. The ones who respond to the situation will be the ones who will survive the next normal instead of the ones who react instead. Thinking beyond the pandemic we all shall live with this new next normal till we know where we are heading and what's waiting for us (Naseem, et al, 2020; Inkster, et al, 2020).

THE ROAD AHEAD

It was an AI-driven algorithm which was the first to in fact spot the virus crisis named COVID-19. Even before WHO released a statement on 9th January 2020, an artificial intelligence platform called BlueDot alerted its clients on December 31, 2019, about a cluster of pneumonia cases in Wuhan, China. The global business landscape then evolved at an unprecedented pace. It became highly unpredictable and uncertain due to constant changes in market demand, regulations, social trends, customer expectations, due to the emergence of pandemic. Businesses had no choice but to adapt or leave (Inkster, et al, 2020.

It seems with whatever can be observed as the situation worldwide, that building continuity, building strong operational resilience, efficient adaptation and subsequent recovery, slowly embracing the next normal is the road ahead. There is a need to deftly manage to blend AI elements with traditional Business Intelligence (Xu et al, 2021).

With augmented financial analytics along with AI based algorithms businesses can:

Figure 2.

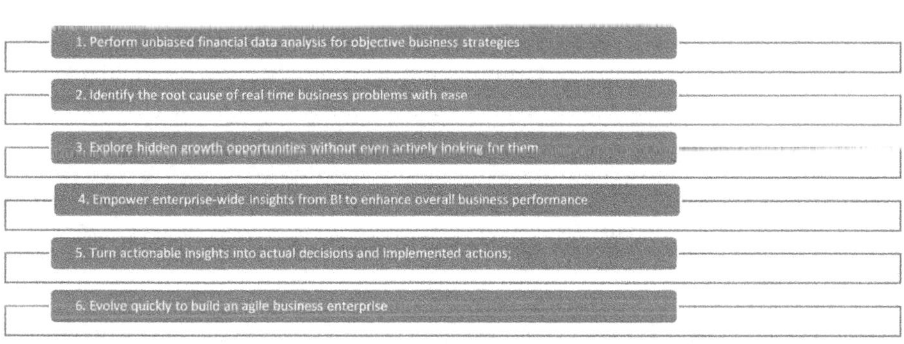

This research has highlighted leveraging artificial intelligence and financial analytics as an inherent capability by businesses to transform into a competitive advantage by many business organisations in the future. Also, it will be a sustainability factor in the long run.

Application of artificial intelligence will be immensely valuable in helping businesses adapt to new trends. Advanced robots that can recognize objects and handle tasks that previously required humans will promote effective and quick decision making through data analysis. Through machine learning and advanced financial data analytics, AI will help firms detect changing consumption patterns and deliver "hyper personalized" products to customers who shop online. Most companies already have previous extensive experience with digital applications such as automation and basic data analytics. But AI, which enables machines to solve problems and take actions that in the past could only be done by humans, goes far beyond that. It will be very valuable for businesses to implement. According to joint BCG and MIT research, to a good rule of thumb is to dedicate around 10 percent of AI investment to algorithms, 20 percent to technology, and 70 percent to business process transformation. To conclude, financial analytics combined with appropriate AI algorithms would further enhance decision making, analysis and strategy formulation by business organisations in future beyond the pandemic. Winning businesses will reinvent themselves by putting both at the core of their organizations.

REFERENCES

Ågerfalk, P. J., Conboy, K., & Myers, M. D. (2020). *Information systems in the age of pandemics: COVID-19 and beyond*. Academic Press.

Akter, S., Michael, K., Uddin, M. R., McCarthy, G., & Rahman, M. (2020). Transforming business using digital innovations: The application of AI, blockchain, cloud and data analytics. *Annals of Operations Research*, 1–33. doi:10.100710479-020-03620-w

Arga, K. Y. (2020). COVID-19 and the Futures of Machine Learning. *OMICS: A Journal of Integrative Biology*, *24*(9), 512–514. doi:10.1089/omi.2020.0093 PMID:32511048

Bhushan, R., & Ghosh, S. (2020). *AI: An opportunity amidst a crisis*. Accessed at: www.pwc.in/assets/pdfs/data-and-analytics/ai-an-opportunity-amidst-a-crisis.pdf

Bragazzi, N. L., Dai, H., Damiani, G., Behzadifar, M., Martini, M., & Wu, J. (2020). How big data and artificial intelligence can help better manage the COVID-19 pandemic. *International Journal of Environmental Research and Public Health*, *17*(9), 3176. doi:10.3390/ijerph17093176 PMID:32370204

Candelon, F., Duranton, S., De Bondt, M., Reichert, T., & Charme Di Carlo, R. (2020). *The Rise of the AI-Powered Company in the Postcrisis World.* Accessed at www.bcg.com/en-in/publications/2020/business-applications-artificial-intelligence-post-covid

Coombs, C., & Chopra, R. (2019). *Artificial intelligence and data analytics: Emerging opportunities and challenges in financial services.* Academic Press.

Day, M. Y., Cheng, T. K., & Li, J. G. (2018, August). AI robo-advisor with big data analytics for financial services. In *2018 IEEE/ACM International Conference on Advances in Social Networks Analysis and Mining (ASONAM)* (pp. 1027-1031). IEEE. 10.1109/ASONAM.2018.8508854

Deloitte. (2020). *Reinventing FP&A for the pandemic and beyond.* Accessed at: https://www2.deloitte.com/us/en/pages/finance/articles/cfo-insights-reinventing-fpa-for-the-pandemic-and-beyond.html.html

Henke, N., Puri, A., & Saleh, T. (2020). *Accelerating analytics to navigate COVID-19 and the next normal.* Accessed at: https://www.mckinsey.com/business-functions/mckinsey-analytics/our-insights/accelerating-analytics-to-navigate-COVID-19-and-the-next-normal

Inkster, B., O'Brien, R., Selby, E., Joshi, S., Subramanian, V., Kadaba, M., Schroeder, K., Godson, S., Comley, K., Vollmer, S. J., & Mateen, B. A. (2020). Digital health management during and beyond the COVID-19 pandemic: Opportunities, barriers, and recommendations. *JMIR Mental Health*, *7*(7), e19246. doi:10.2196/19246 PMID:32484783

Malali, A. B., & Gopalakrishnan, S. (2020). Application of Artificial Intelligence and Its Powered Technologies in the Indian Banking and Financial Industry: An Overview. *IOSR Journal Of Humanities And Social Science*, *25*(4), 55–60.

Naseem, M., Akhund, R., Arshad, H., & Ibrahim, M. T. (2020). Exploring the Potential of Artificial Intelligence and Machine Learning to Combat COVID-19 and Existing Opportunities for LMIC: A Scoping Review. *Journal of Primary Care & Community Health*, *11*. doi:10.1177/2150132720963634 PMID:32996368

Sachdeva, R. (2020). *Our response to Covid-19 pandemic and beyond.* Accessed at: www.datamaticsbpm.com/blog/our-response-to-COVID-19-pandemic-and-beyond

Xu, D., Guo, Y., & Huang, M. (2021). Can Artificial Intelligence Improve Firms' Competitiveness during the COVID-19 Pandemic: International Evidence. *Emerging Markets Finance & Trade*, 1–14. doi:10.1080/1540496X.2021.1967740

ADDITIONAL READING

Athey, S. (2019). 21. The impact of machine learning on economics. In *The Economics of Artificial Intelligence* (pp. 507–552). University of Chicago Press.

Athey, S., & Imbens, G. W. (2017). The state of applied econometrics: Causality and policy evaluation. *The Journal of Economic Perspectives, 31*(2), 3–32. doi:10.1257/jep.31.2.3

Evans, J. R., & Lindner, C. H. (2012). Business analytics: The next frontier for decision sciences. *Decision Line, 43*(2), 4–6.

Fang, B., & Zhang, P. (2016). Big data in finance. In *Big Data Concepts, Theories, and Applications* (pp. 391–412). Springer. doi:10.1007/978-3-319-27763-9_11

Shah, N. D., Steyerberg, E. W., & Kent, D. M. (2018). Big data and predictive analytics: Recalibrating expectations. *Journal of the American Medical Association, 320*(1), 27–28. doi:10.1001/jama.2018.5602 PMID:29813156

Yang, R., Yu, L., Zhao, Y., Yu, H., Xu, G., Wu, Y., & Liu, Z. (2020). Big data analytics for financial Market volatility forecast based on support vector machine. *International Journal of Information Management, 50*, 452–462. doi:10.1016/j.ijinfomgt.2019.05.027

KEY TERMS AND DEFINITIONS

Algorithmic Transformation: These are small processes that *transform* a given value into another according to algorithm that is created by analysts.

Artificial Intelligence: The ability of a computer to perform tasks that are usually done by human beings because they require human intelligence and skills to conduct these tasks.

Causality: Given a relationship between two or more variables, it looks the relationship between cause and effect or what variables cause what.

Financial Analytics: A financial analysis that refers to an assessment of the viability, stability, and profitability of a business or a project undertaken by a business using data mining tools to analyze the data with a goal to make financial decisions.

Machine Learning: The use of computer systems that can learn and adapt without following instructions via algorithms and statistical models to analyze the patterns that occur in the data.

Pandemic: A disease that is prevalent over a whole country or throughout the world.

Predictive Analytics: It uses a variety of statistical methods from data mining, predictive modelling, and machine learning. It analyzes the current and historical data to make predictions about the future.

Chapter 8
COVID-19 and the Livelihoods of the Migrant Workers:
A Study in Rural West Bengal, India

Sebak Kumar Jana
https://orcid.org/0000-0002-3532-4350
Vidyasagar University, India

Subrata Naru
Vidyasagar University, India

Pranjit Kr Paul
Vidyasagar University, India

ABSTRACT

The spread of the corona-virus disease 2019 (COVID-19) and subsequent nationwide lockdown in India from March 22, 2020 to control its further outbreak brought turmoil in the lives of millions who are primarily involved in the informal sector. A primary survey was conducted in the District of South 24 Pgs. in the state of West Bengal, India to know the effects of COVID-19 on rural livelihood, particularly of the migrant workers. Types of disruptions of rural livelihood of the households have been explored in the study. Perceptions of the effects of shocks of COVID-19 on the rural households have been assessed in terms of the following variables: loss of assets, loss of income, food insecurity/shortage, death of livestock, decline in consumption, decline in health conditions, socialization, effects on education, problems in accessing health facilities. Types of government supports provided to the households have been found for the study area. The role of the government in overcoming the crisis of livelihood has also been assessed.

DOI: 10.4018/978-1-7998-6900-9.ch008

INTRODUCTION

The spread of the Corona-virus Disease 2019 (COVID-19), and subsequent nationwide lockdown in India from March 22, 2020 to control its further outbreak brought turmoil in the lives of millions who are primarily involved in the informal sector. With the growing joblessness in India, International Labour Organisation (ILO) stated that with a vast share of people working in the informal economy in India, millions of workers in the informal economy are at the risk of falling deeper into poverty during the crisis.

Interstate and district borders were sealed on 29th March, 2020, transportation got stopped, factories, shops, restaurants and all types of the economic activities were shut, barring only the essential services. Most of the migrant workers are daily wage earners and work in MSMEs and construction sector. In both these sectors, they are not protected by good health facilities and proper shelter. They altogether remain outside the legal cover under the name 'The Inter-State Migrant Workmen (Regulation of Employment and Conditions of Service) Act, 1979. Almost forty millions of workers in India went jobless because of lockdown. COVID-19 is impacting global food systems, disrupting regional agricultural value chains, and posing risks to household food security. COVID-19 has affected the Indian economy as well as the livelihood of the migrant workers working in the informal sector.

In this chapter, we conducted a survey in the district of South 24 Pgs. in the state of West Bengal India, to know the of COVID-19 on rural livelihood, particularly of the migrant workers. The data have been collected from the households where the main occupations of the heads of the households are migrant workers and daily laborers. The number of sample households taken for the present study is 150. The blocks in the district where the primary survey were conducted are Patharpratima, Kakdwip and Namkhana.

The major objectives of this chapter are as follows: (i) The effects of COVID-19 on migrant workers in India, (ii) Types of disruptions rural livelihood, (iii) Effects of shocks, (iv) Types of government support provided to the households.

There are few studies on the effect of COVID-19 in the informal sector of the economy. Mitra (2020) highlighted the livelihood losses and increase in unemployment in India due to COVID-19 outbreak mainly due of huge reverse migration of the informal workers. Shegunshi & Hiremath (2020) studied on employment situation and income condition of the households in both the pre and post pandemic period and mainly expecting consequences on the informal sector economy in India. Srivastava & Sivaramane (2020) examine how the household's consumption pattern changed from non-essential to most essential commodities for livelihood in India during the economic slowdown period for COVID-19. Singh (2020) investigate the condition of migrant workers during pandemic and finds excess pressure on agriculture sector for returning the migrant workers. Lahiri & Sinha (2021) studies the impact of pandemic on household consumption and occupation. Reddy & Mamgain (2020) analyse the policy response to the pandemic induced economic crisis towards faster and inclusive recovery and reconstruction of rural livelihood in India through short-term measures for stimulating effective demand in rural areas. Khanna (2020) suggests relooking the migration related policies when a migrant has to leave the working place for the health crisis. Some other important studies related to the present study are Choudhari (2020), Breman, Rajan et al (2020), Khanna (2020), Rajan et al (2020), Khanna (2020), de Haan (2020), Singh (2020), Pal et al (2021), Ramakumar (2020), Lusome & Bhagat (2020) Gopalan & Misra (2020), Sengupta & Jha (2020), Suresh et al (2020), Mishra (2021), Shakya (2020), Miyamura (2021), Ranjan (2021), Kumar (2020), Barhate (2021), Jha et al (2020)., Choolayil & Putran (2021), Jalan & Sen (2020), Mohan& Mishra (2021), Ruthven (2021), Choudhury et al (2020), Padhee & Pingali (2020), Kumar & Choudhury (2021), Shah & Lerche (2020). Lele, Bansal, & Meenakshi (2020), Mookerjee et al (2021), Kumar et al (2021). Ullah et al (2021).

STUDY AREA AND METHODOLOGY

The present study is based on the data collected from the district of South 24 Parganas which is one of the largest districts of West Bengal. A major percentage of population of the district live in rural areas and are economically backward with agricultural activities as main occupation and in some areas people earn their livelihood as migrant workers. In this study three blocks have been chosen from the district of South 24 Parganas namely Kakdwip, Namkhana and Patharpratima. From the each block 50 households have been selected with total sample size being 150 households. Out of the households surveyed 72 percent of the households belong to the caste of general category and remaining 28 percent households belong to scheduled category. About 80 percent households are small in size and most of the families are Hindu. Some other characteristics of the households surveyed as shown in Table 1 are as follows: 76 percent of the households are job card holders of MGNREGS which is the major employment programme in India, 97 percent belongs to Hindu religion, 83 percent belong to BPL (Below the Poverty Line) status, 89 percent belong to migrant workers, 18 percent of households were found micro family, workers had to changes their occupation after the start of nationwide lockdown due to COVID-19 outbreak. At the time of survey it was found that at least one of the members in 102 households was infected with corona virus.

Table 1. Characteristics of the households surveyed

		No of Households	% of households
	Total Households	150	100
Social Category	Non Schedule	108	72
	Schedule	42	28
Family Type	Joint	27	18
	Small	123	82
Religion	Hindu	146	97
	Muslim	4	3
Economic Status	APL	25	17
	BPL	125	83
Workers Type	Migrant Workers	134	89
	Non-Migrant Workers	16	11
MGNREGS Job Card	No	36	24
	Yes	114	76
Occupation Changes for COVID-19	No	18	12
	Yes	132	88

Source: Primary Survey

Types of disruptions of rural livelihood of the households have been measured by the perceptions of the households relating the following variables: major source of income, government procurement of paddy, monthly family income, monthly family expenditure, MGNREGA employment, agricultural production, sale of assets, livestock price, price of vegetables, access to water, access to health institutions, health issues, children, borrowing/loan, food consumption (items), benefits from government scheme, ration, savings (measured in Rs. or INR). Effects of shocks of COVID-19 on the rural households has been assessed in terms of the following variables: loss of assets, loss of income, food insecurity/shortage, death of livestock, decline in consumption, decline in health conditions, socialization, effect on education, problems in accessing health facilities. The role of the government in overcoming the crisis of livelihood has also been assessed.

MAJOR FINDINGS OF THE STUDY

The findings of the study relate to overall impact on households as perceived by the households, impact of COVID-19 on income, expenditure and savings of the Households, Impact of COVID-19 on indebtedness of the households.

Overall Impact on Households

After the nationwide lockdown it has been the slowdown of economic activity in both urban and rural areas. A large number of rural households in the selected sample are mainly engaged as migrant workers and daily wage earners. With the shutdown of the informal industry the significant portion of rural workers lost their jobs and returned to the village and as a result the income of the rural people fell enormously. Here it has been attempted to understand how much rural people affected level by the COVID-19 pandemic in rural Bengal considering the South 24 Parganas district.

Figure 1. COVID-19 impact on rural HHs in south 24 Parganas District
Source: Primary Survey

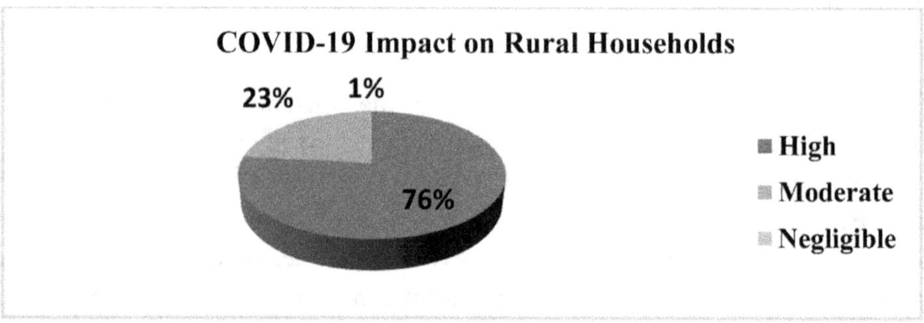

The figure 1 reveals the COVID-19 has impacted hugely the rural households in South 24 Parganas district with 76 percent households has high impact on their livelihood for the pandemic. COVID-19 impacts are moderate among 23 percent households and remaining only 1 percent rural households says that their impact is very negligible.

The figure 2 presents the pandemic impact on rural households as per types of workers and it is observed that households with migrant workers are badly affected as compared to non-migrant workers. The details of impacts of pandemic have been presented in Table 2 for different categories: Social Category, Family Type, Religion, Economic Status, Workers Type and Job Card holding status. It has also been found that those who have been impacted highly are found to change their occupations also.

Figure 2. Workers type-wise Covid-19 impact in South 24 Parganas District
Source: Primary Survey

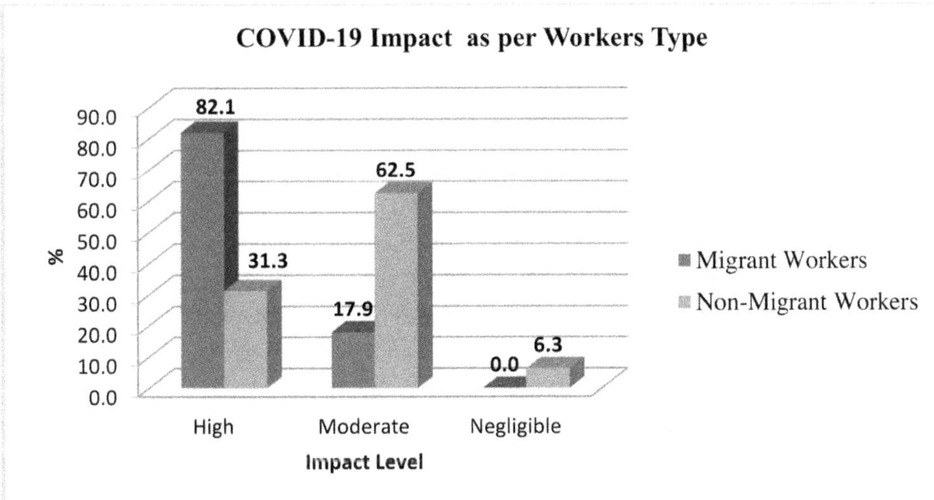

Table 2. Category-wise COVID-19 impact on rural HHs in South 24 Parganas District

Category		COVID-19 Impact Level		
		High	Moderate	Negligible
	Overall	76.7	22.7	0.7
Social Category	Non Scheduled	77.8	21.3	0.9
	Scheduled	73.8	26.2	0.0
Family Type	Joint	63.0	33.3	3.7
	Small	79.7	20.3	0.0
Religion	Hindu	76.0	23.3	0.7
	Muslim	100.0	0.0	0.0
Economic Status	APL	76.0	20.0	4.0
	BPL	76.8	23.2	0.0
Workers Type	Migrant Workers	82.1	17.9	0.0
	Non-Migrant Workers	31.3	62.5	6.3
Job Card	No	83.3	13.9	2.8
	Yes	74.6	25.4	0.0
Occupation Changes for COVID-19	No	33.3	61.1	5.6
	Yes	82.6	17.4	0.0

Source: Primary Survey

Table 2 shows the overall impact on household due to the COVID-19 outbreak of different categories of people in the South 24 Parganas district in West Bengal. It is observed that more than 70 percent households both from schedule or non-schedule category are highly affected by the nationwide lockdown and remaining percentages are moderately affected. COVID-19 impact is high among the small family as compared with joint family, and 100 percent Muslim households are highly affected as per our study though in the sample size it was very less in number. Economic status-wise households have no significant differences in COVID-19 impact level in South 24 Parganas district and here the table 2 clearly shows that impact level is high for migrant workers, households with non-migrant workers mainly engaged with agriculture, daily wage earner in rural area also affected but the level is moderate. Due to lockdown the large number of household changed their occupation particularly those households overall impact is very high in the study area.

In the time of COVID-19 outbreak it has been seen that the people got not only shock of income but they also faced other different types of shocks in India as well as in West Bengal. The present study identified the different kinds of shocks as per the perception of the people like loss of household assets, shortages of available food items storage which reduced the consumption level, affect on health and education, problems in accessibility in local government health facilities for other than COVID-19 issues etc. A large number of households (67percent) had to sell the household assets to run the family during the pandemic time while each and every household faced crisis of income shortage which is presented in figure 3.

Figure 3. Status of shocks during Covid-19 in South 24 Parganas District

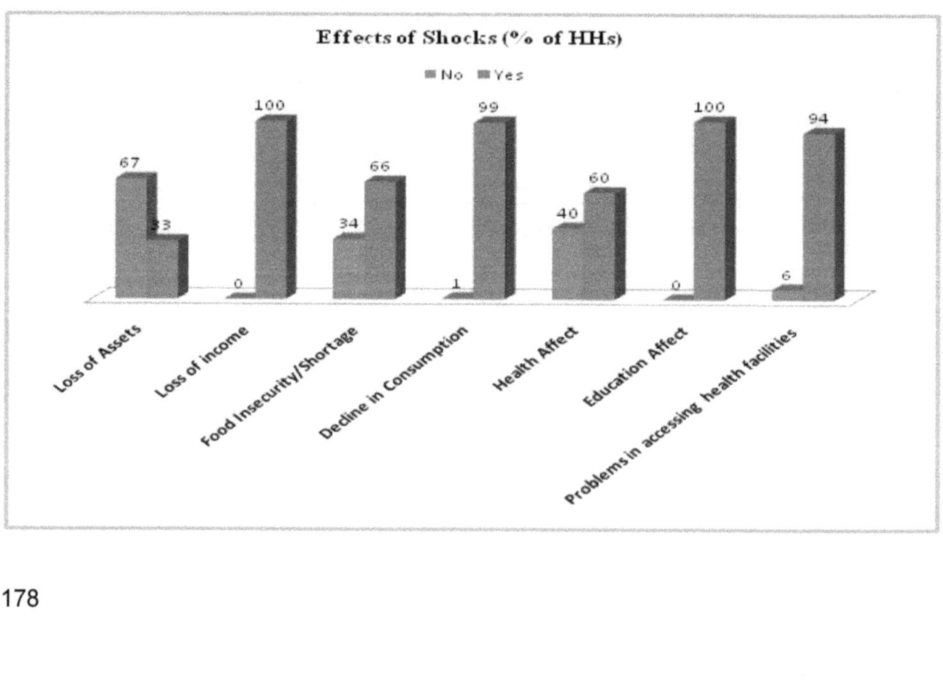

Impact on Income, Expenditure and Savings of the Households

Here we have presented the impact of pandemic on the rural sample households in terms of their impacts on Average Monthly HHs Income (Rs.), Average Monthly HHs Expenditure (Rs.), Average HHs Monthly Savings (Rs.). It is found that both the average monthly income and expenditure have declined in the pandemic period by a substantial amount. As a result savings of the households have declined heavily.

It is necessary to keep in mind that the COVID-19 outbreak in India has experienced high and continuously rising unemployment. The consumption and savings of different categories of households have been presented in Table 3. Taking all the categories into account before the COVID-19 time period average household income was nearly INR 13000/- but during the pandemic period average income reduced to more than 50 percent.

Table 3. COVID-19 lockdown impact on income, expenditure and savings of rural HHs in South 24 Parganas

Category		Average Monthly HHs Income (Rs.)		Average Monthly HHs Expenditure (Rs.)		Average HHs Monthly Savings (Rs.)	
		Before COVID-19	During COVID-19	Before COVID-19	During COVID-19	Before COVID-19	During COVID-19
Social Category	Non Schedule	14357	3990	6236	5051	8121	-2095
	Schedule	12374	3864	5738	4905	6636	-1869
Family Type	Joint	17111	7159	8074	6630	9037	-796
	Small	13076	3178	5663	4654	7413	-2303
Religion	Hindu	13810	3975	6106	5027	7704	-2005
	Muslim	13500	2750	5750	4375	7750	-3000
Economic Status	APL	16060	7087	6740	5620	9320	-1368
	BPL	13350	3473	5968	4888	7382	-2165
Workers Type	Migrant	13756	3359	5996	4914	7760	-2457
	Non-Migrant	14188	7833	6938	5813	7250	1531
Job Card	No	13175	5313	5764	4819	7411	-1425
	Yes	14000	3606	6202	5070	7798	-2224
Occupation Changes for COVID-19	No	13250	7528	6500	5389	6750	2139
	Yes	13877	3276	6042	4958	7836	-2601

Source: Primary Survey

Figure 4. COVID-19 Impact on Income, Expenditure and Savings on Rural HHs in South 24 Parganas District
Source: Primary Survey

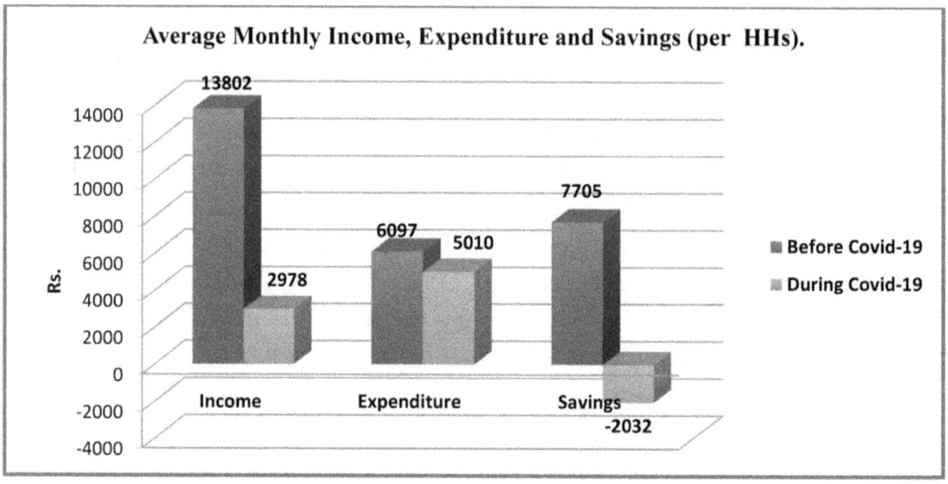

Figure 4 reveals the average income, average expenditure and average savings of the households surveyed. Figure 4 clearly shows that before the pandemic the average household monthly income was in between INR 12000/- to INR 14000/- but after the start of COVID-19 outbreak the income of the sample households falls to INR 2000/- to INR 3000/-. Before the pandemic has started household monthly expenditure was 6265/- but during the COVID-19 period it is falls to INR 5151/- per month and it is found that during the pandemic period savings were found negative. In this period households fulfil the income and expenditure gap from their previous savings or taking loan.

Borrowing by the Households

With the losses of job and fall of income across the nation during the COVID-19 outbreak, mainly the rural lower and middle-income group household has been badly affected. Household primarily borrowed money to survive and run their family in India. The pandemic impact is still unfolding in the household and experienced difficult time. People are forced to take loan to survive. The present study also looks into the scenario of borrowing status of the households where it shows the COVID-19 impact on loans taken by the households through different sources.

Figure 5. Scenario of loan taken by the households during Covid-19 period in rural south 24 Parganas District
Source: Primary Survey

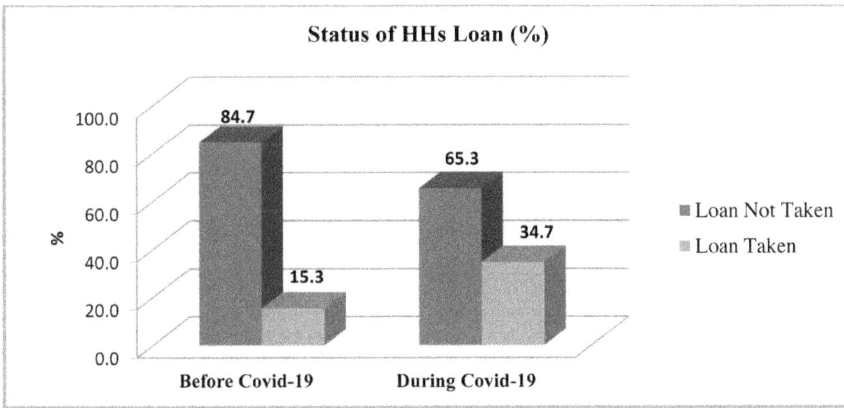

The figure 5 presents the household loan status in during COVID-19 Period in Rural South 24 Parganas District and found that the pandemic has significant role on loan taking by the households to run the livelihood. As per the study more or less 15 percent households took loan from the bank or any other source like money lender, Swarnajayanti Gram Sarojgar Yojana (SGSY) etc. and remaining portion not taken any type of loan. The situation has changed after the pandemic has come that 34.7 percent household took loan during the COVID-19 period which also shown in the figure 5.

Figure 6. Percentage of loan sources by the HHs during Covid-19 in South 24 Parganas District
Source: Primary Survey

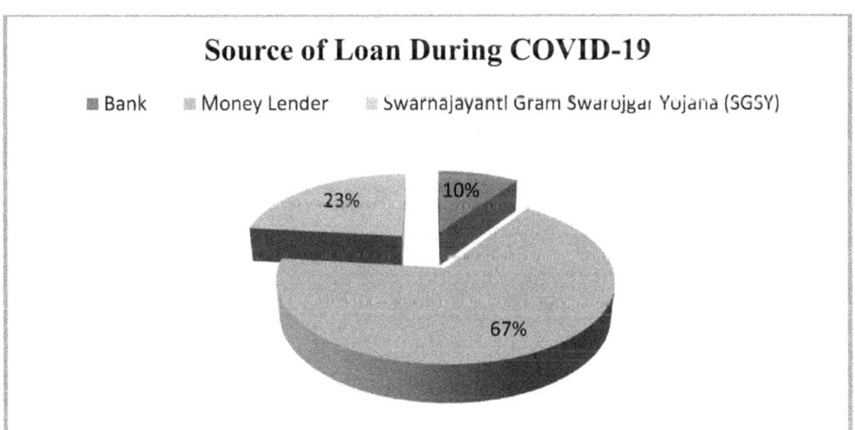

The present study reveals that during pandemic period, highest percentage (67percent) of households borrowed from money lenders, 23 percent households get loan from Bank and remaining 10 percent received from Swarnajayanti Gram Swarojgar Yojana (SGSY) which is presented in Figure 6. The Swarnajayanti Gram Swarojgar Yojana (SGSY) is programme through Self Help Groups (SHGs), where the main focus is to remove poverty of the rural people providing by providing micro-credit.

Table 4. The number of HHs taken loans before and after Covıd-19

Category		Percent of HHs Taken Loan	
		Before COVID-19	During COVID-19
	Overall	15.3	34.7
Social Category	Non Schedule	12.0	36.1
	Schedule	23.8	31.0
Family Type	Joint	14.8	18.5
	Small	15.4	38.2
Religion	Hindu	14.4	35.6
	Muslim	50.0	0.0
Economic Status	APL	8.0	36.0
	BPL	16.8	34.4
Workers Type	Migrant Workers	15.7	34.3
	Non-Migrant Workers	12.5	37.5
Job Card	No	13.9	27.8
	Yes	15.8	36.8
Occupation Changes for COVID-19	No	16.7	33.3
	Yes	15.2	34.8

Source: Primary Survey

Financial Support from Government

During the pandemic situation, both the Central and State Government provide various kinds of support to the people. The figure 7 presents the scenario of financial support by the government (both state and central government) to rural households in South 24 Parganas district of West Bengal. The study finds that before pandemic started the percentage of household got financial support from the government was 14percent but during the COVID-19 period it increased to 20.7percent.

Figure 7. Percentage of HHs get financial support from government in South 24 Parganas District
Source: Primary Survey

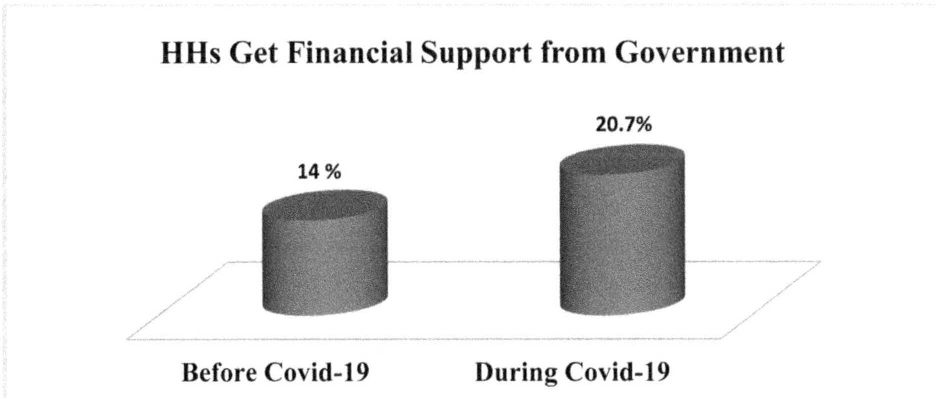

It has been seen from the analysis that maximum households benefited with the government financial support whose family member engaged as a migrant workers. In both time periods it is seen that 80 to 90 percent migrant workers got support, but during pandemic time government gives more importance to migrant workers in the mention district that is shown by the figure 8.

Figure 8. Workers type wise percent of HHs get financial support from government in South 24 Parganas District
Source: Primary Survey

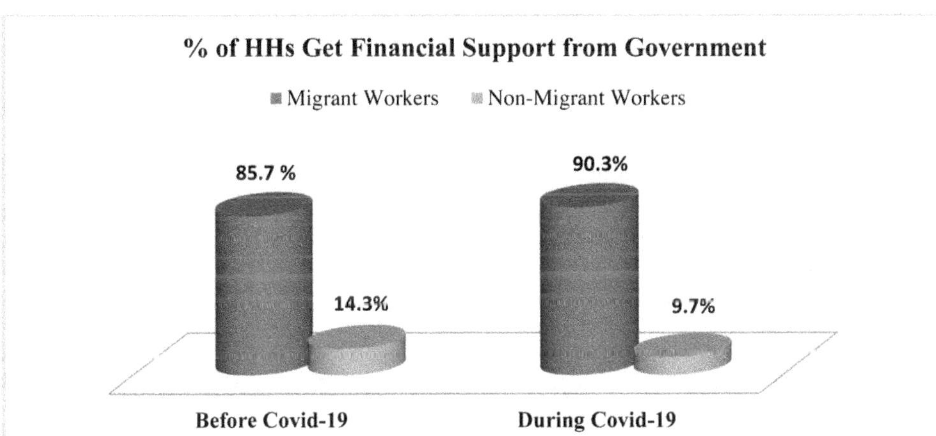

Suggestions by the Households

During the survey the households were asked to suggest ways how their problems can be tackled from this nationwide ongoing crisis due to COVID-19. From the responses of the sample households it is found that 11.3 percent households suggest for continuation of free ration to the people till the pandemic ends, 36percent of households demand creation of employment opportunities for the rural people where unemployed and migrant labour who return to the village due to pandemic they can get jobs and earn to run the livelihood. Since some of the rural households are engaged with agricultural activities, they demand free agricultural inputs to the farmers for coming Rabi season cultivation in the South 24 Parganas district. In this period people also face the problems of accessibilities of government hospitals for patients, where health support services are required to be strengthened so that patients other than COVID-19 get appropriate treatment in local hospital. As the migrant workers lost their jobs, some households demand to the government to provide bank loan with subsidy to the affected household relating guarantee provisions for self employment and starting a new small business to survive with family. Some of them also suggest to increase the scope of public employment programme like MGNREGA in the badly affected area.

Table 5. Suggestions by the households to tackle the pandemic situation

Perception of the HHs (Suggestion)	Percentage of HHs
• Continuation of free supply of Ration till the pandemic ends	11.3
• Create employment opportunities so that unemployed and migrant labour can have jobs and earn for their families	36.0
• Direct cash transfer to the bank accounts of migrant labours already lost their employment and returned home	13.3
• Free distribution of agricultural inputs to all farmers families for coming Rabi season cultivation.	11.3
• Health support services are required to be strengthened so that patients other than COVID-19 get appropriate treatment in local hospital.	3.3
• Provide bank loan with subsidy to the affected HHs relating guarantee provisions for self employment and starting small business	12.0
• Registration of Migrant Labours at Grampanchayat level so that they can be tracked and saved from distress if any.	6.0
• Scope of MGNREGA should be extended	6.7

Source: Primary Survey

CONCLUSION

The COVID-19 has caused a huge shock across the nation after announced the lockdowns. Many economic activities were disrupted and different factories were shutting down. Those who were involved in the industry and in the informal sector outside had to return to homes and as a result their income levels have been affected in a very big way. It is reported that nearly 90 percent of the labour force in India is engaged in the informal sector in India which is true for the state of West Bengal also. Due to pandemic this portion of workers are badly affected. In the present study it is found how these migrant workers due to loss of income and sometimes they have been forced to change their occupation. The study revealed the different shocks during the period in terms of loss of household assets, affect on health and education, problems in accessibility in local government health facilities. As a result of huge losses of their income, the households were forced to use previous savings and increase borrowing from local money lenders to meet the crisis. The study also reports some suggestions by the sample households to tackle the pandemic situation like financial support to the affected people specially the migrant, creation of agro based employment opportunities, direct cash transfer to the household; increasing the scope of public employment programme like MGNREGA.

REFERENCES

Barhate, B., Hirudayaraj, M., Gunasekara, N., Ibrahim, G., Alizadeh, A., & Abadi, M. (2021). Crisis Within a Crisis: Migrant Workers' Predicament During COVID-19 Lockdown and the Role of Non-profit Organizations in India. *Indian Journal of Human Development*, *15*(1), 151–164.

Breman, J. (2020). The pandemic in India and its impact on footloose labour. *The Indian Journal of Labour Economics*, *63*(4), 901–919.

Choolayil, A. C., & Putran, L. (2021). The COVID-19 Pandemic and Human Dignity: the Case of Migrant Labourers in India. *Journal of Human Rights and Social Work*, 1-12.

Choudhari, R. (2020). COVID 19 pandemic: Mental health challenges of internal migrant workers of India. *Asian Journal of Psychiatry*, *54*, 102254.

Choudhury, P., Ghosh, R. K., & Sindhi, S. (2020). *COVID-19 Crisis, Pandemic Resilience and Linkages to Land: An Exposition*. Academic Press.

de Haan, A. (2020). Labour migrants during the pandemic: A comparative perspective. *The Indian Journal of Labour Economics*, *63*(4), 885–900.

Gopalan, H. S., & Misra, A. (2020). COVID-19 pandemic and challenges for socio-economic issues, healthcare and National Health Programs in India. *Diabetes & Metabolic Syndrome*, *14*(5), 757–759.

Jalan, J., & Sen, A. (2020). Containing a pandemic with public actions and public trust: The Kerala story. *Indian Economic Review*, *55*(1), 105–124.

Jha, M. K., & Pankaj, A. K. (2020). Insecurity and fear travel as labour travels in the time of pandemic. *Borders of an Epidemic*, 56.

Khanna, A. (2020). Impact of migration of labour force due to global COVID-19 pandemic with reference to India. *Journal of Health Management*, *22*(2), 181–191.

Kumar, K., Mehra, A., Sahoo, S., Nehra, R., & Grover, S. (2020). The psychological impact of COVID-19 pandemic and lockdown on the migrant workers: A cross-sectional survey. *Asian Journal of Psychiatry*, *53*, 102252.

Kumar, P., Singh, S. S., Pandey, A. K., Singh, R. K., Srivastava, P. K., Kumar, M., ... Drews, M. (2021). Multi-level impacts of the COVID-19 lockdown on agricultural systems in India: The case of Uttar Pradesh. *Agricultural Systems*, *187*, 103027.

Kumar, S., & Choudhury, S. (2021). Migrant workers and human rights: A critical study on India's COVID-19 lockdown policy. *Social Sciences & Humanities Open*, *3*(1), 100130.

Lahiri, S., & Sinha, M. (2021). A study of the socio-economic implications of the COVID-19 pandemic. *Australasian Accounting, Business and Finance Journal*, *15*(1), 51–69.

Lele, U., Bansal, S., & Meenakshi, J. V. (2020). Health and nutrition of India's labour force and COVID-19 challenges. *Economic and Political Weekly*, *55*(21), 13.

Lusome, R., & Bhagat, R. B. (2020). Migration in Northeast India: Inflows, outflows and reverse flows during pandemic. *The Indian Journal of Labour Economics*, *63*(4), 1125–1141.

Mishra, D. K. (2021). Migrant Labour during the Pandemic: A Political Economy Perspective. *The Indian Economic Journal*.

Mitra, A., & Singh, J. (2020). COVID-19 Pandemic and Livelihood Loss: Variations in Unemployment Outcomes and Lessons for Future. Institute of Economic Growth, University Enclave, University of Delhi.

Miyamura, S. (2021). Turbulence ahead: Labour and struggles in times of the COVID-19 pandemic in India. *Canadian Journal of Development Studies*, *42*(1-2), 165–177.

Mohan, M., & Mishra, S. (2021). India's Response to the COVID-19 Pandemic: A Frontal Assault on the "Historically Dispossessed." *International Journal of Health Services*, *51*(1), 107–114.

Mookerjee, D., Chakravarty, S., Roy, S., Tagat, A., & Mukherjee, S. (2021). A Culture-Centered Approach to Experiences of the Coronavirus Pandemic Lockdown Among Internal Migrants in India. *The American Behavioral Scientist*.

Padhee, A. K., & Pingali, P. (2020). *Lessons from a pandemic to repurpose India's agricultural policy*. Nature India.

Pal, S. C., Saha, A., Chowdhuri, I., Roy, P., Chakrabortty, R., & Shit, M. (2021). Threats of unplanned movement of migrant workers for sudden spurt of COVID-19 pandemic in India. *Cities (London, England)*, *109*, 103035.

Rajan, S. I., Sivakumar, P., & Srinivasan, A. (2020). The COVID-19 pandemic and internal labour migration in India: A 'crisis of mobility'. *The Indian Journal of Labour Economics*, *63*(4), 1021–1039.

Ramakumar, R. (2020). Agriculture and the COVID-19 Pandemic: An Analysis with special reference to India. *Review of Agrarian Studies, 10*.

Ranjan, R. (2021). Impact of COVID-19 on migrant labourers of India and China. *Critical Sociology*, *47*(4-5), 721–726.

Reddy, W. R., & Mamgain, R. P. (2020). Revival and Reconstruction of Rural Livelihoods amidst COVID-19: Policy Responses, Opportunities and Way Ahead. *SRSC Policy Paper Series, 1*.

Ruthven, O. (2021). 'Blind laws' and the bureaucracy of rights migrant industrial workers in post-lockdown India. *Journal of Agrarian Change*.

Sengupta, S., & Jha, M. K. (2020). Social policy, COVID-19 and impoverished migrants: Challenges and prospects in locked down India. *The International Journal of Community and Social Development*, *2*(2), 152–172.

Shah, A., & Lerche, J. (2020). Migration and the invisible economies of care: Production, social reproduction and seasonal migrant labour in India. *Transactions of the Institute of British Geographers*, *45*(4), 719–734.

Shakya, M. (2020). The politics of border and nation in Nepal in the time of pandemic. *Dialectical Anthropology*, *44*(3), 223–231.

Shegunshi, M. P., & Hiremath, G. N. (2020). *COVID-19 Impact on Indian Labour Class*. Academic Press.

SinghB. P. (2020). *Impact of COVID-19 on rural economy in India*. doi:10.2139/ssrn.3609973

Singh, O. P. (2020). Mental health of migrant laborers in COVID-19 pandemic and lockdown: Challenges ahead. *Indian Journal of Psychiatry*, *62*(3), 233.

Srivastava, S. K., & Sivaramane, N. (2020). Income-induced effects of COVID-19 on the food consumption pattern of Indian households. *Agricultural Economics Research Review, 33*, 15–24. doi:10.5958/0974-0279.2020.00014.2

Suresh, R., & James, J., & RSj, B. (2020). Migrant Workers at Crossroads–The COVID-19 Pandemic and the Migrant Experience in India. *Social Work in Public Health*, *35*(7), 633–643.

Ullah, A. A., Nawaz, F., & Chattoraj, D. (2021). Locked up under lockdown: The COVID-19 pandemic and the migrant population. *Social Sciences & Humanities Open*, *3*(1), 100126.

KEY TERMS AND DEFINITIONS

Border Management: It is the facilitation of authorized flows of individuals such as tourists, refugees, business travelers, across a country's border with the goal to detect and prevent the admission of non-citizens into the country.

Human Rights: These are the rights that is believed to belong to each and every person.

Labor Migration: It is the movement of people from one region to another region or from area within a country to another area of the country for the purpose of employment.

Migration: It represents the movement of people from one country to another country because of economic, social, or political reasons.

Pandemic: It is an epidemic of an infectious disease which has spread over many regions and affects numerous individuals.

Push-Pull Factors: Migration is often assessed by "push-pull." Push are factors that cause people to leave their country because of economic, political, or social problems while the pull factors are the reasons that attract people to the new country.

Rural Areas: It is a geographic area that is located outside of towns and urbanized areas.

Survey Research: It is the process of conducting research using a survey in which the researchers send to respondents. After the respondents complete the survey, the researchers collect the data to analyze and to draw meaningful conclusions.

Chapter 9
The Impact of COVID-19 on the Size Distribution of New Firms in Turkey

Yigit Aydogan
https://orcid.org/0000-0002-1823-0352
Kirklareli University, Turkey

ABSTRACT

A surge in new firm registrations have been one of the most intriguing outcomes of the economic turbulence caused by the COVID-19 pandemic. Turkey followed a similar pattern to many other economies that observed an initial drop and a rapid V-shaped recovery of entry when the virus hit the country. However, the size distribution of new firms has been very different. While others experience a strong rise in smaller entrants, larger firms have dominated the pack in Turkey. As a widely-known long-term problem of the Turkish economy, which has been accused of causing the stagnation of growth, miniscule firms have been losing their weight rapidly among the entrants. It revives lost hopes for the future of the economy and also motivates questions regarding the other determinants of such transformation in new firm formation.

INTRODUCTION

Encouraging new firm formation is the magic wand of an open liberal economy which suffers from long-term high unemployment rate accompanied with a relatively young population and continuing inbound population movements from less developed countries/regions. Turkey is the unspoken subject of the previous statement. Turkey

DOI: 10.4018/978-1-7998-6900-9.ch009

has a large undereducated population carried from the 20th century and higher educated millions of youngsters. There are 8 million students (almost 10 percent of the population) enrolled to tertiary education (Kalyoncuoglu, 2020). Moreover, the country has been historically subject to migration of millions of people from underdeveloped regions such as Iraq, Iran, Syria, Central Asia, Africa, and lately Afghanistan, which are geographically close or human trafficking happen to be easy due to landscape. Apart from industrial economies, influx of unskilled (potential) workers to a developing economy with staggering growth can be fatal. On the other hand, piling up such people without economic integration (*i.e.* not being able to employ due to lack of unskilled jobs, and/or, employing immigrants and laying off Turkish citizens) resuscitate lost businesses or force them to become entrepreneurs at any scale starting from zero. When investigating the last 11 and a half years of business formation data in Turkey, it is imperative to remember this swift multidimensional transformation that involves tens of millions of people.

Governments subsidize distressed firms in order to maintain the overall functioning of the economy and prevent job losses during crises. Like many others, Turkish government also provided many protective measures to back firms up during the COVID-19 pandemic (a brief summary of the support program can be found in Aydogan (2021)). However, certain measures in unique occasions might have adverse effects. Acemoglu et al. (2018) points to the fact that long run business dynamism/ growth can be harmed with subsidizing incumbent firms during crises via blocking entry. COVID-19 related economic crisis is a new challenge for policymakers and taken measures' effects are hard to calculate. For example, there is an unprecedented measure of lockdown which has heterogeneous effects on different parties. Other temporary measures had been to impose bans on specific business actions: it was forbidden to declare bankruptcy, take debtors to the court for not paying when its due, lay off workers. There were options provided to (and mainly benefited by) firms such as imposing involuntary unpaid leaves for employees and benefiting from short-time work subsidies. The net outcome from a combination of such powerful and open-to-abuse measures is extremely hard to estimate by taking all into account. Modeling such measures into a single framework would be cumbersome, if even possible at all. Due to the need for a starting point, simpler models as exampled here would be invaluable.

Examining the size distribution of firms has been an important and popular venture in the literature, starting with the pioneering work of Gibrat (1931) and becoming more popular after Simon & Bonini (1958). It has been shown to be highly skewed to the right, meaning that most of the operating firms are rather small (Cabral & Mata, 2003). However, the distribution of entering firms' sizes are not widely investigated. New firm sizes are found to be highly dependent on the entrepreneurial characteristics, sector to be worked, location of the firm, and the number of owners (Barkham, 1994). The unique case of COVID-19 related global health crisis can be considered to affect almost all of the mentioned factors. Entrepreneurs as human beings have been living in a world surrounded by a deadly virus which can easily transmit over a basic social encounter. Sectors have been ordered to shut down, or significantly alter their way of business for an unknown period. Regarding the location, supply-chains have got broken up, office works have been abandoned to be replaced by home-offices, and popular locations for daily businesses shaken up with needs of social distance. Manufacturers', service employees' and consumers' choices might be altered regarding the location of their firm. The number of founders can get affected due to the same measures of social distancing. Regression of the social life and all kinds of travel opportunities might make getting different entrepreneurs together harder. Therefore, a possible anomaly of new firm size distribution during the COVID-19 pandemic would be of high interest to both researchers and policymakers.

Reynolds & Maki (1990) asserts that as the researchers and policy-makers gain more insight about economic activity, the importance of new firm formation, along with new branches of existing firms, in predicting the volatility of economic progress is to be increased. Firms are one of the main agents in the economy. In a normal period of time, many firms enter and others exit the market in a typical economy, creating a dynamic and fertile business environment. Firm dynamics can be investigated for diagnosing impact of certain shocks, such as the ongoing health and economic crisis of COVID-19 pandemic. Newly formed firms' capital structures are highly sensitive to shocks of any kind. Determining the effect of the COVID-19 pandemic on capital levels on entry is important because the initial size of a firm and the economic environment that it was born sets the firm's characteristics throughout its lifetime. Firms that have entered the market during a turmoil tend to be smaller in terms of size and they stay stagnant over time (Moreira, 2017; Aydogan, 2020). There can be solutions offered to such disadvantaged firms in order to make them prosper in the long run. So, if there is even a temporary shrinkage in the size of new firms during the COVID-19 pandemic, it needs to be addressed properly for effective policymaking.

This chapter aims to investigate the size distribution of monthly new firm formation in Turkey, focusing on the comparison of the recent past with the pandemic period. Smaller entrants during the pandemic would mean that the recovery from the economic downturn might be troublesome and the future economic growth might be endangered. Instead, a surprising result of larger-than-before new firms would indicate that the near future in the economy can be fruitful, if the dark days end. The chapter is organized as follows: the second section includes a literature survey. The third section presents the data of monthly entrance in Turkey and provides regression model with results. The fourth section proposed excerptions from the research. The fifth one includes future research directions and the last part concludes.

BACKGROUND

Research on the effects of the COVID-19 crisis on firm entry has piled up within several months as this paper is being written and the data has been accumulated for other nations. Haltiwanger (2021) finds that the US new business formation decreased sharply in the early pandemic period, then accelerated with an unprecedented pace starting from the second half of 2020 and continuing in 2021. Buffington et al. (2021) reports that new firm registrations decreased significantly in the US during March and April 2020, then increased sharply starting in May 2020 and continuing into 2021. They claim that non-employer firm registrations are higher than potential employer registrations. It can be translated into this chapter's framework as smaller firms' entry has been increasing more than larger firms during the COVID-19 pandemic. Dinlersoz et al. (2021) finds that the response from potential entrepreneurs on entry decision is different during the COVID-19 recession from the post-Lehman period: a sharp decline followed by a V-shaped recovery and depict all-time-highs in terms of total entry. They also find that most of the increased pandemic entrants to the US economy are non-employers and they are not expected to alter this position.

Kurmann et al. (2021) note that although small firms' entry is crucial to make up for job creation during COVID-19 job losses, new business registrations remained at half of the previous year's value in Canada. Fritsch et al. (2021) asserts that new firm registrations was mildly decreased then recovered during the initial year of the COVID-19 pandemic in Germany. They claim that the recovery of the entry might be due to personal work efforts who just became unemployed or life experimentations from newly emerged home-office workers. Ayres and Raveendranathan (2021) demonstrate that credit shocks and social distance/lockdown measures decrease entry. Fazio et al. (2021) investigates the spatial determinants of volatility of entry and show that new firm registration differs among locations based on race and socioeconomic code. Government incentivized credit expansion has been shown to be a dimmer for new firm formation (Morgan et al., 2020). Anokhin et al. (2021) conclude that while clustering entrepreneurships discourage new firm entry locally, high unemployment rates diminish the effect.

Size of a new firm depends on many factors including interest rates, financial-or non-financial- incentives, entrepreneur's social capital and networks, risk perception, socioeconomic status. The seminal work of Evans & Jovanovic (1989) ties the act of establishing a firm to the entrepreneur's initial capital and note that liquidity constraints are measurably binding. Davidsson et al. (1994) take the institutional point of view to classify new firms, following Reynolds & Maki (1990): *simples*, *tops* and *branches* while simples mostly being small firms. It was noted that small firms provide more than 50 percent of the job creation in Sweden.

Estrin & Prevezer (2010) investigates the effects of institutions to the entry in emerging markets. They find that while the interaction between the strength of formal rules and deficiency caused by informal mechanisms work together to support entry for some countries, their co-existence sabotage the new firm formation in others. Klapper & Love (2011) investigates how new firm formation gets affected by financial crises by looking at 93 countries data. Finally, Bloom et al. (2021) investigate the impact of the COVID-19 pandemic on US firms.

In the microeconomics literature, classical approaches to entry by studying competition in specific industries over capital levels are abundant. Chevalier (1995) shows that entry is encouraged by competitive takeovers. Capital structure is a determinant of production decisions, and increased output is associated with increased debt in industries with low entry barriers (Phillips, 1995). Mackay and Phillips (2005) asserts that industry-median reverting behavior of size for entrants is not important for economic purposes. The rankings within an industry is expected to last despite the suggested dynamism. Miao (2005) claims that new firm formation increases along with the debt ratios of operating firms. (One can refer to other works that investigates the relation between capital and firm dynamics such as Dixit (1989), Fries et al. (1997).

SIZE DISTRIBUTION OF NEW FIRMS IN TURKEY

In this part, the data of entering firms to the Turkish economy will be examined using monthly entry data. First, an overview of the data and the summary statistics will be presented. Then, the COVID-19 pandemic's impact on different size classes of entrants will be assessed using Ordinary Least Squares (OLS) regression method.

Data

In this study, size of new firms will be based on their initial capital levels at the registry date. There are different size definitions for firms in the literature, *e.g.* number of employees (Axtell, 2001), sales (Cefis et al., 2002), mainly depending on data availability. The Union of Chambers and Commodity Exchanges of Turkey (TOBB) collects and shares the initial capital data of new firms in each month, and it is publicly available from their website (TOBB, 2021). The new firm registry data considered in this chapter spans 138 months between 01-2010 and 06-2021. There have been 777,858 new firms entered to the Turkish economy. Distributions of monthly data of entrants are to be depicted in order to capture a divergence during the COVID-19 pandemic. Stylized facts and summary statistics are to be tabulated in detail for comparison with the earlier time period. Comparing also with the pandemic data, possible interactions of new firm size related to peaks of the infection are to be assessed.

The reported size classifications of firms have been constant for the considered time period. One may question the reliability of retaining a TRY based scaling system for more than a decade long period since the Turkish national currency is open to sharp decreases in real value. The primary reason to use the scale chart at hand is that it is the official one in place. In fact, the Turkish Lira has lost significant (approximately 83%) value against the US Dollar between 2010 and 2021 (1 USD floats around 8.5 TRY as of June, 2021 (CBRT, n.d.)). A small firm in 2010 would correspond to a large firm in 2021 in USD terms. As an alternative measure, Consumer Price Index Based Real Effective Exchange Rate has decreased from 119.07 in January 2010 to 59.65 in June 2021, nearly halved. On the other hand, the micro firms have kept their pace which warns about the disconnected nature of the local economy from the world. There are new firms registering each month which has very little capital in real terms. For example, 621 firms entered to the market in June 2021 that has less than or equal to only one thousand USD in terms of capital. The long-term average for such firms with very little capital is 834 firms/month during the period under investigation. Therefore, maintaining a stable TRY based scale has additional explanatory power in terms of economic framework in the country.

Panels (a) and (b) of Table 1 serves as a legend for the size labels in use throughout this part. TOBB provides the new firm capital data under two sections divided as limited liability companies and corporations where the former have 21 size classes while the latter have 14. Those 21 and 14 size classes' widths generally do not match and need to be combined at compatible capital levels in order to provide a meaningful classification. Therefore, the group (a) in the Table 1 is a mere combination of the originally reported size classes to match each other at the closest value, referred as the *narrow grouping*. The second grouping is denoted under the panel (b) in Table 1. It was suggested here in order to propose a solution to the rightful concerns about the original size classification's practical value, due the significant depreciation of Turkish Lira during the period. The second classification mentioned above with three size groups is to be called *the wide grouping* thereafter.

Table 1. Proposing three different size classifications of new firms in Turkey

(a)		
Label	**Size**	
Micro	Up to 50,000TRY	
Micro+	50,001TRY - 100,000TRY	
Small	100,001TRY - 200,000TRY	
Small+	200,001TRY - 300,000TRY	
Medium	300,001TRY - 400,000TRY	
Medium+	400,001TRY - 500,000TRY	
Large	500,001TRY - 1,000,000TRY	
Large+	1,000,001TRY - 2,000,000TRY	
Giant	2,000,001TRY and above	
(b)		
Label	**Size**	
Tiny	Up to 100,000TRY	
Regular	100,001TRY - 1,000,000TRY	
Big	1,000,001TRY and above	
(c)		
Label	**Size**	
	Employees	**Net Sales or Assets**
Micro	0-9	Up to 3,000,000TRY
Small	10-49	Up to 25,000,000TRY
Medium	50-249	Up to 125,000,000TRY
Non-SME	250 and above	125,000,001 and above

Panel (c) in Table 1 is reported in order to point out the ambiguity on the official data handling of different organizations in Turkey and not to be referred again later on. It contains another official firm size categorization concerning a completely different data source regarding incumbent firms, provided by the Ministry of the Industry and Technology under the name Entrepreneur Information System (EIS). It is based on decomposing the Small and Medium Enterprises (SMEs). Micro, small and medium enterprises are categorized according to their employment, net sales or assets whichever being the highest according to the thresholds in the table. The data set lags approximately two years behind and contain micro data of all firms in Turkey, representing a total of 1,358,065 firms in 2018. Relating to the paper at hand, 82 percent of incumbent firms (a total of 1,118,078 firms) were categorized as micro depending on their employment being lower than 10, or, net sales or assets below 3 million TRY, according to the EIS. The average of the assets of all firms, according to the figures on their official balance sheets as reported to the Revenue Administration of Turkey, was equal to 6,202,161TRY in 2018. On the other hand, the mean assets of the micro firms according to the EIS classification is 1,349,428TRY. An average firm is 4.6 times larger than an average micro firm based on assets, despite the micro firms constitute the vast majority of the total. Therefore, there is a big size disparity regarding the incumbent firms which puts additional importance on the current quest on investigating the new firm sizes.

Table 2. Summary statistics of monthly new firm size classes in Turkey between January 2010 - June 2021

	Mean	Std. Dev.	Median	Skewness	Kurtosis
Micro	2,107	569	2071	0.24	4.02
Micro+	1,689	605	1589	0.43	2.31
Small	530	218	473	0.53	2.32
Small+	325	185	266	0.96	3
Medium	140	145	88	2.2	6.81
Medium+	388	345	251	1.81	5.4
Large	306	280	184	1.87	5.5
Large+	79	72	52	1.97	6.05
Giant	71	59	47	2	6.47
Tiny	3,798	1,031	3,926	0.05	2.94
Regular	1,690	1,123	1,253	1.54	4.57
Big	150	130	98	1.99	6.19
All	5,637	1,991	5,207	0.87	0.24

Table 2 presents summary statistics of all size classes of entrants that are proposed earlier. It can be seen that the new firm size distribution is skewed to the right, meaning that smaller size groups are usually more crowded than larger ones (except for *small+* and *medium* which might indicate that the current classification is unnecessarily detailed or at least it can be improved by getting hands on firm level data). The metrics in the Table 2 refers to the "in-group" statistics. Skewness and kurtosis of the size groups do not bear information about the actual entry distribution. It is seen from Table 2 that smaller groups are less skewed and have less kurtosis (except *micro*), meaning that in a given month the expected influx of smaller firms is more uniformly distributed. As the size class grow, skewness and kurtosis increases.

It indicates that the probability of observing an extreme number of entrants within a typical larger size class is higher. Basically, monthly entry of larger firms may vary significantly. The *wider grouping* with three classes is easier to the eye. *Tiny* firms' entry in a given month is almost normally distributed throughout the period with skewness close to zero and kurtosis close to 3. *Regular* and *big* firms have a more meaningful mean to be clustered around (high skewness) and more likely to draw extreme values (high kurtosis).

Figure 1. Total entry between January 2010 - June 2021, logarithmic scale

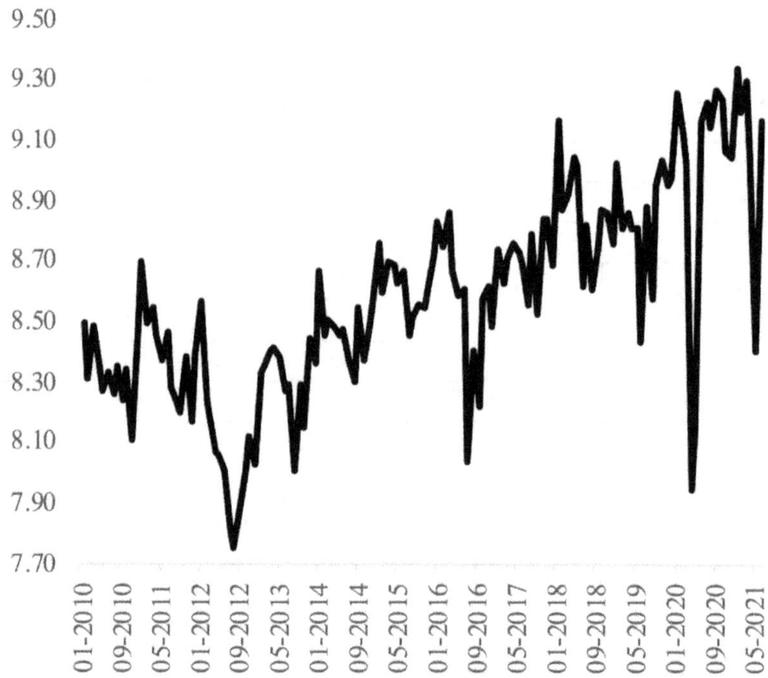

Figure 1 depicts the line graph of the number of new firms in Turkey between January 2010 and June 2021 on a logarithmic scale. The upward trend in the figure is evident yet it has been accompanied with great volatility. Visual inspection of the data shows that there is no seasonal movement except a positive impact of the month of January (for a similar *January Effect*, please refer to the literature of financial studies provided in the Additional Reading section to this chapter). The sharp declines in the graph coincides different months of the year. It can be said that monthly entry data might be subject to mild seasonality because of the certain accounting or tax advantages during some periods in a particular year. However, a monthly dummy variable should adequately capture the important part of it. It can be seen that entry has been collapsed first but then rapidly and significantly increased during the pandemic period, similar to the assertions by Haltiwanger (2020) using the US business formation statistics.

Figure 2. Distribution of monthly entry among size classes and in total between January 2010 and June 2021

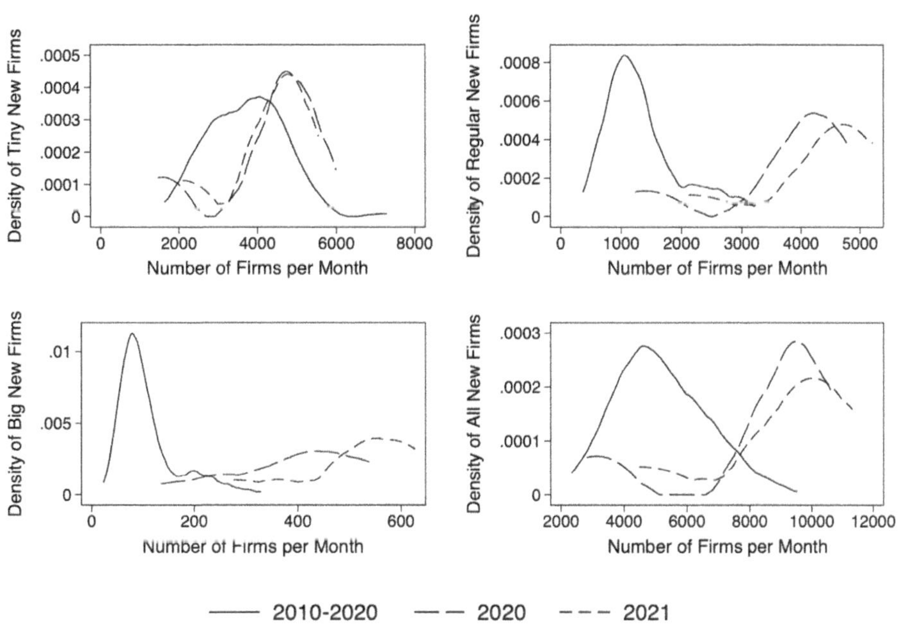

Distribution of monthly new firms in each of the *wider* size groups and the overall entry are depicted in Figure 2 (similar looking distributions of the narrow groups are reported as Figures 4-6 in the Appendix to this chapter). A surprising fact is revealed in Figure 2 which happens to be a sharp increase in entry of new firms in Turkish economy during the pandemic period. Increase in the regular and big firms' entry is immense. Moreover, as the world continues its voyage through the pandemic, this shift continues. There is more entry of larger firms in 2021 against 2020 whilst 2020 entry had been opulent, too.

Table 3. Robustness of the new firm size distribution when Covid-19 hits Turkey, % of total

Date	Total #	Micro	Micro+	Small	Small+	Medium	Medium+	Large	Large+	Giant	Tiny	Regular	Big
02-2020	9,154	27%	30%	10%	7%	4%	10%	9%	2%	1%	56%	40%	3%
03-2020	8,275	25%	30%	10%	7%	5%	11%	8%	2%	2%	55%	41%	4%
04-2020	2,812	24%	28%	9%	8%	5%	12%	9%	2%	2%	51%	44%	5%
05-2020	3,438	21%	28%	8%	8%	5%	13%	11%	3%	2%	49%	45%	6%
06-2020	9,594	21%	27%	9%	8%	5%	13%	11%	3%	2%	48%	46%	5%

Intriguing analysis of the new firm size distribution in Turkey during the pandemic can be enhanced by taking a closer look at the arrival time of the Sars-Cov-2 which is dated in March of 2020 (Zorlu, 2020). Table 3 tabulates the initial impact of the pandemic on entry statistics. With the pandemic measures, entry in April and May 2020 dropped significantly. However, despite the total number of entries has suddenly decreased 66% monthly in April, the size distribution of new firms according to the size categories had been altered only by a few percent. It highlights the value of the new firm size distribution as an important regularity that must be examined thoroughly.

Model

Measuring the impact of COVID-19 on the size distribution of new firms is no easy task to model. The subject matter is closely related to different branches in the literature such as business financing, behavioral economics or labor economics. The purpose of this research is to isolate the relevant part and present a clear-cut quantitative output. Here, the model is built in a similar fashion as Klapper & Love (2011) used to detecting the effect of the Global Financial Crisis on new firm formations. Therefore, the main regression model can be defined as

$$entry_t = \alpha + \beta_1 covid_t + \beta_2 january_t + \beta_3 trend_t + \epsilon_t . \qquad (1)$$

where α .is the intercept, *entry* is the number of new firms in each size class, *january* is the dummy to capture the expected positive effect of the first month of each year to eliminate seasonality, *trend* is the term to capture any long-term trends affecting the new firm formation with consecutive values starting from 1 and ϵ .is the error term. There is an approximately three-months delay from the global COVID-19 outbreak and the first infected individual's announcement in Turkey on March 10, 2020 (Zorlu, 2020 March 11). Therefore, the dummy variable of *covid* is treated differently in two separate estimations: the first one starts on January 2020 and called *covid-19 global*. The second *covid* dummy variable takes the value of 1 starting from March 2020 and called *covid-19 Turkey* in the following part. Models with these two pandemic dummy variables are estimated separately.

The natural logarithm of the monthly data of new firms in each size class has been used in the regressions one at a time, hence the model is log-linear. A serial correlation is unlikely within the entry statistics simply because of the independence of the entry decisions of the entrepreneurs in each period. Moreover, adding a dummy variable for the first month of each year contributes to the suitability of the data structure. As stated in the Data section, the main problem with the new firm data in Turkey is its meaningfulness in classifying by size in current real value due to the outdated size categories. Due to the reservations mentioned above regarding the decay of the size classifications' economic meaning, estimations can be diversified to compare. The narrow and wider size groupings are going to be estimated separately to investigate the model's explanatory power.

Estimation Results

The following tables present the estimation output of Equation 1 considering two bi-parted reporting. The difference between the Tables 4 and 5 is the size classification on new firms, *i.e.* narrow or wider grouping. Additionally, panels (a) and (b) of each Table is based on the usage of the COVID-19 dummy, regarded as either the global advent of the pandemic or its appearance in Turkey.

Table 4 presents the effect of the COVID-19 pandemic on Turkish new firm size distribution, based on the narrow grouping. It can be seen that the estimated values are highly statistically significant with a few exceptions. Panel (a) shows the impact of global outbreak. The pandemic has negative effect on the micro and micro+ size classes, former being more severe. Specifically, micro firms' entry during the pandemic are expected to be 39% and micro+ entry is 12% lower than usual. On the other hand, there is a clear positive effect on the larger size classes. Medium and medium+ firms' entry have increased 96% and 94% respectively. Entry of large+, large, giant and small+ firms also increased significantly by 85%, 84%, 79% and 54% in an orderly fashion. The global COVID-19 dummy variable has returned to be statistically insignificant for the total new firms per month, and for small firms. The dummy variable for the first month of each year has returned a similar value for most of the size classes except when it was statistically insignificant for medium+ and giant firms. The month of January is expected to yield around 30% more firms for most of the size classes.

Table 4. Estimation output of equation 1 with narrow size classification (a)

	Micro	Micro+	Small	Small+	Medium	Medium+	Large	Large+	Giant	All
covid-19 global	-0.39***	-0.12*	0.05	0.54**	0.96***	0.94***	0.84***	0.85***	0.79***	0.07
january	0 31***	0.28***	0.30***	0.32*	0.30***	0.23	0.21*	0.28**	0.09	0.28***
trend	0 01***	0.01***	0.01***	0.01***	0.01***	0.01***	0.01***	0.01***	0.01***	0.01***
constant	7 39***	6.83***	5.71***	5.23***	3.75***	5.00***	4.62***	3.31***	3.33***	8.13***
R-squared	0 25	0.61	0.42	0.35	0.81	0.58	0.70	0.68	0.68	0.59

Table 5. (b)

	Micro	Micro+	Small	Small+	Medium	Medium+	Large	Large+	Giant	All
covid-19 Turkey	-0.43***	-0.17**	-0.01	0.45***	0.88***	0.86***	0.78***	0.82***	0.75***	0.03
january	0.28***	0.27***	0.30***	0.36***	0.37***	0.29**	0.27**	0.34***	0.14	0.28***
trend	0.01***	0.01***	0.01***	0.01***	0.01***	0.01***	0.01***	0.01***	0.01***	0.01***
constant	7.40***	6.83***	5.70***	5.20***	3.70***	4.95***	4.59***	3.27***	3.29***	8.12***
R-squared	0.26	0.62	0.42	0.33	0.79	0.56	0.68	0.67	0.66	0.59

***99%, **95%, *90% statistical significance

Panel (b) in Table 4 reports a modified version of the *covid* dummy in Equation 1, starting on March instead of January, as the virus arrived in Turkey three months later. It is evident that the overall significance of the coefficients has been improved. Associated with weaker significance, micro+, small+, medium+ and large firms' coefficients from Panel (a) is better described with Turkish pandemic dummy variable in Panel (b). All subjected coefficients are statistically significant with a p-value of less than 5% except for small firms' entry and total entry which returned as statistically insignificant. Comparing with the global COVID-19 dummy, local pandemic dummy has more negative and less positive effect on the variables. The negative effect on micro and micro+ firms is increased along with the statistical significance when focused on local spread of the virus, from -39% to -43% and from -12% to -17% respectively. The positive effect on small+, medium, medium+, large, large+ and giant firms are reduced by a few percentage points, varying between 3% to 9%. January dummy is also highly significant except giant firms and estimated around 30%.

Table 5 reports the estimation output of Equation 1 in accordance with the wider size groups proposed in Panel (b) of Table 1. Panel (a) of Table 5 depicts that global

Table 6. Estimation output of equation 1 with wider size classification (a)

	Tiny	Regular	Big
covid-19 global	-0.26***	0.60***	0.82***
january	0.30***	0.27**	0.19*
trend	0.01***	0.01***	0.01***
constant	7.84***	6.66***	4.02***
R-squared	0.43	0.58	0.70

Table 7. (b)

	Tiny	Regular	Big
covid-19 Turkey	-0.30***	0.54***	0.79***
january	0.28***	0.31***	0.25**
trend	0.01***	0.01***	0.01***
constant	7.84***	6.63***	3.99***
R-squared	0.44	0.56	0.68
***99%, **95%,*90% statistical significance			

pandemic has negative effect on tiny firms' entrance and positive effect on regular and big firms. A global pandemic month is expected to yield a 26% lower entry of tiny firms, 60% more entry of regular sized firms and 82% more entry of big firms. January dummy is less and less significant as the firm size increase which is a more obvious result than Table 4 where the decrease in significance is not as straightforward while moving towards larger firm groups.

Panel (b) of Table 5 yields the estimations of Equation 1 with Turkish pandemic dummy. It can be seen that local pandemic variable has more negative effect on smaller firms and less positive effect on larger firms. Tiny firms' entry is expected to be 30% less (from 26% calculated with global pandemic dummy) while regular sized firms' entry is expected to be increased by 54% (from 60% calculated with global pandemic dummy) and big firms' entry is estimated to be increased by 79% (from 82% calculated with global pandemic dummy) more than a typical month. In Panel (b), the estimation with dummy variable for the first month of each year is returned statistically more significant than the coefficients in Panel (a). Here, being in the month of January increases the expectation of entry of tiny firms 28%, regular firms 31% and big firms 25%.

SOLUTIONS AND RECOMMENDATIONS

It is evident from the estimations that exceptionally small firms are hit hard by the pandemic. Both global and local advent of the pandemic is found to be highly important. The negative effect of the COVID-19 on the micro and micro+ firms' (together combined to form *tiny*) entry is found to be multiplied when the virus hit Turkey. On the other hand, entry by the larger firms are exceptionally increased during the pandemic. Regarding the flood of new firms during certain times, financing can be examined. De Meza & Webb (1987) models *overinvestment* as profitable investments create financing opportunities for the bad ones which in turn decrease social efficiency. If the expected returns differ among projects, more than socially optimal amount of investment might occur. One can expect that during volatile and undirected periods, such difference in investment projects shall occur more frequently. Turkish economy had been passing through an uncharted period of economic turmoil even before the COVID-19 pandemic hit (Orhangazi & Yeldan, 2021) where income disparities surge both for businesses and employees.

It can be expected from a period of social distance with increasing home-office and freelance working conditions, micro firms' entry might be expected to be boosted. However, that did not turn out to be true for Turkish case. Moreover, it seems that people with low amount of capital have been proportionately discouraged to enter to the market as the near future is unpredictable with temporary shut-down measures from the government as the pandemic grows periodically.

It can be said that both *narrow* and *wider* size classifications are valuable for economic research. Using *narrow* size categories provide more insight on the smaller but more crowded firm groups. However, it does not provide much extra information for larger firms. On the other hand, for a study with a macro perspective, utilization of wider size groups bear adequate information for many purposes. In an inflationary economy, data categorization in official reports must be updated periodically in accordance with the economic developments. Altering the size groups similar to the current proposition should be a concern for the data sharing authority. Moreover, the original data is reported in a strangely cumulative nature via multiple Microsoft Excel® files. The data can be distributed more conveniently to facilitate more research by the TOBB. An obvious method would be setting up a basic interactive database website, similar to the contemporary data sharing standards.

FUTURE RESEARCH DIRECTIONS

This paper has shown the strange and swift transformation of the size distribution of new firms in favor of the larger ones. Building upon the findings, the first thing to do should be investigating the underlying dynamics leading to this outcome in order to support the progress. Sectoral decomposition of new firms is an important source of information regarding the expectations and experiences of the owner/founder of new larger firms. It is also important to depict the socioeconomic characteristics of contemporary entrepreneurs. The theories of immigrants' impact on increasing entry and their specific impact on size distribution of new firm registrations can be investigated. Putting aside the scientific anxiety to shed light on this strange observation, it can also be said that *everything* should be kept as it is in order not to disturb the flow even if it is a lucky outcome from unintentional interventions.

As mentioned earlier, current paper is only a beginning of an important quest on identifying the effects of the COVID-19 pandemic on the firm dynamics. One of the most important aspect of becoming an entrepreneur is the decision on how to finance the new business. Types of financing of new businesses in Turkey, whether credit or equity, is an intriguing topic. As seen from the Figure 3, private sector credits issued by the banks have surged and collapsed from time to time. The effect, or existence, of credit rationing in Turkey can be re-analyzed following Guncavdi et al. (1998). Comprising a high volume of work age people with different nationalities, access to finances in Turkish economy has become an important topic to survey.

The evident risk appetite of banks reflected on the continuous high credit expansion depicted in Figure 3 brings several other questions. Considering the birth and death statistics of Turkish firms, optimum capital level for entry can be calculated if the data of TURKSTAT and TOBB can be matched. Barriers to entry in Turkey should be a prioritized research subject.

Figure 3. Total private sector credit issued by the banks in Turkey, Bn TRY

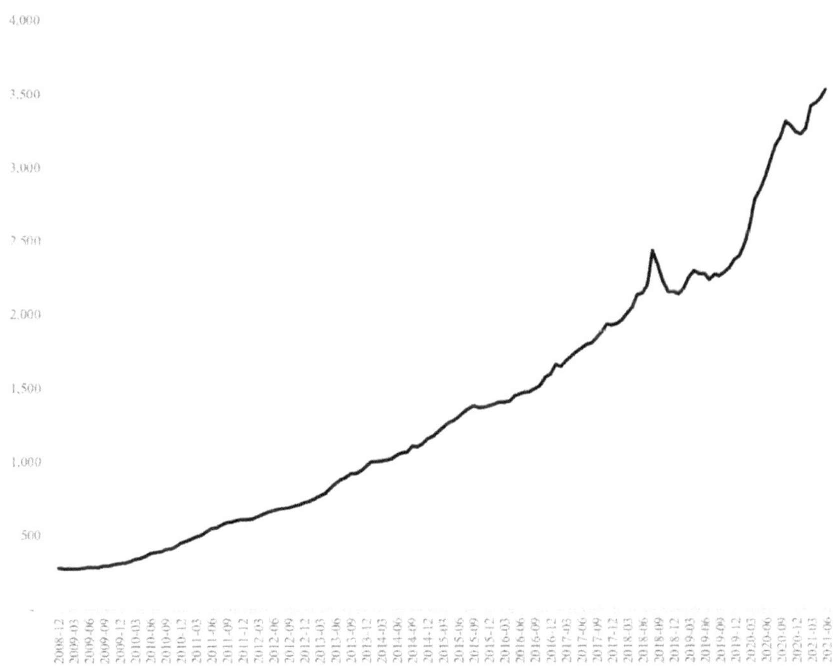

As noted by Davidsson et al. (1994), regional effects of job creation by different size classes of new firms vary considerably. Therefore, investigating the relationship between regional job creation and new firm formation will be invaluable. City based statistics of new firm capital is available at TOBB website. Moreover, sectoral decomposition of entry during COVID 19 pandemic is of high importance. Infrastructural development throughout Turkey has been an important argument which is stressed out regularly by many parties. Certain monumental high-cost and low-return infrastructure elements have become abundant in remote corners of the country such as airports and bridges. Detecting the effect of such elements on new firm formation and especially on the evolution of its size distribution by incorporating them into flexible models would draw attention. A model with regional new firm registrations, sizes and sectors would feature significant information about the transformation of the local economic activity.

CONCLUSION

New firm creation is a vital dynamism source for any economy at all times. It gains importance for countries with high unemployment and increasing labor force, just like Turkey. Shocks and crises like COVID-19 pandemic make the continuum of entry indispensable for successful governance during downturns. The focus is not only on the total number of entrants, but also on the size distribution of new firms. Smaller entrants tend to keep it that way during their lifetime, and it can be a long period in economies lacking selection like Turkey. Formation of many larger firms are preferred with expectations of contributing to the long-term growth of the economy. However, it is only at an indirect reach for policymakers since the entrepreneurs are the ones making the decision and putting up the effort. It would not be an overstatement to call the current figures of entry put forward earlier is a dream for any government around the world during the COVID-19 crisis. Despite the widespread increase in entry around the world as reported earlier, size distribution of new firms is much more balanced in Turkey in favor of the larger size groups. It can be expected that such improvement in the new firm size distribution would have a positive impact on the near future of the Turkish economy.

This study has been focusing on pointing out the effects of the advent of the COVID-19 pandemic on the size distribution of new firms. Surely, mentioning capital as the criterion of the firm size brings up the need for multidimensionality as the subject unveils. However, it is also important to depict the issue plain and simple with a macro perspective. It was shown in this paper that smaller firm creation have lost a huge momentum in Turkey right after the COVID-19 hits. The deterioration is so powerful that there is no urgent need for a sectoral or regional work to prove its economic importance. Moreover, larger firms' entry has surged during the same period. As majority of long-lived small firms have been stated one of the main problems of Turkish firm size distribution in the related literature mentioned above, recent events must have brought up positive feelings for all relevant parties. The lowering of the smaller firm registrations and increase of entry by the larger firms is an important finding regarding the future of the Turkish economy as mentioned earlier.

The new firm registration data has been reported by TOBB for more than a decade. Turkey has experienced a severe inflationary period lately and the value of TRY against USD has been deteriorated significantly. Yet, the official size classification of firms did not change at all. One can easily assert that the official classifications had lost economic value. In this paper, a broader size definition was proposed against such complaints. Surprisingly enough, extremely smaller size classes have been found worthy of investigation econometrically. They continue to embody large number of members and make up large portions of the total entrants. The reason of continuing importance of micro size firms might be due to the economics of influx of low skilled workers. Putting aside the reason behind it, it seems that researchers and policymakers concerned with Turkish economy is likely to continue putting up much effort to studying the economics of miniscule firms.

ACKNOWLEDGMENT

This research received no specific grant from any funding agency in the public, commercial, or not-for-profit sectors.

REFERENCES

Acemoglu, D., Akcigit, U., Alp, H., Bloom, N., & Kerr, W. (2018). Innovation, reallocation, and growth. *The American Economic Review*, *108*(11), 3450–3491. doi:10.1257/aer.20130470

Anokhin, S., Chistyakova, N., Antonova, I., Spitsina, L., Wincent, J., & Parida, V. (2021). Flagship enterprises, entrepreneurial clusters, and business entry rates: Insights from the knowledge spillover theory of entrepreneurship. *Entrepreneurship and Regional Development*, *33*(3-4), 353–367. doi:10.1080/08985626.2021.1872942

Axtell, R. (2001). Zipf Distribution of U.S. Firm Sizes. *Science*, *293*(5536), 1818–1820. doi:10.1126cience.1062081 PMID:11546870

Aydogan, Y. (2020). Evolution of the Firm Size Distribution in Turkey. *Oneri Journal*, *15*(53). Advance online publication. doi:10.14783/maruoneri.676735

Aydogan, Y. (2021). Evolution of the Firm Structure in the Post-COVID-19 Era: A Roadmap for Turkish SMEs. In *Handbook of Research on Strategies and Interventions to Mitigate COVID-19 Impact on SMEs* (pp. 245–266). IGI Global. doi:10.4018/978-1-7998-7436-2.ch012

Ayres, J., & Raveendranathan, G. (2021). *Firm Entry and Exit during Recessions* (No. 11353). Inter-American Development Bank.

Barkham, R. J. (1994). Entrepreneurial characteristics and the size of the new firm: A model and an econometric test. *Small Business Economics*, *6*(2), 117–125. doi:10.1007/BF01065184

Bloom, N., Fletcher, R. S., & Yeh, E. (2021). The impact of COVID-19 on US firms (No. w28314). National Bureau of Economic Research.

Cabral, L., & Mata, J. (2003). On the evolution of the firm size distribution: Facts and theory. *The American Economic Review*, *93*(4), 1075–1090. doi:10.1257/000282803769206205

CBRT. (n.d.). *Indicative Exchange Rates* [Database]. Central Bank of Republic of Turkey. https://www.tcmb.gov.tr/kurlar/kurlar_en.html

Cefis, E., Ciccarelli, M., & Orsenigo, L. (2002). From Gibrat's legacy to Gibrat's fallacy. A Bayesian Approach to Study the Growth of Firms. *Working papers at the Hyman Minsky Department of Economic Studies*, 19.

Chevalier, J. A. (1995). Capital structure and product-market competition: Empirical evidence from the supermarket industry. *The American Economic Review*, 415–435. https://www.jstor.org/stable/2118181

Davidsson, P., Lindmark, L., & Olofsson, C. (1994). New firm formation and regional development in Sweden. *Regional Studies*, *28*(4), 395–410. doi:10.1080/00343409412331348356

De Meza, D., & Webb, D. C. (1987). Too much investment: A problem of asymmetric information. *The Quarterly Journal of Economics*, *102*(2), 281–292. doi:10.2307/1885064

Dinlersoz, E., Dunne, T., Haltiwanger, J., & Penciakova, V. (2021, May). Business Formation: A Tale of Two Recessions. *AEA Papers and Proceedings. American Economic Association*, *111*, 253–257. doi:10.1257/pandp.20211055

Dixit, A. (1989). Entry and exit decisions under uncertainty. *Journal of Political Economy*, *97*(3), 620–638. doi:10.1086/261619

Estrin, S., & Prevezer, M. (2010). A survey on institutions and new firm entry: How and why do entry rates differ in emerging markets? *Economic Systems*, *34*(3), 289–308. doi:10.1016/j.ecosys.2010.01.003

Evans, D. S., & Jovanovic, B. (1989). An estimated model of entrepreneurial choice under liquidity constraints. *Journal of Political Economy*, *97*(4), 808–827. doi:10.1086/261629

Fries, S., Miller, M., & Perraudin, W. (1997). Debt in industry equilibrium. *Review of Financial Studies*, *10*(1), 39–67. doi:10.1093/rfs/10.1.39

Fritsch, M., Greve, M., & Wyrwich, M. (2021). The COVID-19 Pandemic and Entrepreneurship in Germany: First Observations and Interpretations. *Jena Economic Research Papers*, 7.

Gibrat, R. (1931). *Les inégalites économiques*. Sirey.

Günçavdı, Ö., Bleaney, M., & McKay, A. (1998). Financial liberalisation and private investment: Evidence from Turkey. *Journal of Development Economics*, *57*(2), 443–455. doi:10.1016/S0304-3878(98)00097-2

Haltiwanger, J. C. (2021). Entrepreneurship During the COVID-19 Pandemic: Evidence from the Business Formation Statistics (No. w28912). National Bureau of Economic Research.

Hodrick, R. J., & Prescott, E. C. (1997). Postwar US business cycles: An empirical investigation. *Journal of Money, Credit and Banking*, *29*(1), 1–16. doi:10.2307/2953682

Kalyoncuoglu, Y. (2020, May 6). *Yükseköğrenimdeki öğrenci sayısı 8 milyonu buldu*. Anatolian Agency. https://www.aa.com.tr/tr/egitim/yuksekogrenimdeki-ogrenci-sayisi-8-milyonu-buldu/1830726

Klapper, L., & Love, I. (2011). The impact of the financial crisis on new firm registration. *Economics Letters*, *113*(1), 1–4. doi:10.1016/j.econlet.2011.05.048

Kurmann, A., Lalé, E., & Ta, L. (2021). *The Impact of Covid-19 On Small Business Dynamics and Employment: Real-Time Estimates with Homebase Data*. Cirano, 2021s-26.

MacKay, P., & Phillips, G. M. (2005). How does industry affect firm financial structure? *Review of Financial Studies*, *18*(4), 1433–1466. doi:10.1093/rfs/hhi032

Miao, J. (2005). Optimal capital structure and industry dynamics. *The Journal of Finance*, *60*(6), 2621–2659. doi:10.1111/j.1540-6261.2005.00812.x

MoreiraS. (2017). Firm Dynamics, Persistent Effects of Entry Conditions, and Business Cycles (October 1, 2016). SSRN. doi:10.2139/ssrn.3037178

Morgan, T., Anokhin, S., Ofstein, L., & Friske, W. (2020). SME response to major exogenous shocks: The bright and dark sides of business model pivoting. *International Small Business Journal*, *38*(5), 369–379. doi:10.1177/0266242620936590

Orhangazi, Ö., & Yeldan, A. E. (2021). The Re-making of the Turkish Crisis. *Development and Change*, *52*(3), 460–503. doi:10.1111/dech.12644

Phillips, G. M. (1995). Increased debt and industry product markets an empirical analysis. *Journal of Financial Economics*, *37*(2), 189–238. doi:10.1016/0304-405X(94)00785-Y

Reynolds, P. D., & Maki, W. R. (1990). *Business volatility and economic growth.* US Small Business Administration.

Simon, H. A., & Bonini, C. P. (1958). The size distribution of business firms. *The American Economic Review*, *48*(4), 607–617.

TOBB. (2021). *Company Establishment and Liquidation Statistics* [Database]. Available at: https://tobb.org.tr/BilgiErisimMudurlugu/Sayfalar/Eng/KurulanKapananSirketistatistikleri.php

Zorlu, F. (2020, March 11). *Turkey confirms first case of coronavirus.* Anatolian Agency. https://www.aa.com.tr/en/latest-on-coronavirus-outbreak/turkey-confirms-first-case-of-coronavirus/1761522

ADDITIONAL READING

Armington, C., & Acs, Z. J. (2002). The determinants of regional variation in new firm formation. *Regional Studies*, *36*(1), 33–45. doi:10.1080/00343400120099843

Audretsch, D. B., & Mahmood, T. (1995). New firm survival: New results using a hazard function. *The Review of Economics and Statistics*, *77*(1), 97–103. doi:10.2307/2109995

Coleman, S., & Robb, A. (2009). A comparison of new firm financing by gender: Evidence from the Kauffman Firm Survey data. *Small Business Economics*, *33*(4), 397–411. doi:10.100711187-009-9205-7

Dörr, J. O., Licht, G., & Murmann, S. (2021). Small firms and the COVID-19 insolvency gap. *Small Business Economics*, 1–31. doi:10.100711187-021-00514-4

Eaton, B. C., & Lipsey, R. G. (1980). Exit barriers are entry barriers: The durability of capital as a barrier to entry. *The Bell Journal of Economics*, *11*(2), 721–729. doi:10.2307/3003391

Geroski, P. A. (1995). What do we know about entry? *International Journal of Industrial Organization*, *13*(4), 421–440. doi:10.1016/0167-7187(95)00498-X

Kuckertz, A., & Brändle, L. (2021). Creative reconstruction: a structured literature review of the early empirical research on the COVID-19 crisis and entrepreneurship. *Management Review Quarterly*, 1-27. doi:10.1007/s11301-021-00221-0

Lee, S. Y., Florida, R., & Acs, Z. (2004). Creativity and entrepreneurship: A regional analysis of new firm formation. *Regional Studies*, *38*(8), 879–891. doi:10.1080/0034340042000280910

Luo, Y. (2001). Determinants of entry in an emerging economy: A multilevel approach. *Journal of Management Studies*, *38*(3), 443–472. doi:10.1111/1467-6486.00244

Rozeff, M. S., & Kinney, W. R. Jr. (1976). Capital market seasonality: The case of stock returns. *Journal of Financial Economics*, *3*(4), 379–402. doi:10.1016/0304-405X(76)90028-3

Thaler, R. H. (1987). Anomalies: The January effect. *The Journal of Economic Perspectives*, *1*(1), 197–201. doi:10.1257/jep.1.1.197

KEY TERMS AND DEFINITIONS

Consumer Price Index-Based Real Effective Exchange Rate: A calculation method of real effective exchange rate, based on a weighted average value of a currency against its major trade partners, adjusted for to the relative price changes of a similar product basket.

Corporation: A common type of business establishment of which owners are considered as shareholders, employing professional executives, and also has limited liability in accordance to its assets.

January Effect: A financial market phenomenon referring to the abnormally high returns during the first month of each year without a good reason.

Limited Liability Company: A popular type of business establishment of which equity is owned/provided by the partners and liable for its debts and obligations as its assets.

Nonemployer Firm: A business establishment lacking any paid employees.

APPENDIX

Figure 4. Distribution of monthly entry in micro, micro+, small and small+ size classes between January 2010 and June 2021

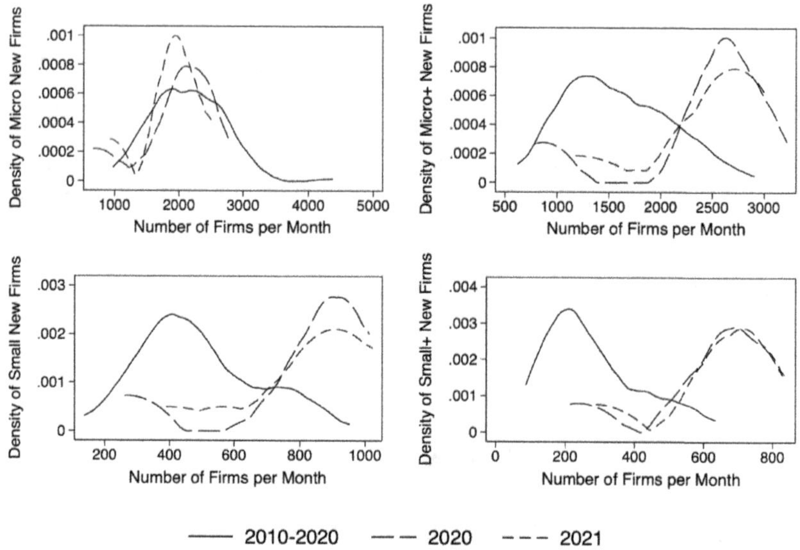

Figure 5. Distribution of monthly entry in medium, medium+, large and large+ size classes between January 2010 and June 2021

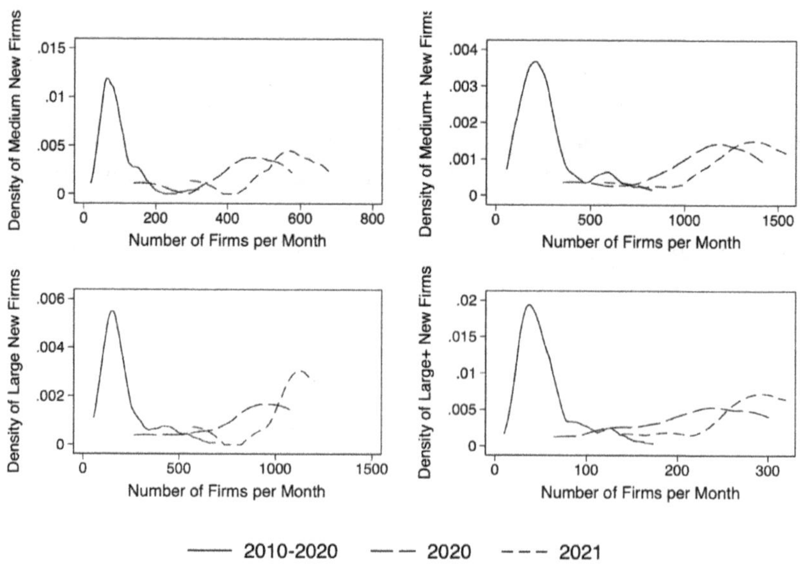

Figure 6. Distribution of monthly entry in giant size classes between January 2010 and June 2021

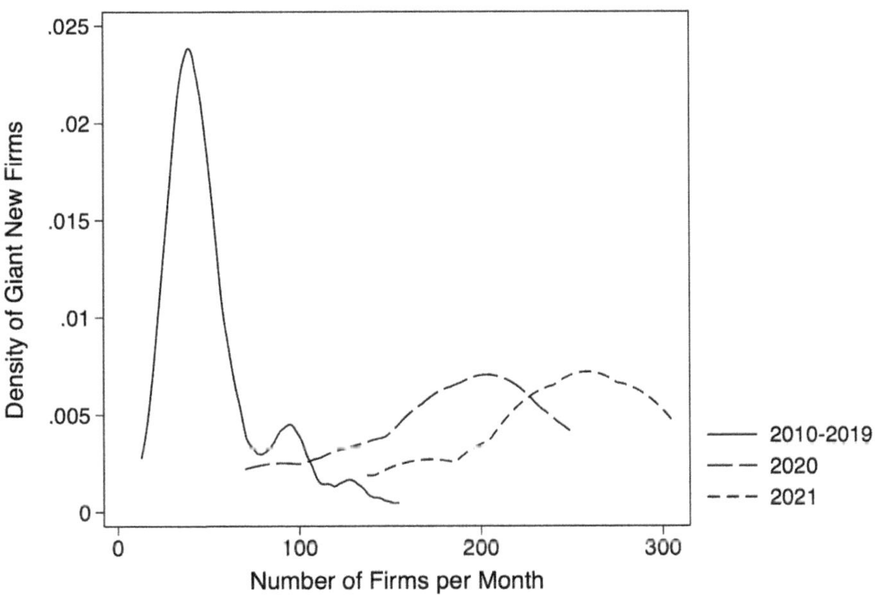

Conclusion

INTRODUCTION

This book illustrated the transformational effects of the COVID-19 pandemic, and a range of themes were discussed in this book. The content of these chapters was presented to generate new research that could provide additional answers to the economic effects of the COVID-19 pandemic. Some chapters were more technical and attempted to show that data as well as statistical methods can be used to analyze the specific research questions regarding the COVID-19 pandemic. The reader must remember that the COVID-19 pandemic is still ongoing, and we do not know precisely when this pandemic may end. To that end, we do not know the full impacts of the COVID-19 pandemic and what the post-pandemic world will look like.

ROLE OF UNCERTAINTY

The suddenness and enormity of the massive job losses and the severity of the economic contraction relative to the size of the mortality shock are unprecedented in March 2020. Given the nature of the COVID-19 pandemic and the continuing nature of the pandemic, we can see why it has generated such an extraordinary surge in economic uncertainty as mentioned in a quote by Jerome Powell in the Introduction of this book. Barro et al. (2020) and Altig et al. (2020) echo the sentiment of Jerome Powell. They too also stressed the increasing uncertainty levels that make it difficult to determine when the pandemic will end, and no one knows for sure what the full impacts of this pandemic will have on economies (more on developed countries and less on developing countries). More importantly, on a policy level, the uncertainty surrounding these policy responses is important because policymakers are not sure if these economic impacts will be transitory or permanent and how these interventions would influence investment and consumption decisions as well as how long it will take for these economies to recover (Altig et al., 2020).

We should note that these continuing high levels of uncertainty do not bode well for a rapid economic recovery. This higher level of uncertainty generally makes it more difficult for firms and consumers because they will proceed in a cautious manner that inhibits investment, impacts hiring, and affects consumption by consumers for durable goods, among other reasons. The economics literature shows no dearth of the impacts of uncertainty on economic decisions. Examples include Bernanke (1983), Dixit and Pindyck (1994), Abel and Eberly (1996), and Bertola, Guiso and Pistafferi (2005). Also, Altig et al. (2020) stressed that given the scale of the impacts of COVID-19 on the economies, the recent job losses and the collapse in investment, a strong recovery would require a huge surge in new activity. Consequently, this surge in economic activity will outweigh the persisting uncertainty and enable a robust economic recovery to occur.

In a crisis such as the COVID-19 pandemic, policymakers and others would be interested in the real-time tracking concerning the perceptions of economic uncertainty that can be used to develop the appropriate policy to ameliorate the problems associated with uncertainty. Motivated by these observations, Baker et al. (2021) developed a measure to track the perception about economic uncertainty using messages transmitted on the social platform Twitter. Why do we use text messages from Twitter? The following three reasons explain the use of Twitter:

1. The volume of available tweets is enormous because 22 percent of US adults use Twitter.
2. It can capture the beliefs of a broad cross-section of those on social media rather than just the focus on experts and journalists.
3. They come with a precise timestamp that cannot be modified. This will enable the researchers to develop high frequency or related data.
4. The relevancy of each message can be captured by its number of retweets and would enable for a construction of weighted indices which can be used as an input to the index.

Their results show the time-series correlation between the monthly Twitter Economic Uncertainty (TEU-USA) and the Economic Policy Uncertainty (EPU-USA)[1] measures is 0.73, which is rather high. This correlation means that those on Twitter and journalists are rather similar in the assessment of uncertainty. Of course, the inputs used to estimate the uncertainty levels via the TEU-USA are enormous and change quickly. Baker et al. (2021) carefully present the details to develop the TEU-USA.

DATA AND STATISTICAL IMPLICATIONS OF COVID-19 ON FUTURE RESEARCH

COVID-19 resulted in social and economic disruptions, but it now presents challenges for the modeling of economic time series. For example, if we plot a macroeconomic time series, we will often see a spike or a massive decline around March 2020. The sudden drop or spike is so large that it would dwarf decades of data preceding it. Without any adjustment, the data would look odd or out of place. The historical data provides really no guidance to help understand the economic implications of global health shocks and to model these sudden changes in the data in statistical models. Foroni et al. (2020) corrects post-COVID-19 forecasts using information from the 2008 financial crisis. Primiceri and Tambalotti (2020) assume that COVID-19 is a one-period shock that functions differently from a standard shock in macroeconomics. They then model these dynamic responses using calibrated functions to trace out the impacts of COVID-19. Other researchers will incorporate information via priors which can be tricky in itself. Knowing what the priors should be is not an easy task. Just ask any Bayesian statistician, and they can tell you the difficulties to estimate the priors. As an example, Huber et al. (2020) estimate an additive regression tree to approximate these priors and use these priors to deal with the extreme values that exist in the data as a result of the COVID-19 pandemic. These methods, which appear to be robust, are early approaches to statistically model the effects of the COVID-19. Now the question becomes, will these methods work in the long-term? Nobody knows for sure at this point.

Ng (2021) considers an approach not used by others. Specifically, Ng (2021) uses a starting point that COVID-19 is not an economic shock but just a persistent health event that provides major economic impacts. In other words, the variations that exist in economic data after COVID-19 are large not because of changes in distribution of variables already in the economic model but because the economic data are no longer driven purely by these economic shocks. The latter is tedious to model in order to obtain reasonable forecasts and statistical results. Consequently, Ng (2021) knew of these complexities and used COVID-19 indicators as controls in regressions to "decovid" the data so the economic impacts can be identified. Ng (2021) used the COVID-19 indicators as explored in the paper to incorporate additional information relevant for an economic scenario that would enable to the impacts of COVID-19 to be carefully told by the data. The measures of COVID-19 indicators that are incorporated into the models by Ng (2021) are hospitalization (H), positive cases (P), and deaths (D).

CONCLUSION

The challenge of this book is that COVID-19 pandemic is still ongoing, and we do not know when the COVID-19 pandemic will end. Likewise, we do not know what the implications will be. Uncertainty continues to be a problem and provides some skepticism to the consumers and businesses. The challenge for the end of the COVID-19 pandemic is to overcome the high level of uncertainty, and this is the major challenge for most economies. There are unique ways to measure uncertainty in real time that serve as impetus for the crafting of the appropriate policies to ameliorate uncertainty (see Baker et al. (2021)). In addition to the uncertainty problem, there are data issues that could distort statistical analysis. There are several suggested approaches that normally treat COVID-19 as standard economic shock, but the effectiveness of these statistical approaches is uncertain. Ng (2021) suggests that COVID-19 could be treated as a health shock rather than an economic shock. The new twist is to treat the COVID-19 as a health shock rather than a standard economic shock would allow greater clarity to examine the true impacts of the statistical impacts of the COVID-19. However, the approach is rather new. It does offer promising assessment of the economic impacts that could lead to greater clarity of these impacts and how to analyze such data. In the end, we will be examining the full implications of COVID-19 for many years to come.

REFERENCES

Abel, A., & Eberly, J. (1996). Optimal investment with costly reversibility. *The Review of Economic Studies*, *63*(4), 581–593. doi:10.2307/2297794

Altig, D., Baker, S., Barrero, J. M., Bloom, N., Bunn, P., Chen, S., Davis, S. J., Leather, J., Meyer, B., Mihaylov, E., Mizen, P., Parker, N., Renault, T., Smietanka, P., & Thwaites, G. (2020). Economic uncertainty before and during the COVID-19 pandemic. *Journal of Public Economics*, *191*, 104274. doi:10.1016/j.jpubeco.2020.104274 PMID:32921841

Baker, S. R., Bloom, N., & Davis, S. J. (2016). Measuring economic policy uncertainty. *The Quarterly Journal of Economics*, *131*(4), 1593–1636. doi:10.1093/qje/qjw024

Baker, S. R., Bloom, N., Davis, S. J., & Renault, T. (2021). *Twitter-Derived Measures of Economic Uncertainty*. Academic Press.

Barro, R. J., Ursua, J. F., & Weng, J. (2020). *The Coronavirus and the Great Influenza Pandemic: Lessons from the 'Spanish Flu' for the Coronavirus's Potential Effects on Mortality and Economic Activity*. NBER Working Paper 26866.

Bernanke, B. (1983). Irreversibility, uncertainty, and cyclical investment. *The Quarterly Journal of Economics*, *98*(1), 85–106. doi:10.2307/1885568

Bertola, G., Guiso, L., & Pistaferri, L. (2005). Uncertainty and consumer durables adjustment. *The Review of Economic Studies*, *72*(4), 973–1007. doi:10.1111/0034-6527.00358

Dixit, A., & Pindyck, R. (1994). *Investment under uncertainty*. Princeton University Press. doi:10.1515/9781400830176

Foroni, C., Marcellino, M., & Stevanovic, D. (2020). *Forecasting the Covid-19 Recession and Recovery: Lessons from the Financial Crisis*. Unpublished Manuscript.

Huber, F., Koop, G., Onorante, L., Mfarrhofer, M., & Schreiner, J. (2020). Nowcasting in a Pandemic Using Non-Parametric Mixed Frequency VAR. *Journal of Econometrics*. Advance online publication. doi:10.1016/j.jeconom.2020.11.006

Ng, S. (2021). *Modeling Macroeconomic Variations after Covid-19*. NBER Working Paper No. 29060.

Primiceri, G., & Tambalotti, A. (2020). *Macroeconomic Forecasting the Time of COVID-19*. Northwestern University.

ENDNOTE

1 This is a newspaper-based version (EPU-USA) of the measurement of uncertainty. See Baker, Bloom and Davis (2016) for the development of the EPU-USA approach.

Compilation of References

Aarts, E., Fleuren, H., Sitskoorn, M., & Wilthagen, T. (2021). *The New Common: How the COVID-19 Pandemic is Transforming Society*. Springer. doi:10.1007/978-3-030-65355-2

Abel, A., & Eberly, J. (1996). Optimal investment with costly reversibility. *The Review of Economic Studies*, *63*(4), 581–593. doi:10.2307/2297794

Acemoglu, D., Akcigit, U., Alp, H., Bloom, N., & Kerr, W. (2018). Innovation, reallocation, and growth. *The American Economic Review*, *108*(11), 3450–3491. doi:10.1257/aer.20130470

Adamczyk, A. (2020, August 28). *It's been a month since the extra $600 per week in enhanced unemployment benefits expired. Here's where things stand now.* Retrieved January 1, 2021, from https://www.cnbc.com/2020/08/28/its-been-a-month-since-enhanced-unemployment-benefits-ended.html

Adegboye, F. S. (2020). Food prices in Nigeria have shot through the roof. But is the pandemic to blame? *The Conservation*. https://theconservation.com/food-prices-in

Africa News. (2020). *Africa COVID-19 stats: 874, 036cases; 18,498 deaths; 524, 577 recoveries*. https://www.africanews.com

Ågerfalk, P. J., Conboy, K., & Myers, M. D. (2020). *Information systems in the age of pandemics: COVID-19 and beyond*. Academic Press.

Aidi, W., Fatai, R., & Karingi, S. (2020). COVID-19 and migrant remittances: Supporting this essential lifeline under threat. *Brookings: Africa in Focus*. https://www.brookings.edu/blog/africa-in-focus/2020/10/26/COVID-19-and-migrnt-remittances-supporting-this-essential-lifeline-under-thereat

Akat, M., & Karanta, K. (2020). Psychological effects of COVID-19 pandemic on society and its reflections on education. *Turkish Studies*, *15*(14), 1–13. https://dx.do.org/10.7827/TurskishTudies.44336

Aktan, S. (2020). Tarihteki en ölümcül salgın hastalıklar neden ortaya çıktı ve nasıl sona erdi? *Euornews*. https://tr.euronews.com/2020/05/12/tarihteki-en-olumcul-salginlar-hangileriydi-neden-olustular-ve-nasil-sona-erdiler

Akter, S., Michael, K., Uddin, M. R., McCarthy, G., & Rahman, M. (2020). Transforming business using digital innovations: The application of AI, blockchain, cloud and data analytics. *Annals of Operations Research*, 1–33. doi:10.100710479-020-03620-w

Alam, M. N., Alam, M. S., & Chavali, K. (2020). Stock Market Response during COVID-19 Lockdown Period in India: An Event Study. *The Journal of Asian Finance, Economics, and Business*, *7*(7), 131–137. doi:10.13106/jafeb.2020.vol7.no7.131

Al-Awadhi, A. M., Al-Saifi, K., Al-Awadhi, A., & Alhamadi, S. (2020). Death and contagious infectious diseases: Impact of the COVID-19 virus on stock market returns. *Journal of Behavioral and Experimental Finance*, *27*, 100326. doi:10.1016/j.jbef.2020.100326 PMID:32292707

All Africa. (2020). *Africa: Over 2milliom COVID-19 recoveries across the continent.* https://allafrica.com/stories/202012130022.html

Allen, G. (2020, November 11). *Floridians Vote To Increase State's Minimum Wage To $15 Per Hour.* Retrieved January 1, 2021, from https://www.npr.org/2020/11/11/933937204/floridians-vote-to-increase-states-minimum-wage-to-15-per-hour

Altig, D., Baker, S., Barrero, J. M., Bloom, N., Bunn, P., Chen, S., ... Mizen, P. (2020). Economic uncertainty before and during the COVID-19 pandemic. *Journal of Public Economics*, *191*, 104274. doi:10.1016/j.jpubeco.2020.104274 PMID:32921841

Andam, K., Edeh, H., Oboh, V., Pauw, K., & Thurlow, J. (2020). Impacts of COVID-19 on food system and poverty in Nigeria. *Advances in Food Security and Sustainability*, *15*, 145–173. doi:10.1016/bs.af2s.2020.09.002

Anokhin, S., Chistyakova, N., Antonova, I., Spitsina, L., Wincent, J., & Parida, V. (2021). Flagship enterprises, entrepreneurial clusters, and business entry rates: Insights from the knowledge spillover theory of entrepreneurship. *Entrepreneurship and Regional Development*, *33*(3-4), 353–367. doi:10.1080/08985626.2021.1872942

Arga, K. Y. (2020). COVID-19 and the Futures of Machine Learning. *OMICS: A Journal of Integrative Biology*, *24*(9), 512–514. doi:10.1089/omi.2020.0093 PMID:32511048

Arndt, C., Davies, R., Babriel, S., Harris, L., Makrelove, K., Robinson, S., ... Anderson, L. (2020). COVID-19 lockdowns, income distribution, and food security: An analysis for South Africa. *Global Food Security*, *26*, 100410. doi:10.1016/j.gfs.2020.100410 PMID:32834955

Artiga, S., Corallo, B., & Pham, O. (2020, August 17). *Racial Disparities in COVID-19: Key Findings from Available Data and Analysis - Issue Brief.* https://www.kff.org/report-section/racial-disparities-in-COVID-19-key-findings-from-available-data-and-analysis-issue-brief/

Asadullah, M. N., & Bhula-or, R. (2020, April 28). *Why COVID-19 will worsen inequality in Thailand.* The Diplomat. https://thediplomat.com/2020/04/why-COVID-19-will-worsen-inequality-in-thailand/

Asian Development Bank. (2020, March). *The Economic Impact of the COVID-19 Outbreak on Developing Asia.* ADB briefs No. 128. doi:10.22617/BRF200096

Ataguba, J. E. (2020). COVID-19 pandemic, a war to be worn: Understanding its economic implications for Africa. *Applied Health Economics and Health Policy, 18*(3), 325–328. doi:10.100740258-020-00580-x PMID:32249362

Au, A. K., Ramasamy, B., & Yeung, M. C. (2005). The effects of SARS on the Hong Kong tourism industry: An empirical evaluation. *Asia Pacific Journal of Tourism Research, 10*(1), 85–95. doi:10.1080/1094166042000330236

Auxier, B., & Anderson, M. (2020, July 27). *As schools close due to the coronavirus, some U.S. students face a digital 'homework gap'.* https://www.pewresearch.org/fact-tank/2020/03/16/as-schools-close-due-to-the-coronavirus-some-u-s-students-face-a-digital-homework-gap/

Axtell, R. (2001). Zipf Distribution of U.S. Firm Sizes. *Science, 293*(5536), 1818–1820. doi:10.1126cience.1062081 PMID:11546870

Aydogan, Y. (2020). Evolution of the Firm Size Distribution in Turkey. *Oneri Journal, 15*(53). Advance online publication. doi:10.14783/maruoneri.676735

Aydogan, Y. (2021). Evolution of the Firm Structure in the Post-COVID-19 Era: A Roadmap for Turkish SMEs. In *Handbook of Research on Strategies and Interventions to Mitigate COVID-19 Impact on SMEs* (pp. 245–266). IGI Global. doi:10.4018/978-1-7998-7436-2.ch012

Ayres, J., & Raveendranathan, G. (2021). *Firm Entry and Exit during Recessions* (No. 11353). Inter-American Development Bank.

Bagus, P., Peña-Ramos, J. A., & Sánchez-Bayón, A. (2021). A. COVID-19 and the Political Economy of Mass Hysteria. *International Journal of Environmental Research and Public Health, 18*(4), 1376. doi:10.3390/ijerph18041376 PMID:33546144

Baker, S. R., Bloom, N., Davis, S. J., & Renault, T. (2021). *Twitter-Derived Measures of Economic Uncertainty.* Academic Press.

Baker, S. R., Bloom, N., & Davis, S. J. (2016). Measuring economic policy uncertainty. *The Quarterly Journal of Economics, 131*(4), 1593–1636. doi:10.1093/qje/qjw024

Bangkok Post Online Reporters. (2020, June 12). *Curfew ending, country remains closed to outsiders.* Bangkok Post. https://www.bangkokpost.com/thailand/general/1933820/curfew-ending-country-remains-closed-to-outsiders

Bank of Thailand. (2020). *BOT press release – Monetary policy report, June 2020.* Monetary Policy Strategy Division, Bank of Thailand.

Barbieri, P. N., & Bonini, B. (2021). Political orientation and adherence to social distancing during the COVID-19 pandemic in Italy. *Economics and Politics, 38*(2), 483–504. doi:10.100740888-021-00224-w

Barhate, B., Hirudayaraj, M., Gunasekara, N., Ibrahim, G., Alizadeh, A., & Abadi, M. (2021). Crisis Within a Crisis: Migrant Workers' Predicament During COVID-19 Lockdown and the Role of Non-profit Organizations in India. *Indian Journal of Human Development, 15*(1), 151–164.

Barkham, R. J. (1994). Entrepreneurial characteristics and the size of the new firm: A model and an econometric test. *Small Business Economics*, *6*(2), 117–125. doi:10.1007/BF01065184

Barro, R. J., Ursua, J. F., & Weng, J. (2020). *The Coronavirus and the Great Influenza Pandemic: Lessons from the 'Spanish Flu' for the Coronavirus's Potential Effects on Mortality and Economic Activity*. NBER Working Paper 26866.

Barua, Z., Barua, S., Aktar, S., Kabir, N., & Li, M. (2020). Effects of misinformation on COVID-19 individual responses and recommendations for resilience of disastrous information consequences of misinformation. *Progress in Disaster Science*, *8*, 100119. doi:10.1016/j.pdisas.2020.100119 PMID:34173443

Bashir, M. F., Benjiang, M. A., & Shahzad, L. (2020). A brief review of socio-economic and environmental impact of COVID-19. *Air Quality, Atmosphere & Health*, *13*(12), 1–7. doi:10.100711869-020-00894-8 PMID:32837620

Bassey, J. (2020). CACOVID launches 23bn food palliative for 1.7m households. *Business Day*. https://businessday.ng/coronavirus/article/cacovid-launches-n23bn-food-palliative-for-1-7m-households/

Bassier, I., Joala, R., & Vilankazi, T. (2020). South Africa needs better food price controls to shield poor people from COVID-19 fallout. *The Conservation*. https://theconservation.com/south-africa-needs-better-food-price-controls-to-shield-poor-people-from-COVID-19-fallout-143288

Basu, R. (2021). *Democracy and Public Policy in the post-COVID-19 World: Choices and Outcomes*. Routledge.

Bateman, N., & Ross, M. (2021, January 6). *Why has COVID-19 been especially harmful for working women?* Brookings. https://www.brookings.edu/essay/why-has-COVID-19-been-especially-harmful-for-working-women/

Bauer, L. (2020). *About 14 million children in the US are not getting enough to eat.* [web log]. https://www.brookings.edu/blog/up-front/2020/07/09/about-14-million-children-in-the-us-are-not-getting-enough-to-eat/

Baum, F., Freeman, T., Musolino, C., Abramovitz, M., De Ceukelaire, W., Flavel, J., Friel, S., Giugliani, C., Howden-Chapman, P., Huong, N. T., London, L., McKee, M., Popay, J., Serag, H., & Villar, E. (2021). Explaining COVID-19 performance: What factors might predict national responses? *BMJ (Clinical Research Ed.)*, *372*, n91. Advance online publication. doi:10.1136/bmj.n91 PMID:33509924

BBC. (2020). *Virüs bulaştırma katsayısı R0 nedir, nasıl hesaplanır?* bbc.com/turkce/haberler-dunya-52197229

Ben Achour, S. (2019). *How to value a life, statistically speaking*. Marketplace. https://www.marketplace.org/2019/03/20/how-value-life/popout/

Bergsen, P. (2020). A new political economy for Europe post-COVID-19. *European View.*, *19*(2), 131–137. doi:10.1177/1781685820968301

Bernanke, B. (1983). Irreversibility, uncertainty, and cyclical investment. *The Quarterly Journal of Economics*, *98*(1), 85–106. doi:10.2307/1885568

Bertola, G., Guiso, L., & Pistaferri, L. (2005). Uncertainty and consumer durables adjustment. *The Review of Economic Studies*, *72*(4), 973–1007. doi:10.1111/0034-6527.00358

Bhushan, R., & Ghosh, S. (2020). *AI: An opportunity amidst a crisis*. Accessed at: www.pwc.in/assets/pdfs/data-and-analytics/ai-an-opportunity-amidst-a-crisis.pdf

Bieszk-Stolorz, B., & Dmytrów, K. (2020). Survival analysis in assessment of influence of the SARS-CoV-2 pandemic on probability and intensity of decline in the value of stock indices. Research Square, 1-9. doi:10.21203/rs.3.rs-41942/v1

Blanke, J. (2020). Economic impact of COVID-19: Protecting Africa's food systems from farm to fork. *Brookings: Africa in Focus*. https://www.brookings.edu/blog/africa-in-focus/2020/06/economic-impact-of-COVID-19-protecting-africas-food-systems-from-farm-to-fork

Bloom, N., Fletcher, R. S., & Yeh, E. (2021). The impact of COVID-19 on US firms (No. w28314). National Bureau of Economic Research.

Blundell, R., Costa Diaz, M., Joyce, R., & Xu, X. (2020). COVID-19 and inequalities. *Fiscal Studies*, *41*(2), 291–319. doi:10.1111/1475 5890.12232 PMID:32836542

Board of Governors of the Federal Reserve System. (2020). *Report on the Economic Well-Being of U.S. Households in 2018-May 2019*. Board of Governors of the Federal Reserve System. https://www.federalreserve.gov/publications/2019-economic-well-being-of-us-households-in-2018-banking-and-credit.htm

Bodwig, C., Gentilini, U., Usman, Z., & Williams, P. (2020). *COVID-19 in Africa: How can social safety nets help mitigate the social and economic impacts?* World Bank Blogs. https://blogs.worldbank.org/african/COVID-19-africa-how-can-social-safety-nets-help-mitigate-social-and-economic-impacts

Boettke, P., & Powell, B. (2021). The political economy of the COVID-19 pandemic. *Southern Economic Journal*, *87*(4), 1090–1106. doi:10.1002oej.12488 PMID:33821055

Bontemps, T. (2020, December 21). *NBA commissioner Adam Silver says league won't 'jump the line' to get vaccines*. ESPN. https://www.espn.com/nba/story/_/id/30573657/nba-commissioner-adam-silver-says-league-jump-line-get-vaccines

Bontemps, T., & Lowe, Z. (2020, June 14). *NBA to test players and staff for coronavirus every other day before going to Orlando*. ESPN. https://www.espn.com/nba/story/_/id/29309011/nba-test-players-staff-coronavirus-every-other-day-going-orlando

Booth, A., & Stern, O. (2020). Social and economic impacts of COVID-19 across sub-Saharan Africa. *Kroll*. https://www.kroll.com/en/insights/publications/africa/social-economic-impact-COVID-19-sub-saharan-africa

Bragazzi, N. L., Dai, H., Damiani, G., Behzadifar, M., Martini, M., & Wu, J. (2020). How big data and artificial intelligence can help better manage the COVID-19 pandemic. *International Journal of Environmental Research and Public Health, 17*(9), 3176. doi:10.3390/ijerph17093176 PMID:32370204

Brands, H., & Gavin, F. J. (Eds.). (2020). *COVID-19 and World Order. The Future of Conflict, Competition, and Cooperation*. John Hopkins University Press.

Breman, J. (2020). The pandemic in India and its impact on footloose labour. *The Indian Journal of Labour Economics, 63*(4), 901–919.

Buheji, M. (2020). Psychological resilience and poor communities coping with COVID-19 pandemic. *International Journal of Psychology and Behavioral Sciences, 10*(4), 100–108. doi:10.5923/j.ijpbs.20201004.03

Bump, J. B., Baum, F., Sakornsin, M., Yates, R., & Hofman, K. (2021). Political economy of COVID-19: Extractive, regressive, competitive. *BMJ (Clinical Research Ed.)*, n73. Advance online publication. doi:10.1136/bmj.n73 PMID:33483317

Buonsenso, D., Cinicola, B., Rafaelli, F., Sollena, P., & Iodice, F. (2020). Social consequences of COVID-19 in a low resource setting in Sierra Leone, West Africa. *International Journal of Infectious Diseases, 97*, 23–26. doi:10.1016/j.ijid.2020.05.104 PMID:32497794

Bureau of Labor Statistics. (2021, January 8). *The Employment Situation-December 2020.* https://www.bls.gov/news.release/pdf/empsit.pdf

Bureau of Transportation Statistics. (2020, May 17). *Household, Individual, and Vehicle Characteristics*. Household, Individual, and Vehicle Characteristics | Bureau of Transportation Statistics. https://www.bts.gov/archive/publications/highlights_of_the_2001_national_household_travel_survey/section_01

Cabral, L., & Mata, J. (2003). On the evolution of the firm size distribution: Facts and theory. *The American Economic Review, 93*(4), 1075–1090. doi:10.1257/000282803769206205

Caitlin, S. B., & Ravallion, M. (2020). *Inequality and the coronavirus: Socioeconomic covariates of behavioral responses and viral outcomes across US counties*. NBER Working Paper 27549.

Calefati, J. (2020, April 21). Still going in to work in Pennsylvania amid the coronavirus? Chances are, you're a low-wage worker, data show. *The Philadelphia Enquirer*. https://www.inquirer.com/politics/essential-grocery-work-home-pennsylvania-true-false-20200421.html

Callaway, E. (2020, September). *The Coronavirus is Mutating - Does it Matter?* Nature. https://www.nature.com/articles/d41586-020-02544-6

Candelon, F., Duranton, S., De Bondt, M., Reichert, T., & Charme Di Carlo, R. (2020). *The Rise of the AI-Powered Company in the Postcrisis World.* Accessed at www.bcg.com/en-in/publications/2020/business-applications-artificial-intelligence-post-covid

Cao, W., Fang, Z., Hou, G., Han, M., Xu, A., Dong, J., & Zheng, J. (2020). The psychological impact of the COVID-19 epidemic on college students in China. *Psychiatry Research*, *287*, 112934. doi:10.1016/j.psychres.2020.112934 PMID:32229390

Carminati, D. (2020, September 23). *Thailand's Economy and the Pandemic: Facing Delays and Difficult Choices.* Global Risk Insights. https://globalriskinsights.com/2020/09/thailands-economy-and-the-pandemic-facing-delays-and-difficult-choices/

CBRT. (n.d.). *Indicative Exchange Rates* [Database]. Central Bank of Republic of Turkey. https://www.tcmb.gov.tr/kurlar/kurlar_en.html

Cefis, E., Ciccarelli, M., & Orsenigo, L. (2002). From Gibrat's legacy to Gibrat's fallacy. A Bayesian Approach to Study the Growth of Firms. *Working papers at the Hyman Minsky Department of Economic Studies*, 19.

Cennimo, D. J. (n.d.). Coronavirus disease 2019 (COVID-19). *Medscape.* https://emedicine.medscape.com/article/2500114-overview#

Centre for Strategic and International Studies. (2020). *Southeast Asia COVID-19 tracker.* CSIS. https://www.csis.org/programs/southeast-asia-program/southeast-asia-COVID-19-tracker-0

Chang, C. C., Lee, D. H., Lin, H. C., & Hsu, S. S. (2007). *The potential economic impact of avian flu pandemic on Taiwan* (No. 381-2016-22318). Academic Press.

Chang, C. L., McAleer, M., & Wang, Y. A. (2020). Herding behavior in energy stock markets during the Global Financial Crisis, SARS, and ongoing COVID-19. *Renewable & Sustainable Energy Reviews*, *134*, 110349. doi:10.1016/j.rser.2020.110349 PMID:34234619

Chan, K. H., Peiris, J. S., Lam, S. Y., Poon, L. L., Yuen, K. Y., & Seto, W. H. (2011). The effects of temperature and relative humidity on the viability of the SARS coronavirus. *Advances in Virology*, *2011*, 1–7. Advance online publication. doi:10.1155/2011/734690 PMID:22312351

Channel News Asia. (2020, August 6). *Tourism-reliant Thailand shelves "Travel Bubble" Plan as Asia COVID-19 cases rise.* https://www.channelnewsasia.com/news/asia/thailand-COVID-19-tourism-travel-bubble-asia-cases-12995474

Chen, C. D., Chen, C. C., Tang, W. W., & Huang, B. Y. (2009). The positive and negative impacts of the SARS outbreak: A case of the Taiwan industries. *Journal of Developing Areas*, *43*(1), 281–293. doi:10.1353/jda.0.0041

Chen, M. H. (2007). Macro and non-macro explanatory factors of Chinese hotel stock returns. *International Journal of Hospitality Management*, *26*(4), 991–1004. doi:10.1016/j.ijhm.2006.04.002 PMID:32287850

Chen, M. H., Jang, S. S., & Kim, W. G. (2007). The impact of the SARS outbreak on Taiwanese hotel stock performance: An event-study approach. *International Journal of Hospitality Management*, *26*(1), 200–212. doi:10.1016/j.ijhm.2005.11.004 PMID:32287849

Chen, M. P., Lee, C. C., Lin, Y. H., & Chen, W. Y. (2018). Did the SARS epidemic weaken the integration of Asian stock markets? Evidence from smooth time-varying cointegration analysis. Economic research-. *Ekonomska Istrazivanja, 31*(1), 908–926. doi:10.1080/1331677X.2018.1456354

Chevalier, J. A. (1995). Capital structure and product-market competition: Empirical evidence from the supermarket industry. *The American Economic Review*, 415–435. https://www.jstor.org/stable/2118181

Chiang Rai Times. (2020, September 11). *Thailand's real crisis is its contracting economy not COVID-19.* https://www.chiangraitimes.com/economy-business/thailands-real-crisis-is-its-contracting-economy-not-COVID-19/

Chilufya, C. (2020). *The African economy is "infected": The economic impacts of COVID-19 is worsening poverty in Africa.* Xavier. https://xavier.network/news/the-african-economy-is-infected-the-economic-impacts-of-COVID-19-is-worsening-poverty-in-africa

Choolayil, A. C., & Putran, L. (2021). The COVID-19 Pandemic and Human Dignity: the Case of Migrant Labourers in India. *Journal of Human Rights and Social Work*, 1-12.

Choudhari, R. (2020). COVID 19 pandemic: Mental health challenges of internal migrant workers of India. *Asian Journal of Psychiatry*, *54*, 102254.

Choudhury, P., Ghosh, R. K., & Sindhi, S. (2020). *COVID-19 Crisis, Pandemic Resilience and Linkages to Land: An Exposition*. Academic Press.

Control Risks. (2020). *Sub-Saharan Africa: COVID-19 mitigation measures*. https://www.controrisk.com/COVID-19-mitigation-measures-across-sub-saharan-africa

Convay, E. (2018). Gerçekten Bilmeniz Gereken 50 Ekonomi Fikri. İstanbul: Domingo Yayınevi.

Coombs, C., & Chopra, R. (2019). *Artificial intelligence and data analytics: Emerging opportunities and challenges in financial services*. Academic Press.

Cooper, I., Mondal, A., & Antonopoulos, C. G. (2020). A SIR model assumption for the spread of COVID-19 in different communities. *Chaos, Solitons, and Fractals*, *139*, 110057. doi:10.1016/j.chaos.2020.110057 PMID:32834610

Corbet, S., Hou, Y., Hu, Y., Lucey, B., & Oxley, L. (2020). Aye Corona! The contagion effects of being named Corona during the COVID-19 pandemic. *Finance Research Letters*, 101591. PMID:32837362

Cox, J., Greenwald, D. L., & Ludvigson, S. C. (2020). What Explains the COVID-19 Stock Market? (No. w27784). National Bureau of Economic Research.

Crowder, L. V., Lindley, W., Trulove, W., Ilboudo, J. P., & Castello, R. D. (1998). *Knowledge and information for food security in Africa: From traditional media to the internet.* Food and Agriculture Organisation. https://www.fao.org/3/w9290e/w9290e00.htm

Czech, K., Wielechowski, M., Kotyza, P., Benešová, I., & Laputková, A. (2020). Shaking Stability: COVID-19 Impact on the Visegrad Group Countries' Financial Markets. *Sustainability*, *12*(15), 6282. doi:10.3390u12156282

Das, A. K., & Gopalan, S. A. (2020). Epidemiology of COVID-19 and predictors of recovery in the Republic of Korea. *Pulmonary Medicine*, *2020*, 1–6. Advance online publication. doi:10.1155/2020/7291698 PMID:32774918

David, S. A., Inácio, C. M. C. Jr, & Machado, J. A. T. (2020). The recovery of global stock markets indices after impacts due to pandemics. *Research in International Business and Finance*, 101335. PMID:34173412

Davidsson, P., Lindmark, L., & Olofsson, C. (1994). New firm formation and regional development in Sweden. *Regional Studies*, *28*(4), 395–410. doi:10.1080/00343409412331348356

Day, B., Mckay, R. B., Ishman, M., & Chung, E. (2004). The new normal: Lessons learned from SARS for corporations operating in emerging markets. *Management Decision*, *42*(6), 794–806. doi:10.1108/00251740410542357

Day, M. Y., Cheng, T. K., & Li, J. G. (2018, August). AI robo-advisor with big data analytics for financial services. In *2018 IEEE/ACM International Conference on Advances in Social Networks Analysis and Mining (ASONAM)* (pp. 1027-1031). IEEE. 10.1109/ASONAM.2018.8508854

de Haan, A. (2020). Labour migrants during the pandemic: A comparative perspective. *The Indian Journal of Labour Economics*, *63*(4), 885–900.

De Meza, D., & Webb, D. C. (1987). Too much investment: A problem of asymmetric information. *The Quarterly Journal of Economics*, *102*(2), 281–292. doi:10.2307/1885064

Deaton, A. (2021). *COVID-19 and global income inequality*. NBER Working Paper.

Dechsupa, S., Assawakosri, S., Phakham, S., & Honsawek, S. (2020). Positive impact of lockdown on COVID-19 outbreak in Thailand. *Travel Medicine and Infectious Disease*, *36*(4), 101802. doi:10.1016/j.tmaid.2020.101802 PMID:32569811

Deloitte. (2020). *Reinventing FP&A for the pandemic and beyond*. Accessed at: https://www2.deloitte.com/us/en/pages/finance/articles/cfo-insights-reinventing-fpa-for-the-pandemic-and-beyond.html.html

Department of Disease Control, Thai Government. (2020, October 29). *COVID-19 situation reports*. https://covid19.ddc.moph.go.th/en

Dessalegn, B.-W. S., & Frissa, S. (2020). *Combating the mental health impact of COVID-19 in SubSaharan Africa*. ASSET. https://healthasset.org/combatting-the-mental-health-impact-of-COVID-19-sub-saharan-africa/

Ding, W., Levine, R., Lin, C., & Xie, W. (2020). *Corporate immunity to the COVID-19 pandemic (No. w27055)*. National Bureau of Economic Research. doi:10.3386/w27055

Dinlersoz, E., Dunne, T., Haltiwanger, J., & Penciakova, V. (2021, May). Business Formation: A Tale of Two Recessions. *AEA Papers and Proceedings. American Economic Association, 111*, 253–257. doi:10.1257/pandp.20211055

Dixit, A. (1989). Entry and exit decisions under uncertainty. *Journal of Political Economy, 97*(3), 620–638. doi:10.1086/261619

Dixit, A., & Pindyck, R. (1994). *Investment under uncertainty*. Princeton University Press. doi:10.1515/9781400830176

Dodo, M. K. (2002). *Understanding Africa's food security challenges*. doi:10.5772/intechopen.91773

Doyle, O. (2020). *COVID-19: Exacerbating Educational Inequalities?* UCD Geary Institute for Public Policy.

Duangdee, V. (2020, October 6). *"Golden week" ghost town: Thailand's Pattaya party zone struggles with no Chinese tourists*. South China Morning Post. https://www.scmp.com/week-asia/economics/article/3104289/golden-week-ghost-town-thailands-pattaya-party-zone-struggles

Dubner, S. (2016, August 8). *Who Decides How Much a Life Is Worth? (Ep. 344)*. Freakonomics. https://freakonomics.com/podcast/kenneth-feinberg/

ECDC. (2020). *COVID-19 situation update worldwide as of 12 December 2020*. European Centre for Disease Prevention and Control. https://www.ecdc.europea.eu/en/gographical-distribution-2019-ncocov-cases

English, K. (2020, April). *Chaos at Ministry as protesters demand 5,000 Bhat cash relief.* Khaosod English. https://www.khaosodenglish.com/politics/2020/04/14/chaos-at-ministry-as-protesters-demand-5000-baht-cash-relief/#search/project-syndicate.org/_blank

Eribo, S. (2020). *In Nigeria, philanthropy's COVID-19 response raises questions*. Alliance for Philanthropy and Social Investment Worldwide. https://www.alliancemagazine.org/blog/nigeria-philantropy-COVID-19-response-raises-questions/

Estrin, S., & Prevezer, M. (2010). A survey on institutions and new firm entry: How and why do entry rates differ in emerging markets? *Economic Systems, 34*(3), 289–308. doi:10.1016/j.ecosys.2010.01.003

Evans, D. S., & Jovanovic, B. (1989). An estimated model of entrepreneurial choice under liquidity constraints. *Journal of Political Economy, 97*(4), 808–827. doi:10.1086/261629

FactCheck.org. (2020, December 22). *A Guide to Our Coronavirus Coverage*. https://www.factcheck.org/a-guide-to-our-coronavirus-coverage/

FAO. (2020). Africa: Regional overview of food security and nutrition. Food and Agriculture Organisation.

Feinberg, K. (2008, May 25). *What Is the Value of a Human Life?* NPR. https://www.npr.org/templates/story/story.php?storyId=90760725

Fisher, J., Languilaire, J.-C., Lawthom, R., Nieuwenhuis, R., Petts, R. J., Runswick-Cole, K., & Yerkes, M. A. (2020). Community, work, and family in times of COVID-19. *Community Work & Family*, *23*(3), 247–252. Advance online publication. doi:10.1080/13668803.2020.1756568

Fitch Solutions. (2020). *Thailand tourism report: Includes 5-year forecasts to 2024.* Fitch Solutions Group Limited.

Fleurbaey, M. (2020). *Essay: Should We Save Lives—or Save the Economy?* Princeton University. https://paw.princeton.edu/article/essay-should-we-save-lives-or-save-economy

Foroni, C., Marcellino, M., & Stevanovic, D. (2020). *Forecasting the Covid-19 Recession and Recovery: Lessons from the Financial Crisis.* Unpublished Manuscript.

Freed, M., Cubanski, J., Neuman, T., Kates, J., & Michau, J. (2020). *What Share of People Who Have Died of COVID-19 Are 65 and Older – and How Does It Vary by State?* Kaiser Family Foundation. https://www.kff.org/coronavirus-COVID-19/issue-brief/what-share-of-people-who-have-died-of-COVID-19-are-65-and-older-and-how-does-it-vary-by-state/

Fries, S., Miller, M., & Perraudin, W. (1997). Debt in industry equilibrium. *Review of Financial Studies*, *10*(1), 39–67. doi:10.1093/rfs/10.1.39

Frimpong, O. B., Bihuzo, R. M., & Commodore, R. (2020). *The COVID-19 pandemic in Africa: Impact, responses, and lessons from Ghana, the Democratic Republic of the Congo and Rwanda.* https://www.wilsoncenter.org/publication/COVID-19-afroica-impact-responses-and-lessons-ghana-democratic-republic-congo

Fritsch, M., Greve, M., & Wyrwich, M. (2021). The COVID-19 Pandemic and Entrepreneurship in Germany: First Observations and Interpretations. *Jena Economic Research Papers*, 7.

Fronstin, P., & Woodbury, S. (2020, October 7). *How Many Americans Have Lost Jobs with Employer Health Coverage During the Pandemic?* Commonwealth Fund. https://www.commonwealthfund.org/publications/issue-briefs/2020/oct/how-many-lost-jobs-employer-coverage-pandemic

Furceri, D., Loungani, P., Ostry, J. D., & Pizzuto, P. (2020). Will COVID-19 affect inequality? Evidence from past pandemics. *Covid Economics: Vetted and Real-Time Papers*, (12), 138–157.

Galvao, J. (2020). COVID-19: The deadly threat of misinformation. *The Lancet. Infectious Diseases*. Advance online publication. doi:10.1016/S1473 3099(20)30721-0 PMID:33031753

Garcia, C., & Smith, S. V. (2020, September 8). *Egg Prices Skyrocket During The Pandemic.* NPR. https://www.npr.org/2020/09/08/910788715/egg-prices-skyrocket-during-the-pandemic

Gerszon Mahler, D., Yonzan, N., Lakner, C. R., Castaneda Aguilar, A., & Wu, H. (2021). *Updated Estimates of the Impact of COVID-19 on Global Poverty: Turning the Corner on the Pandemic in 2021?* World Bank Blogs. Retrieved November 21, 2021 from, https://blogs.worldbank.org/opendata/updated-estimates-impact-covid-19-global-povertyturning-corner-pandemic-2021

Gibrat, R. (1931). *Les inégalites économiques*. Sirey.

Giordano, P. (2020). *Contagio*. Giulio Einaudi.

Glaesser, D., Kester, J., Paulos, H., Alizadeh, A., & Valentin, B. (2017). Global travel pattern: An overview. *Journal of Travel Medicine*, *24*(4). Advance online publication. doi:10.1093/jtm/tax007 PMID:28637267

Göktaş, A., Koker, N. E., & Alemdar, Y. M. (2008). How to manage reputation during crisis: An analysis of Turkish white meat sector during the avian influenza (bird flu) crisis. *Journal of Yaşar University*, *3*(12), 1760–1786.

Goldstein, D. (2020, June 10). Research Shows Students Falling Months Behind During Virus Disruptions. *The New York Times*. https://www.nytimes.com/2020/06/05/us/coronavirus-education-lost-learning.html

Gopalan, H. S., & Misra, A. (2020). COVID-19 pandemic and challenges for socio-economic issues, healthcare and National Health Programs in India. *Diabetes & Metabolic Syndrome*, *14*(5), 757–759.

Grasso, J. (2020, June 14). *NBA Players Will Test for COVID-19 'Every Other Day' Before Orlando*. Sports Illustrated Philadelphia 76ers News, Analysis and More. https://www.si.com/nba/76ers/news/nba-players-test-COVID-19-every-day-orlando

Griffith, R., Levell, P., & Stroud, R. (2020). The Impact of COVID-19 on Share Prices in the UK. *Fiscal Studies*, *41*(2), 363–369. doi:10.1111/1475-5890.12226

Grun, R., Semali, A., & Vandeninden, F. (2020). *The virus that spurred Burkina Faso and African nations to scale up its social safety nets*. World Bank Blogs. https://blogs.worldbank.org/nasikiliza/virus-spurred-burkina-faso-and-safrican-nations-scale-its-social-safety-nets

Günçavdı, Ö., Bleaney, M., & McKay, A. (1998). Financial liberalisation and private investment: Evidence from Turkey. *Journal of Development Economics*, *57*(2), 443–455. doi:10.1016/S0304-3878(98)00097-2

Guy, J. S. (2018). Beyond global modernity, global consciousness and global governmentality: The symmetrical anthropology of globalisation. *European Journal of Social Theory*, *19*(4), 451–467. doi:10.1177/1368431016655066

Haltiwanger, J. C. (2021). Entrepreneurship During the COVID-19 Pandemic: Evidence from the Business Formation Statistics (No. w28912). National Bureau of Economic Research.

Hanna, M., & Graham, K. A. (2020, August 18). *Philly-area private schools press ahead on in-person openings: 'Everybody's looking for the best option'*. https://www.inquirer.com. https://www.inquirer.com/education/pennsylvania-archdiocese-philadelphia-private-schools-reopening-20200816.html

Hasnain, M., Paşa, M. F., & Gani, I. (2020). Combined measures to control the COVID-19 pandemic in Wuhan, Hubei, China: A narrative review. *Journal of Biosafety and Biosecurity.*, *2*(2), 51–57. doi:10.1016/j.jobb.2020.10.001 PMID:33521592

Hendrix, C. S. (2021). *The Political Economy of Pandemic Preparedness and Effectiveness.* PIIE Working Paper.

Henke, N., Puri, A., & Saleh, T. (2020). *Accelerating analytics to navigate COVID-19 and the next normal.* Accessed at: https://www.mckinsey.com/business-functions/mckinsey-analytics/our-insights/accelerating-analytics-to-navigate-COVID-19-and-the-next-normal

Higuera, V. (2017). *How are diseases transmitted?* Healthline. https://www.healthline.com/health/disease-transmission

Hodrick, R. J., & Prescott, E. C. (1997). Postwar US business cycles: An empirical investigation. *Journal of Money, Credit and Banking*, *29*(1), 1–16. doi:10.2307/2953682

Horsley, S. (2020, May 26). *For Many, $600 Jobless Benefit Makes It Hard To Return To Work.* NPR. https://www.npr.org/2020/05/26/861906616/when-returning-to-your-job-means-a-cut-in-pay

HRW. (2020). Impact of COVID-19 on children's education in Africa. *The Human Rights Watch.* https://www.hrw.org/news/2020/08/26/impact-COVID-19-childrens-education-africa

Huber, F., Koop, G., Onorante, L., Mfarrhofer, M., & Schreiner, J. (2020). Nowcasting in a Pandemic Using Non-Parametric Mixed Frequency VAR. *Journal of Econometrics.* Advance online publication. doi:10.1016/j.jeconom.2020.11.006

Huddleston, T. (2019, October 22). *These are the highest paid players in the NBA right now.* CNBC. https://www.cnbc.com/2019/10/22/highest-paid-players-in-the-nba-right-now.html

Hung, J. (2020a, October 23). *A trickle of Chinese tourists return to Thailand, with hopes of more to come.* The Diplomat. https://thediplomat.com/2020/10/a-trickle-of-chinese-tourists-return-to-thailand-with-hopes-of-more-to-come/

Hung, J. (2020b, April 1). *Delivery people are risking their lives to keep Asia running. Here's what people are doing to say thank you.* The Diplomat. https://thediplomat.com/2020/04/delivery-people-are-risking-their-lives-to-keep-asia-running-heres-what-people-are-doing-to-say-thank-you/

Iacurci, G. (2020, August 3). *The $600 unemployment boost has ended. What's next?* CNBC. https://www.cnbc.com/2020/07/31/the-600-unemployment-boost-has-ended-whats-next.html

Ihekweazu, C., & Agogo, E. (2020). Africa's response to COVID-19. *BMC Medicine*, *18*(151), 151. Advance online publication. doi:10.118612916-020-01622-w PMID:32438912

ILO. (2020). *COVID-19 and the world of work* (6th ed.). ILO Monitor.

Inkster, B., O'Brien, R., Selby, E., Joshi, S., Subramanian, V., Kadaba, M., Schroeder, K., Godson, S., Comley, K., Vollmer, S. J., & Mateen, B. A. (2020). Digital health management during and beyond the COVID-19 pandemic: Opportunities, barriers, and recommendations. *JMIR Mental Health, 7*(7), e19246. doi:10.2196/19246 PMID:32484783

International Labour Organisation (ILO). (2021). *Triangle in ASEAN Quarterly Briefing Note.* https://www.ilo.org/wcmsp5/groups/public/---asia/---ro-bangkok/documents/genericdocument/wcms_735108.pdf

International Monetary Fund. (2020). *A Crisis Like No Other, An Uncertain Recovery.* World Economic Outlook Update. Retrieved November 21, 2021, from https://www.imf.org/en/Publications/WEO/Issues/2020/06/24/WEOUpdateJune2020

Iqbal, N., Fareed, Z., Shahzad, F., He, X., Shahzad, U., & Lina, M. (2020). Nexus between COVID-19, temperature and exchange rate in Wuhan City: New findings from Partial and Multiple Wavelet Coherence. *The Science of the Total Environment, 729*, 138916. doi:10.1016/j.scitotenv.2020.138916 PMID:32388129

Irby, L. T. (2020, July 21). *Here Is a Look at What a Good Credit Limit Is on a First Credit Card.* The Balance. https://www.thebalance.com/what-s-a-good-credit-limit-on-a-first-credit-card-960003

Ishida, T., Ishikawa, N., & Fukushige, M. (2010). Impact of BSE and bird flu on consumers' meat demand in Japan. *Applied Economics, 42*(1), 49–56. doi:10.1080/00036840701564392

Jagannathan, M. (2020, December 23). *How many people have to get vaccinated against COVID-19 to reach herd immunity? 'The faster we do it, the faster we get back to life.'* MarketWatch. https://www.marketwatch.com/story/how-many-people-have-to-get-vaccinated-against-COVID-19-to-reach-herd-immunity-the-faster-we-do-it-the-faster-we-get-back-to-life-11608740335

Jalan, J., & Sen, A. (2020). Containing a pandemic with public actions and public trust: The Kerala story. *Indian Economic Review, 55*(1), 105–124.

Janeway, C. A. Jr, Travers, P., Walkport, M., & Shlomchik, M. J. (2001). *Immunobiology* (5th ed.). Garland Science.

Jansenn, P. (2020, August 14). *Thailand's COVID success turns economic failure.* Asia Times. https://asiatimes.com/2020/08/thailands-covid-success-turns-economic-failure/

Jayachandran, S. (2020, December 29). Financial Rewards for College Students Could Help Curb the Pandemic. *The New York Times.* https://www.nytimes.com/2020/12/29/business/rewards-college-students-coronavirus.html

Jha, M. K., & Pankaj, A. K. (2020). Insecurity and fear travel as labour travels in the time of pandemic. *Borders of an Epidemic*, 56.

JonungL.RoegerW. (2006). The macroeconomic effects of a pandemic in Europe-A model-based assessment. Available at SSRN 920851. doi:10.2139/ssrn.920851

K. (2021, January 14). *Economic recovery: one step forward, several steps back.* Marketplace. https://www.marketplace.org/shows/marketplace/economic-recovery-one-step-forward-several-steps-back/

Kalyoncuoglu, Y. (2020, May 6). *Yükseköğrenimdeki öğrenci sayısı 8 milyonu buldu.* Anatolian Agency. https://www.aa.com.tr/tr/egitim/yuksekogrenimdeki-ogrenci-sayisi-8-milyonu-buldu/1830726

Kansiime, M. K., Tambo, J. A., Mugambi, I., Bundi, M., Kara, A., & Owuor, C. (2020). COVID-19 implications on household income and food security in Kenya and Uganda: Findings from a rapid assessment. *World Development, 137*, 105199. doi:10.1016/j.worlddev.2020.105199 PMID:32982018

Kaplan, S., Lefler, J., & Zilberman, D. (2021). The political economy of COVID-19. *Applied Economic Perspectives and Policy*, 1–12. doi:10.1002/aepp.13164 PMID:34230850

Karki, S. (2017). Effects of highly pathogenic avian influenza H5N1 outbreak in Nepal from financial and social perspectives: A case study. *Nepalese Veterinary Journal, 34*, 26–35. doi:10.3126/nvj.v34i0.22861

Kartal, M. T., Depren, Ö., & Depren, S. K. (2020). The determinants of main stock exchange index changes in emerging countries: Evidence from Turkey in COVID-19 pandemic age. *Quantitative Finance and Economics, 4*(4), 526–541. doi:10.3934/QFE.2020025

Kashen, J., Glynn, S. J., & Novello, A. (2020, October 30). *How COVID-19 Sent Women's Workforce Progress Backward.* Center for American Progress. https://www.americanprogress.org/article/covid-19-sent-womens-workforce-progress-backward/

Kayhan, M. (2020). İnsanlık Tarihinin Seyrini Değiştiren 11 Salgın Hastalık. *Arkeofili.* https://arkeofili.com/insanlik-tarihinin-seyrini-degistiren-11-salgin-hastalik/

Khanna, A. (2020). Impact of migration of labour force due to global COVID-19 pandemic with reference to India. *Journal of Health Management, 22*(2), 181–191.

Khoon, C. C. (2006). *Risk Perception and coping responses in a SARS outbreak in Malaysia* (Vol. 2006). World Scientific. doi:10.1142/9789812773395_0018

Kim, H. H.-S., & Katelyn Kim, H.-J. (2021). Income inequality, emotional anxiety, and self-rated health in times of the coronavirus pandemic: Evidence from a cross-national survey. *Research in Social Stratification and Mobility, 75*, 100640. Advance online publication. doi:10.1016/j.rssm.2021.100640 PMID:34385741

Klapper, L., & Love, I. (2011). The impact of the financial crisis on new firm registration. *Economics Letters, 113*(1), 1–4. doi:10.1016/j.econlet.2011.05.048

Kochhar, R. (2020, August 26). *Unemployment rose higher in three months of COVID-19 than it did in two years of the Great Recession.* Retrieved January 1, 2021, from https://www.pewresearch.org/fact-tank/2020/06/11/unemployment-rose-higher-in-three-months-of-COVID-19-than-it-did-in-two-years-of-the-great-recession/

Kontoangelos, K., Economou, M., & Papageorgiou, C. (2020). Mental health effects of COVID-19 pandemia: A review of clinical and psychological traits. *Psychological Investigation*, *17*(6), 491–505. doi:10.30773/pi.2020.0161 PMID:32570296

Krugman, P. (2020, June 01). *On the economics of not dying*. Retrieved January 1, 2021, from https://www.palmbeachpost.com/story/opinion/columns/more-voices/2020/06/01/paul-krugman-on-economics-of-not-dying/41744823/

Kumar, K., Mehra, A., Sahoo, S., Nehra, R., & Grover, S. (2020). The psychological impact of COVID-19 pandemic and lockdown on the migrant workers: A cross-sectional survey. *Asian Journal of Psychiatry*, *53*, 102252.

Kumar, P., Singh, S. S., Pandey, A. K., Singh, R. K., Srivastava, P. K., Kumar, M., ... Drews, M. (2021). Multi-level impacts of the COVID-19 lockdown on agricultural systems in India: The case of Uttar Pradesh. *Agricultural Systems*, *187*, 103027.

Kumar, S., & Choudhury, S. (2021). Migrant workers and human rights: A critical study on India's COVID-19 lockdown policy. *Social Sciences & Humanities Open*, *3*(1), 100130.

Kurmann, A., Lalé, E., & Ta, L. (2021). *The Impact of Covid-19 On Small Business Dynamics and Employment: Real-Time Estimates with Homebase Data*. Cirano, 2021s-26.

Kuy, S. R., Tsai, R., Bhatt, J., Chu, Q. D., Ghandi, P., Gupta, R., ... Correa, R. (2020). Focusing on vulnerable populations during COVID-19. Note to the Editor. *Academic Medicine*, *95*(11), e2–e3. Advance online publication. doi:10.1097/ACM.0000000000003571 PMID:32639264

Lahiri, S., & Sinha, M. (2021). A study of the socio-economic implications of the COVID-19 pandemic. *Australasian Accounting, Business and Finance Journal*, *15*(1), 51–69.

Latz, C. A., DeCarlo, C., Boitano, L., Png, C. Y. M., Patell, R., Conrad, M. F., Eagleton, M., & Dua, A. (2020). Blood type and outcomes in patients with COVID-19. *Annals of Hematology*, *99*(9), 1–6. doi:10.100700277-020-04169-1 PMID:32656591

Lederer, A., & Stolow, J. (2020, September 18). *Don't Rely on Student Contracts to Safeguard Your Campus. Student contracts won't do enough to encourage safe behaviors during the pandemic (opinion)*. https://www.insidehighered.com/views/2020/09/18/student-contracts-wont-do-enough-encourage-safe-behaviors-during-pandemic-opinion

Lee, J. W., & McKibbin, W. J. (2004). Globalization and disease: The case of SARS. *Asian Economic Papers*, *3*(1), 113–131. doi:10.1162/1535351041747932

Lee, J. W., & McKibbin, W. J. (2004, April). Estimating the global economic costs of SARS. In *Learning from SARS: preparing for the next disease outbreak: workshop summary* (pp. 92–109). National Academies Press.

Lele, U., Bansal, S., & Meenakshi, J. V. (2020). Health and nutrition of India's labour force and COVID-19 challenges. *Economic and Political Weekly*, *55*(21), 13.

Levine, A. (2020, December 21). *Let the ultra-rich and influential skip the line for COVID-19 vaccines? Hear me out.* STAT. https://www.statnews.com/2020/12/22/let-the-ultra-rich-and-influential-skip-the-line-for-COVID-19-vaccines-hear-me-out/

Lew, A. A. (2018). Why travel? – Travel, tourism and global consciousness. *Tourism Geographies*, *20*(4), 742–749. doi:10.1080/14616688.2018.1490343

Lilkert, D., Coman, I., Gregor, M., & Novelli, E. (Eds.). (2021). *Political Communication and COVID-19. Governance and Rhetoric in Times of Crisis.* Routledge. doi:10.4324/9781003120254

Lipscy, P. Y. (2020). *COVID-19 and the Politics of Crisis.* Cambridge University Press. doi:10.1017/S0020818320000375

Liu, H., Manzoor, A., Wang, C., Zhang, L., & Manzoor, Z. (2020). The COVID-19 outbreak and affected countries stock markets response. *International Journal of Environmental Research and Public Health*, *17*(8), 2800. doi:10.3390/ijerph17082800 PMID:32325710

Lobosco, K., & Luhby, T. (2020, December 28). *Here's what's in the second stimulus package.* CNN. https://www.cnn.com/2020/12/20/politics/second-covid-stimulus-package-details/index.html

Loewenstein, G., & Cryder, C. (2020, December 14). Why Paying People to Be Vaccinated Could Backfire. *The New York Times.* https://www.nytimes.com/2020/12/14/upshot/covid-vaccine-payment.html

Luhby, T. (2020, April 1). *Trump administration won't reopen Obamacare enrollment for uninsured.* CNN. https://www.cnn.com/2020/03/31/politics/affordable-care-act-obamacare-open-enrollment-trump/index.html

Lupton, D., & Willis, K. (Eds.). (2021). *The COVID-19 Crisis: Social Perspective.* Routledge. doi:10.4324/9781003111344

Lusome, R., & Bhagat, R. B. (2020). Migration in Northeast India: Inflows, outflows and reverse flows during pandemic. *The Indian Journal of Labour Economics*, *63*(4), 1125–1141.

MacKay, P., & Phillips, G. M. (2005). How does industry affect firm financial structure? *Review of Financial Studies*, *18*(4), 1433–1466. doi:10.1093/rfs/hhi032

Maclean, R., & Mark, S. (2020). 10 African countries have no ventilators: That's only part of the problem. *The New York Times.* https://www.nytimes.com/2020/04/18/world/africa/ africa-coronavirus-ventillators.html

Malali, A. B., & Gopalakrishnan, S. (2020). Application of Artificial Intelligence and Its Powered Technologies in the Indian Banking and Financial Industry: An Overview. *IOSR Journal Of Humanities And Social Science*, *25*(4), 55–60.

Mankiw, N. G. (2020, September 9). Pay People to Get Vaccinated. *The New York Times.* https://www.nytimes.com/2020/09/09/business/pay-people-vaccine-coronavirus.html

MarketLine. (2020). *Travel & tourism in Thailand.* MarketLine Industry Profile.

Marroquin, B., Vine, V., & Morgan, R. (2020). Mental health during the COVID-19 pandemic: Effects of stay-at-home policies, social distancing behaviours, and social resources. *Psychiatry Research, 293*, 113419. doi:10.1016/j.psychres.2020.113419 PMID:32861098

Mazur, M., Dang, M., & Vega, M. (2020). COVID-19 and the march 2020 stock market crash. Evidence from S&P1500. *Finance Research Letters*, 101690. PMID:32837377

McKibbin, W. J., & Fernando, R. (2020). *The global macroeconomic impacts of COVID-19: Seven scenarios.* Centre for Applied Macroeconomic Analysis, CAMA Working Paper, 1-45.

McKinsey. (2021). *The coronavirus effect on global economic sentiment.* Retrieved November 21, 2021, from https://www.mckinsey.com/business-functions/strategy-and-corporate-finance/our-insights/the-coronavirus-effect-on-global-economic-sentiment

Meechukhun, N. (2020, October 26). *Thailand's centre for COVID-19 situation administration agrees to extend emergency decree nationwide for another month.* The Pattaya News. https://thepattayanews.com/2020/10/26/thailands-center-for-COVID-19-situation-administration-agrees-to-extend-emergency-decree-nationwide-for-another-month/

Menard, J., Thompson, J., English, B. C., Hughes, D., Griffith, A. P., Smith, A., & Jensen, K. (2020). Economic Impacts from an On-Farm Highly Pathogenic Avian Influenza Event in Tennessee. *The Review of Regional Studies, 50*(2), 282–300. doi:10.52324/001c.14168

Mendenhall, E., & Kim, A. W. (2020). People in Soweto told us about their fears in the first weeks of South Africa's lockdown. *The Conservation.* https://theconservation.com/people-in-soweto-told-us-about-their-fears-in-the-first-weeks- of-south-africa-lockdown-142325

Miao, J. (2005). Optimal capital structure and industry dynamics. *The Journal of Finance, 60*(6), 2621–2659. doi:10.1111/j.1540-6261.2005.00812.x

Michler, J., & Kilic, T. (2020). *Socioeconomic impacts of COVID-19 in four African countries: Watch the event recording*. The World Bank. https://www.worldbank.org/en/programs/ lsms/brief/socioeconomic-impacts-of-COVID-19-in-four-african-countries-watch-the-event-recording

Michon, K. (2013, October 3). *Damages in a Wrongful Death Lawsuit.* www.nolo.com. https://www.nolo.com/legal-encyclopedia/wrongful-death-claims-overview-30141-2.html

Miguel, E. (2021). The economics of the COVID-19 pandemic in poor countries. *Annual Review of Economics*, 14.

Miller, C. C. (2020, August 4). In the Same Towns, Private Schools Are Reopening While Public Schools Are Not. *The New York Times.* https://www.nytimes.com/2020/07/16/upshot/coronavirus-school-reopening-private-public-gap.html

Mishra, D. K. (2021). Migrant Labour during the Pandemic: A Political Economy Perspective. *The Indian Economic Journal.*

Mitra, A., & Singh, J. (2020). COVID-19 Pandemic and Livelihood Loss: Variations in Unemployment Outcomes and Lessons for Future. Institute of Economic Growth, University Enclave, University of Delhi.

Miyamura, S. (2021). Turbulence ahead: Labour and struggles in times of the COVID-19 pandemic in India. *Canadian Journal of Development Studies*, *42*(1-2), 165–177.

Moein, S., Nickaeen, N., Roointan, A., Borhani, N., Heidary, Z., Javanmard, S. H., Ghaisari, J., & Gheisari, Y. (2021). Inefficiency of SIR models in forecasting COVID-19 epidemic: A case study of Isfahan. *Scientific Reports*, *11*(1), 4725. doi:10.103841598-021-84055-6 PMID:33633275

Mohan, M., & Mishra, S. (2021). India's Response to the COVID-19 Pandemic: A Frontal Assault on the "Historically Dispossessed." *International Journal of Health Services*, *51*(1), 107–114.

Mookerjee, D., Chakravarty, S., Roy, S., Tagat, A., & Mukherjee, S. (2021). A Culture-Centered Approach to Experiences of the Coronavirus Pandemic Lockdown Among Internal Migrants in India. *The American Behavioral Scientist*.

MoreiraS. (2017). Firm Dynamics, Persistent Effects of Entry Conditions, and Business Cycles (October 1, 2016). SSRN. doi:10.2139/ssrn.3037178

Morgan, T., Anokhin, S., Ofstein, L., & Friske, W. (2020). SME response to major exogenous shocks: The bright and dark sides of business model pivoting. *International Small Business Journal*, *38*(5), 369–379. doi:10.1177/0266242620936590

Moseley, W. G., & Battersby, J. (2020). The vulnerability and resilience of African food systems, food security, and nutrition in the context of the COVID-19 pandemic. *African Studies Review*, *63*(3), 449–461. doi:10.1017/asr.2020.72

Mviena, J. L., Fanne, M., Gondo, R., Mwamelo, A., Esso, L., Epée, E., Mballa, G. A. E., & Boum, Y. (2020). How mental health care is changing Cameroon because of the COVID-19 pandemic. *The Lancet. Psychiatry*, *7*(10), E62–E63. doi:10.1016/S2215-0366(20)30390-4 PMID:32949524

Nania, R. (2019, October 22). *Affordable Care Act Costs, Plans for 2020 Announced*. AARP. https://www.aarp.org/health/health-insurance/info-2019/aca-plans-premium-rates-announced.html

Narayan, P. K., Phan, D. H. B., & Liu, G. (2020). COVID-19 lockdowns, stimulus packages, travel bans, and stock returns. *Finance Research Letters*, 101732. PMID:32843886

Naseem, M., Akhund, R., Arshad, H., & Ibrahim, M. T. (2020). Exploring the Potential of Artificial Intelligence and Machine Learning to Combat COVID-19 and Existing Opportunities for LMIC: A Scoping Review. *Journal of Primary Care & Community Health*, *11*. doi:10.1177/2150132720963634 PMID:32996368

Neergaard, L., & Fingerhut, H. (2020, December 9). *AP-NORC poll: Only half in US want shots as vaccine nears*. AP News. https://apnews.com/article/ap-norc-poll-us-half-want-vaccine-shots-4d98dbfc0a64d60d52ac84c3065dac55

Nelson, L., & Lau, M. (2020, December 18). The wealthy scramble for COVID-19 vaccines: 'If I donate $25,000 ... would that help me?' *Los Angeles Times.* https://www.latimes.com/california/story/2020-12-18/wealthy-patients-scramble-COVID-19-vaccine

Ng, S. (2021). *Modeling Macroeconomic Variations after Covid-19.* NBER Working Paper No. 29060.

Nguyen, T. (2020, April 3). Toilet paper is disappearing from shelves - again. *Vox.* Retrieved January 15, 2021, from https://www.vox.com/the-goods/2020/4/3/21206942/toilet-paper-coronavirus-shortage-supply-chain

Nicola, M., Alsafi, Z., Sohrabi, C., Kerwan, A., Al-Jabir, A., Iosifidis, C., Agha, M., & Agha, R. (2020). The socio-economic implications of the coronavirus pandemic (COVID-19): A review. *International Journal of Surgery*, *78*, 185–193. doi:10.1016/j.ijsu.2020.04.018 PMID:32305533

OECD. (2017). *The Pursuit of Gender Equality: An Uphill Battle.* OECD Publishing.

OECD. (2020a). Learning remotely when schools close: How well are students and schools prepared? Insights from PISA. In *Tackling Coronavirus (COVID-19): Contributing to a Global Effort.* OECD.

OECD. (2020b). The impact of COVID-19 on student equity and inclusion: supporting vulnerable students during school closures and school re-openings. In *Tackling Coronavirus (COVID-19): Contributing to a Global Effort.* OECD.

OECD. (2020c). *How's Life? 2020: Measuring Well-being*. OECD Publishing.

OECD. (2021). *Education at a Glance 2020: OECD Indicators*. OECD Publishing.

Omigbodun, O., & Abdulmalik, J. (2020). The pandemic will affect the mental health of these groups. *African Arguments.* https://africanarguments.org/2020/04/the- pandemic-will-affect-the-mental-health-of-these-groups/

Open Development Thailand. (2020, May 16). *COVID-19 in Thailand.* https://thailand.opendevelopmentmekong.net/topics/pandemics-COVID-19/

Organisation for Economic Co-operation and Development (OECD). (2020). *OECD Economic Surveys Economic Assessment Thailand.* https://www.oecd.org/countries/thailand/oecd economic-surveys-thailand-2020-ad2e50fa-en.htm

Orhangazi, Ö., & Yeldan, A. E. (2021). The Re-making of the Turkish Crisis. *Development and Change*, *52*(3), 460–503. doi:10.1111/dech.12644

Owings, L. (2020). Africa 'not ready' for COVID-19 mental health issues. *Sci. Dev. Net.* https://www.scidev.nt/sub-saharan-africa/news/afric-not-ready-for-COVID-19-mental-health-issue

Ozili, P. K. (2020). COVID-19 in Africa: socioeconomic impact, policy response and opportunities. *Policy Response and Opportunities.*

Padhee, A. K., & Pingali, P. (2020). *Lessons from a pandemic to repurpose India's agricultural policy*. Nature India.

Palomino, J. C., Rodriguez, J. G., & Sebastian, R. (2020). Wage inequality and poverty effects of lockdown and social distancing in Europe. *European Economic Review*, 129. PMID:32836323

Pal, S. C., Saha, A., Chowdhuri, I., Roy, P., Chakrabortty, R., & Shit, M. (2021). Threats of unplanned movement of migrant workers for sudden spurt of COVID-19 pandemic in India. *Cities (London, England)*, *109*, 103035.

Papageorge, N. W., Zahn, M. V., Belot, M., van den Broek-Altenburg, E., Choi, S., Jamison, J. C., & Tripodi, E. (2021). *Socio-demographic factors associated with self-protecting behavior during the COVID-19 pandemic*. NBER Working Paper 27378.

PayScale. (2021). *The State of the Gender Pay Gap in 2021*. PayScale.

PHAC. (n.d.). *Healthy living*. Government of Canada. https://www.canada.ca/en/public-health/services/health-promotion/healthy-living-html#

Phillips, G. M. (1995). Increased debt and industry product markets an empirical analysis. *Journal of Financial Economics*, *37*(2), 189–238. doi:10.1016/0304-405X(94)00785-Y

Phiri, M. Z. (2021). *South Africa's COVID-19 Responses: Unmaking the Political Economy of Health Inequalities. ORF Issue Brief 445* . Observer Research Foundation.

Piper, Y. (2021, January 6). Pa. lags nation in people tested per day, is nowhere near level needed to suppress the virus. *Pittsburgh Post-Gazaette*. Retrieved January 15, 2021, from https://www.post-gazette.com/news/health/2021/01/06/Pennsylvania-lags-nation-people-tested-per-day-COVID-19-falls-short-suppression-testing-pandemic-spread/stories/202101060116

Polizzi, C., & Lynn, S. J. (2020). Your coping and resilience strategies might need to shift as the COVID-19 crisis continues. *The Conservation*. https://theconservation.com/your-coping-and-resilience-strategies-might-need-to-shift-as-the-COVID-19-crisis-continues-140507

Porter, E. (2020, December 14). What Happens to the Unemployed When the Checks Run Out? *The New York Times*. https://www.nytimes.com/2020/12/14/business/economy/unemployment-benefits-economy.html

Posner, E.A., & Sunstei, C.R. (2005, Spring). Dollars and Death. *The University of Chicago Law Review. University of Chicago. Law School*, 537.

Primiceri, G., & Tambalotti, A. (2020). *Macroeconomic Forecasting the Time of COVID-19*. Northwestern University.

Qian, Y., & Fan, W. (2020). Who loses income during the COVID-19 outbreak? Evidence from China. *Research in Social Stratification and Mobility*, *68*, 100522. Advance online publication. doi:10.1016/j.rssm.2020.100522

Quealy, K. (2020, May 15). The Richest Neighborhoods Emptied Out Most as Coronavirus Hit New York City. *The New York Times*. https://www.nytimes.com/interactive/2020/05/15/upshot/who-left-new-york-coronavirus.html

Quinn, D. M., & Polikoff, M. (2017, September 14). *Summer learning loss: What is it, and what can we do about it?* Brookings. https://www.brookings.edu/research/summer-learning-loss-what-is-it-and-what-can-we-do-about-it/

Rajan, S. I., Sivakumar, P., & Srinivasan, A. (2020). The COVID-19 pandemic and internal labour migration in India: A 'crisis of mobility'. *The Indian Journal of Labour Economics*, *63*(4), 1021–1039.

Ramakumar, R. (2020). Agriculture and the COVID-19 Pandemic: An Analysis with special reference to India. *Review of Agrarian Studies, 10.*

Ramelli, S., & Wagner, A. F. (2020). *Feverish stock price reactions to COVID-19.* Discussion Paper DP14511, 7, 1-61.

Ranjan, R. (2021). Impact of COVID-19 on migrant labourers of India and China. *Critical Sociology*, *47*(4-5), 721–726.

Ratten, V. (2020). *Coronavirus (COVID-19) and social value co-creation. International Journal of Sociology and Social Policy*. doi:10.1108/IJSSP-06-2020-0237

Reddy, W. R., & Mamgain, R. P. (2020). Revival and Reconstruction of Rural Livelihoods amidst COVID-19: Policy Responses, Opportunities and Way Ahead. *SRSC Policy Paper Series, 1.*

Reinsdorf, M., Tebrake, J., O'Hanlon, N., & Graf, B. (2020). CPI weights and COVID-19 household expenditure pattern. *Statistics: Special Series on COVID-19.* https://www.imf.org/~/media/files/publications/covid19-special-notes/en-special-series-0n-COVID-19-cpi-weights-and-COVID-19-expenditure-patterns.ashx

Reuters. (2020, May 31). *Thailand's parliament approves $58 billion economic package to east virus impact.* In *Reuters*. https://www.reuters.com/article/us-health-coronavirus-thailand-idUSKBN237047

Reynolds, P. D., & Maki, W. R. (1990). *Business volatility and economic growth.* US Small Business Administration.

Riddell, S., Goldie, S., Hill, A., Eagles, D., & Drew, T. W. (2020). The effect of temperature on persistence of SARS-CoV-2 on common surfaces. *Virology Journal*, *17*(1), 145. doi:10.118612985-020-01418-7 PMID:33028356

Roman, N. V., Mthembu, T. G., & Hoosen, M. (2020). Spiritual care – 'Adeeper immunity' – A response to COVID-19 pandemic. *African Journal of Primary Healthcare and Medicine*, *12*(1), 2456. doi:10.4102/phcfm.v12i1.2456 PMID:32634003

Ruthven, O. (2021). 'Blind laws' and the bureaucracy of rights migrant industrial workers in post-lockdown India. *Journal of Agrarian Change.*

Sachdeva, R. (2020). *Our response to Covid-19 pandemic and beyond.* Accessed at: www.datamaticsbpm.com/blog/our-response-to-COVID-19-pandemic-and-beyond

Salisu, A. A., Akanni, L., & Raheem, I. (2020c). The COVID-19 global fear index and the predictability of commodity price returns. *Journal of Behavioral and Experimental Finance, 27*, 100383. doi:10.1016/j.jbef.2020.100383 PMID:32835013

Salisu, A. A., Ebuh, G. U., & Usman, N. (2020b). Revisiting oil-stock nexus during COVID-19 pandemic: Some preliminary results. *International Review of Economics & Finance, 69*, 280–294. doi:10.1016/j.iref.2020.06.023

Salisu, A. A., & Vo, X. V. (2020a). Predicting stock returns in the presence of COVID-19 pandemic: The role of health news. *International Review of Financial Analysis, 71*, 101546. doi:10.1016/j.irfa.2020.101546

Sandel, M. J. (2012). *What Money Can't Buy: The Moral Limits of Markets.* Farar, Straus and Giroux.

Sansa, N. A. (2020). The Impact of the COVID-19 on the Financial Markets: Evidence from China and USA. *Electronic Research Journal of Social Sciences and Humanities,* 2.

Sasson. (2012). Food security for Africa: an urgent global challenge. *Agriculture and Food Security, 1*(2).

Schumaker, E. (2020, November 19). *Which States Have Mask Mandates: Map.* Retrieved January 1, 2021, from https://abcnews.go.com/Health/states-mask-mandates-map/story?id=74168504

Schwartz, K., Freed, M., Cubanski, J., Dolan, R., Pollitz, K., Michau, J., … Neuman, T. (2020, November 18). *Vaccine Coverage, Pricing, and Reimbursement in the U.S.* KFF. https://www.kff.org/coronavirus-COVID-19/issue-brief/vaccine-coverage-pricing-and-reimbursement-in-the-u-s/

Semuels, A. (2020, May 7). *Life for the Millions of Americans Facing Financial Ruin.* Retrieved January 12, 2021, from https://time.com/5833008/us-unemployment-coronavirus/

Sengupta, S., & Jha, M. K. (2020). Social policy, COVID-19 and impoverished migrants: Challenges and prospects in locked down India. *The International Journal of Community and Social Development, 2*(2), 152–172.

Serafini, G., Parmigiani, B., Amerio, A., Aguglia, A., Sher, L., & Amore, M. (2020). The psychological impact of COVID-19 on the mental health in the general population. *QJM: An International Journal of Medicine, 113*(8), 531–537. doi:10.1093/qjmed/hcaa201 PMID:32569360

Shadmi, E., Chen, Y., Dourado, I., Faran-Perach, I., Fuler, J., Hangoma, P., Hanvoravongchai, P., Obando, C., Petrosyan, V., Rao, K., Ruano, A., Shi, L., Souza, L., Spitzer-Shohat, S., Sturgiss, E., Suphanchaimat, R., Uribe, M., & Willems, S. (2020). Health equity and COVID-19: Global perspectives. *International Journal for Equity in Health, 19*(104), 104. Advance online publication. doi:10.118612939-020-01218-z PMID:32586388

Shah, G.H., Shankar, P., Schwind, J.S., & Sittaramane, V. (2020). The Detrimental Impact of the COVID-19 Crisis on Health Equity and Social Determinants of Health. *Journal of Public Health Management and Practice*, *26*(4). doi:10.1097/PHH.0000000000001200

Shah, A., & Lerche, J. (2020). Migration and the invisible economies of care: Production, social reproduction and seasonal migrant labour in India. *Transactions of the Institute of British Geographers*, *45*(4), 719–734.

Shakya, M. (2020). The politics of border and nation in Nepal in the time of pandemic. *Dialectical Anthropology*, *44*(3), 223–231.

Shegunshi, M. P., & Hiremath, G. N. (2020). *COVID-19 Impact on Indian Labour Class.* Academic Press.

Silberner, J. (2020, December 12). *What You Need To Know As The First COVID-19 Vaccines Head Your Way.* NPR. https://www.npr.org/sections/health-shots/2020/12/12/945288710/what-you-need-to-know-as-the-first-COVID-19-vaccine-heads-your-way

Simon, H. A., & Bonini, C. P. (1958). The size distribution of business firms. *The American Economic Review*, *48*(4), 607–617.

Simpson, E., & Conner, A. (2020). *Fighting coronavirus misinformation and disinformation – Preventive product recommendations for social media platforms.* Technology Policy: Centre for American Progress. https://www.americanprogress.org/issues/technology-policy/reports/2020/08/18/488714/fighting-coronavirus-misinformation-disinformation/

SinghB. P. (2020). *Impact of COVID-19 on rural economy in India.* doi:10.2139/ssrn.3609973

Singh, O. P. (2020). Mental health of migrant laborers in COVID-19 pandemic and lockdown: Challenges ahead. *Indian Journal of Psychiatry*, *62*(3), 233.

Siu, A., & Wong, Y. R. (2004). Economic impact of SARS: The case of Hong Kong. *Asian Economic Papers*, *3*(1), 62–83. doi:10.1162/1535351041747996

Smith, T. (2020, September 17). *Students Accused Of Breaking College COVID-19 Rules Fight Their Punishments.* NPR. https://www.npr.org/2020/09/17/914046958/students-accused-of-breaking-college-COVID-19-rules-fight-their-punishments

Smith, J., Davies, S. E., Feng, H., Gan, C. C. R., Grépin, K. A., Harman, S., Herten-Crabb, A., Morgan, R., Vandan, N., & Wenham, C. (2021). More than a public health crisis: A feminist political economic analysis of COVID-19. *Global Public Health: An International Journal for Research, Policy and Practice*, *16*(8-9), 1364–1380. Advance online publication. doi:10.1080/17441692.2021.1896765 PMID:33705248

Snider, M. (2021, January 14). Coronavirus vaccine incentive: Trader Joe's, Instacart and Dollar General to pay workers to get vaccinated. *USA Today*. https://www.usatoday.com/story/money/business/2021/01/14/covid-vaccine-dollar-general-instacart-pay-employees-getting-vaccine/4160708001/

Sohrabi, C., Alsafi, Z., O'Neill, N., Khan, M., Kerwan, A., Al-Jabir, A., Iosifidis, C., & Agha, R. (2020). World Health Organisation declares global emergency: A review of the 2019 novel coronavirus (COVID-19). *International Journal of Surgery*, *76*, 71–76. doi:10.1016/j.ijsu.2020.02.034 PMID:32112977

Spivack, C. (2020, May 21). *Here's how the coronavirus pandemic is affecting public transit.* Curbed NY. https://ny.curbed.com/2020/3/24/21192454/coronavirus-nyc-transportation-subway-citi-bike-COVID-19

Srivastava, S. K., & Sivaramane, N. (2020). Income-induced effects of COVID-19 on the food consumption pattern of Indian households. *Agricultural Economics Research Review*, *33*, 15–24. doi:10.5958/0974-0279.2020.00014.2

St. Fleur, N. (2020, December 14). *Can celebrities spur acceptance of the COVID-19 vaccine?* STAT. https://www.statnews.com/2020/12/14/the-polio-vaccine-had-elvis-can-celebrities-similarly-spur-acceptance-of-the-COVID-19-vaccine/

Stabile, M., Apouey, B. & Solal, I. (2020). *COVID-19, inequality, and gig economy workers.* VoxEU.org.

Steinberg, L. (2020, June 15). Expecting Students to Play It Safe if Colleges Reopen Is a Fantasy. *The New York Times.* https://www.nytimes.com/2020/06/15/opinion/coronavirus-college-safe.html

Street, F. (2019, December 3). *The most visited cities in the world 2019.* CNN Travel. https://edition.cnn.com/travel/article/most-visited-cities-euromonitor-2019/index.html

Subramaniam, T. (2020, November 1). *Fact Check: Can the President enact a nationwide mask mandate?* CNN. https://www.cnn.com/2020/11/01/politics/mask-mandate-fact-check/index.html

Suder, G., & Inthavong, S. (2008). New health risks and sociocultural contexts: Bird flu impacts on consumers and poultry businesses in Lao PDR. *Risk Analysis: An International Journal*, *28*(1), 1–12. doi:10.1111/j.1539-6924.2008.00997.x PMID:18304102

Suresh, R., & James, J., & RSj, B. (2020). Migrant Workers at Crossroads–The COVID-19 Pandemic and the Migrant Experience in India. *Social Work in Public Health*, *35*(7), 633–643.

Swift, J. (1729). *A Modest Proposal.* https://www.gutenberg.org/files/1080/1080-h/1080-h.htm

Tantrakarnapa, K., Bhopdhornangkul, B., & Nakhaapakorn, K. (2020). Influencing factors of COVID-19 spreading: A case study of Thailand. *Journal of Public Health: From Theory to Practice*. doi:10.1007/s10389-020-01329-5

Thailand, S. C. B. (2020). *Thailand after COVID-19 prepare to get through the Economist's perspective. Part 1: The impact of the economy and the Thai labour market.* https://www.scb.co.th/en/personal-banking/stories/business-maker/thailand-after-covid-ep1.html

Thaler, R. (2020, December 9). Getting Everyone Vaccinated, With 'Nudges' and Charity Auctions. *The New York Times.* https://www.nytimes.com/2020/12/09/business/coronavirus-vaccination-auctions-celebrities.html

Thaler, R. (2020, May 20). The Law of Supply and Demand Isn't Fair. *The New York Times*. https://www.nytimes.com/2020/05/20/business/supply-and-demand-isnt-fair.html

The Nation Thailand. (2020, September 14). *SCB forecasts greater contraction of Thai economy in aftermath of COVID-19*. https://www.nationthailand.com/business/30394513?utm_source=homepage&utm_medium=internal_referral

The National Academies. (n.d.). Encountering microbes – Entering the human host. *Infectious Diseases*.https://needtoknow.nas.edu/id/infection/encountering-microbes/entering-the-human-host/#

Thompson, D. (2020, April 27). There Aren't Enough Coronavirus Test Kits to Safely Reopen America, Experts Warn. *U.S. News & World Report*. https://www.usnews.com/news/health-news/articles/2020-04-27/there-arent-enough-coronavirus-test-kits-to-safely-reopen-america-experts-warn

Thurlow, J. (2010). *Implications of avian flu for economic development in Kenya (No. 951). International Food Policy Research Institute*. IFPRI.

TOBB. (2021). *Company Establishment and Liquidation Statistics* [Database]. Available at: https://tobb.org.tr/BilgiErisimMudurlugu/Sayfalar/Eng/KurulanKapananSirketistatistikleri.php

Topcu, M., & Gulal, O. S. (2020). The impact of COVID-19 on emerging stock markets. *Finance Research Letters*, *36*, 101691. doi:10.1016/j.frl.2020.101691 PMID:32837378

Tull, M. T., Edmonds, K. A., Scamaldo, K. Y., Richmond, J. R., Rose, J. P., & Gratz, K. L. (2020). Psychological outcomes associated with stay-at-home orders and the perceived impact of COVID-19 on daily life. *Psychiatry Research*, *287*, 113098. doi:10.1016/j.psychres.2020.113098

Tunçdemir, C. (2020). Çin'e virüs komplosunu kim kurdu? *T24*.

Turner, C. (2020, September 8). *'Children Are Going Hungry': Why Schools Are Struggling To Feed Students*. NPR. https://www.npr.org/2020/09/08/908442609/children-are-going-hungry-why-schools-are-struggling-to-feed-students

U.S. Department of Health and Human Services. (2021, January 8). *Poverty Guidelines*. ASPE. https://aspe.hhs.gov/poverty-guidelines

Ullah, A. A., Nawaz, F., & Chattoraj, D. (2021). Locked up under lockdown: The COVID-19 pandemic and the migrant population. *Social Sciences & Humanities Open*, *3*(1), 100126.

UN Women Headquarters. (2020). *Policy Brief: The Impact of COVID-19 on Women*. United Nations.

UNDP. (2020). *COVID-19: Socio-economic impact*. United Nations Development Program. https://www.undp.org/content/undp/en/coronavirus/socio-economic-impact-of-COVID-19.html

UNESCO (2020). *Socio-economic and cultural impacts of COVID-19 on Africa – UNESCO responses*. United Nations Scientific and Cultural Organisation.

UNICEF. (2020). *Key messages and actions for COVID-19 prevention and control in schools.* United Nations Children Education Fund/World Health Organisation. https://www.who.int/key-messages-and-actions-for-COVID-19-preventiopn-and-control-in-schools

United Nations Thailand. (2020). *Socio-economic response to COVID-19.* https://reliefweb.int/report/thailand/socio-economic-response-COVID-19

USDA Food and Nutrition Service. (2020). *SNAP COVID-19 Waivers.* USDA. https://www.fns.usda.gov/programs/fns-disaster-assistance/fns-responds-COVID-19/snap-COVID-19-waivers

Vargas, C., & Hanna, M. (2020, March 24). *Free breakfast and lunch begins, but not many students in North Philly bite.* https://www.inquirer.com. https://www.inquirer.com/health/coronavirus/coronavirus-philadelphia-schools-free-lunches-grab-and-go-20200316.html

Vesoulis, A. (2020, October 17). Women's COVID-Fueled Exodus From the Workforce Hurts Us All. *Time.* https://time.com/5900583/women-workforce-economy-covid/

Vigdor, N. (2020, April 23). Tennessee Brothers Who Hoarded Hand Sanitizer Settle to Avoid Price-Gouging Fine. *The New York Times.* https://www.nytimes.com/2020/04/22/us/hand-sanitizer-matt-colvin-noah-coronavirus.html

Voinsky, I., Baristaite, G., & Gurwitz, D. (2020). Effects of age and sex on recovery from COVID-19: Analysis of 5769 Israeli patients. *The Journal of Infection, 81*(2), e102–e103. doi:10.1016/j.jinf.2020.05.026 PMID:32425274

Vos, J. (2021). *The Psychology of COVID-19: Building Resilience for Future Pandemics.* SAGE Publications. doi:10.4135/9781529757156

Walque, D., Friedman, J., Gatti, R., & Mattoo, A. (2020, April). How Two Tests Can Help Contain COVID-19 and Revive the Economy. *Research & Policy Briefs*, (29), 8. doi:10.1596/33583

Weekly, T. T. R. (2020, September 28). *Thailand's tourism recovery four years away.* https://www.ttrweekly.com/site/2020/09/thailands-tourism-recovery-four-years-away/

WEF. (2020). *Fighting COVID-19 could cost 500 times as much as pandemic prevention measures.* World Economic Forum. https://www.weforum.org/agenda/2020/08/pandemic-fight-costs-500x-morethen-preventing-one-futurity

WHO. (2020a). *Impact of COVID-19 on people's livelihoods, their health and our food system.* Joint statement by ILO, FAO, IFAD and WHO: World Health Organisation. https://www.who.int/news/item/13-10-2020-impact-of-COVID-19-on-people's-livelihoods-their-health and our-food-systems

WHO. (2020b). *COVID-19 cases top 10 000 in Africa.* World Health Organisation: Regional Office for Africa. https://www.afro.who.int/news/COVID-19-cases-top-10000-africa#

WHO. (2020c). *A second COVID-19 case is confirmed in Africa.* World Health Organisation: Regional Office for Africa. https://www.afro.who.int/news/secon-COVID-19-cases-confirmed-in-africa

WHO. (2020d). *Weekly bulletin on outbreaks and other emergencies*. World Health Organisation: Regional Office for Africa. https://apps.who.int/iris/bitstream/handle/10665/331892/OEW17-2026042020.pdf

WHO. (2020e). *COVID-19: vulnerable and high risk group*. World Health Organisation. https://www.who.int/westernpacific/emergencies/COVID-19information/high-risk-group#

WHO. (2020f). *COVID-19 in Africa: Marking six months of response*. World Health Organisation: Regional Office for Africa. https://www.afro.who.int/COVID-19-africa-marking-six-months-response

WHO. (2020g). *Managing the COVID-19 infodemic: Promoting healthy behaviours and mitigating the harm from information dissemination*. World Health Organisation: https://www.who.int/news/iten/23-09-2020-managing-the-COVID-19-infodemic-promoting-healthy-behaviours-and-mitigating-the-harm-from-misinformation-and-disinformation

WHO. (2021). *WHO Coronavirus disease (COVID-19) pandemic*. https:// www.who.int/emergencies/diseases/novel-coronavirus-2019

Wong, G. (2008). Has SARS infected the property market? Evidence from Hong Kong. *Journal of Urban Economics*, *63*(1), 74–95. doi:10.1016/j.jue.2006.12.007 PMID:32287489

Wooley, S., Sattiraju, N., & Moritz, S. (2020, March 26). *U.S. Schools Trying to Teach Online Highlight a Digital Divide*. Bloomberg. https://www.bloomberg.com/news/articles/2020-03-26/COVID-19-school-closures-reveal-disparity-in-access-to-internet

World Bank Group. (2020). *Thailand economic monitor: Thailand in the time of COVID-19*. The World Bank.

World Bank. (2020). *World Bank predicts sharpest decline of remittance in recent history*. https://www.wordbank.org/en/news/press-relase/2020/04/22/world-bank-predicts-sharpest-decline-of-remittances-in-recent-history

Wright, S. (2020, June 5). *The world's most visited countries*. https://www.worldatlas.com/articles/10-most-visited-countries-in-the-world.html

Wu, Y., Jing, W., Liu, J., Ma, Q., Yuan, J., Wang, Y., Du, M., & Liu, M. (2020). Effects of temperature and humidity on the daily cases and new deaths of COVID-19 in 166 countries. *The Science of the Total Environment*, *729*, 139051. Advance online publication. doi:10.1016/j.scitotenv.2020.139051 PMID:32361460

Wyper, G. M. A., Assuncao, R., Cuschieri, S., Devleesschauwer, B., Fletcher, E., Haagsma, J. A., & Grant, I. (2020). Population vulnerability to COVID-19 in Europe: A burden of disease analysis. *Archives of Public Health*, *78*, 27. doi:10.118613690-020-0043-y

Wyplosz, C. (2020). The good thing about Coronavirus. In Economics in the Time of COVID-19. CEPR Press.

Xu, D., Guo, Y., & Huang, M. (2021). Can Artificial Intelligence Improve Firms' Competitiveness during the COVID-19 Pandemic: International Evidence. *Emerging Markets Finance & Trade*, 1–14. doi:10.1080/1540496X.2021.1967740

Yang, C., Sha, D., Liu, Q., Li, Y., Lan, H., Guan, W. W., ... Wang, Z. (2020). Taking the pulse of COVID-19: A spatiotemporal perspective. *International Journal of Digital Earth*, *13*(10), 1–26. doi:10.1080/17538947.2020.1809723

Ziet, M., Zucker, J., & Tatonetti, N. P. (2020). Associations between blood type and COVID-19 infection, incubation and death. *Nature Communications*, *11*(1), 5761. doi:10.103841467-020-19623-x PMID:33188185

Zorlu, F. (2020, March 11). *Turkey confirms first case of coronavirus*. Anatolian Agency. https://www.aa.com.tr/en/latest-on-coronavirus-outbreak/turkey-confirms-first-case-of-coronavirus/1761522

About the Contributors

Hakan Altin was born in Ankara in 1971. He completed his undergraduate education in Anadolu University, Department of Economics in 1996. He completed his postgraduate education at Ankara University with a withstanding degree in 2010 and received his Ph.D. in Business Administration. He is currently working as a Professor Doctor in the Faculty of Economics and Administrative Sciences, Department of Business Administration at Aksaray University. The author has penned numerous articles and book chapters in finance.

Yigit Aydogan was graduated from Koc University with BS degree in Economics in 2010. After working at multinational companies, he has begun his academic career at the Economics Department of Ege University in 2012. He received a master's degree in Economics from Ege University in 2013. He has received his Ph.D. from Yildiz Technical University in the field of Economics, in 2019. He is a faculty member of Economics Department at Kirklareli University, since 2013.

Nancy Ruth Fox is Associate Professor of Economics at Saint Joseph's University in Philadelphia. She holds an A.B. from Princeton University and a Ph.D. from the University of Pennsylvania, both in economics. Her teaching interests are Ethics and Economics, Poverty, Economics in the News, and Antitrust and Regulation. Her book, Profits and Prophets: Market Economics and Jewish Social Ethics, was published by Palgrave Macmillan in 2020.

Jason Hung is a doctoral candidate in Sociology at the University of Cambridge. He held research attachments at Stanford University (2019), King's College, London (2018-19), University of California, Berkeley (2018) and the University of Warwick (2017, 2016). He works as a columnist at *South China Morning Post* and *The Diplomat*.

İrfan Kalaycı received his BE in economics from Çukurova University (Adana), MSc and Ph.D in economics from İnönü University (Malatya), and associate professorship in macroeconomics from the TR Higher Education Institution-Inter Universities Board (Ankara). His main scientific studies are about economic policy, bioeconomy and Turkey - Europe - World economies. In addition to more than 100 articles and papers, he has 5 books that he edited and wrote chapters, 2 copyright books and 21 awards he received in various scientific and literary competitions. He is currently a professor of economic policy at İnönü University.

Okanlade Adesokan Lawal-Adebowale holds a PhD in Agricultural Communication and is a Professor of Agri-knowledge development and innovation communication. His research focus cuts across a number sub-disciplines in agriculture, rural livelihood, and societal social change and development. Emanating from his research tasks are 37 journal articles, 11 chapters in books and 13 conference proceeding. He is a member of profession bodies such as Rural Sociological Association of Nigeria (RuSAN), Nigerian Forum for Agricultural Advisory Services (NIFAAS), and Farm Management Association of Nigeria (FAMAN).

A. Eren Yıldırım is an Assistant Professor of Economics at Uşak University, Uşak, Turkey. He holds a B. A. in Economics, a MSc in Economics, and a Ph.D. in Economics from Ege University. He has been in Berlin for the Post- Keynesian Summer School from Forum for Macroeconomics and Macroeconomic Policies (FMM). His research focuses on post-Keynesian macroeconomics. His research interests includes income distribution, economic growth, and development economics.

Index

L

M

N

O

P

R

S

T

V

W

www.ingramcontent.com/pod-product-compliance
Lightning Source LLC
LaVergne TN
LVHW061537290926
849162LV00004B/822